A Road Runs Through It

A Road Runs Through It

Reviving Wild Places

Edited by Thomas Reed Petersen

Foreword by Annie Proulx

Wood engravings by Claire Emery © 2006

Johnson Books
BOULDER

Published by Johnson Books, a division of Big Earth Publishing, 3005 Center Green Drive, Suite 220, Boulder, CO 80301.
E-mail: books@bigearthpublishing.com.
www.johnsonbooks.com

Cover photo: Mark Alan Wilson, www.picturetomorrow.org
Cover design: Constance Bollen, cbgraphics
Composition: Michel Reynolds

9 8 7 6 5 4 3 2 1

Library of Congress Cataloging-in-Publication Data
A road runs through it: reviving wild places / edited by Thomas Reed
    Petersen.
    p. cm.
    ISBN 1-55566-371-0
    1. Roads—Environmental aspects. 2. Wilderness areas. I. Petersen,
    Thomas Reed.
    333.78'2140973—dc22

2006005662

Printed in the United States of America on Environmentally Preferable Book Papers, made with recycled fiber and containing 50% Post Consumer Waste.

Contents

Foreword

Annie Proulx

The essays in this collection are varied: poetic, terse, rational, long-winded, slightly crazy, sentimental, sardonic, bitter, peppery, exalted, informed, heartbreaking, angry. Some are in the mode of the requiem, others describe rebirths; some mourn and some give us advice based on hard experience.

We have all had the road-where-there-shouldn't-be-one experience. A few years ago, four of us drove into Wyoming's Red Desert at the start of a project to make a history of the place. We were an archaeologist, a historian, a photographer, a prospector. This region, the largest unfenced area in the lower forty-eight states, a high-desert basin in the arms of the Continental Divide where wild horses still exist, covers roughly 6,000 square miles and is spotted with archaeological sites; Indian corrals; the remains of early oil exploration; outlaw hideout cabins; strange geological formations; trails of historic importance; coal, uranium, and trona mines; ghost towns; rare species of animals; insect mysteries; and an estimated 50,000 antelope. The Red Desert has massive deposits of coalbed methane gas lying beneath its sagebrush, and as we started our project, was just entering the boom phase of major energy extraction. Everywhere we looked we saw new roads. We traveled down one, twice swerving out of the way of a speeding energy company truck, and saw an antelope lying on the roadside, unable to rise. It could neither lift its head nor get up. We stopped. The injury was a large bloody gash on its rear flank, likely a broken pelvis. It was obvious the animal had been hit by a truck. It was a terrifically hot day and the blood of the wound had dried to a black crust but had already attracted a ring of flies. Efforts to call Game and Fish or the sheriff were useless—no reception. It was our problem. The prospector was the only one who had brought a gun, a replica of an old black-powder pistol, but he did not want to fire it, saying he could lose his hunting license forever. The archaeologist, who was not a hunter and had no license, said he didn't care and would do it. So he fired. The antelope quivered slightly and died. Two hours later when we came back, a golden eagle rose from the carcass.

That road and hundreds of others, along with pipelines, thumper trucks, well pads, and compression stations, now interlace and fragment the desert. The traffic is heavy and fast, the noise considerable. Recently some gas field workers were arrested for illegally poaching antelope and deer, and our archaeologist found one of his dig sites deliberately destroyed. It does seem that in many humans—maybe all of us—runs the red urge to ruin and smash.

But also built into every human being is a need to assign meaning to life. We can't help it—it's part of human existence, deep in our psyches, in our ancient sense that there is an overarching ethos that orders all that we are and do. For some this primary force takes the shape of religion; for some it is a connection with other species and the natural world. The outrage and pain many of the essayists in this collection feel when they see that world despoiled may echo the violated feelings of the seventeenth-century pueblo dwellers whose sacred masks and ritual paraphernalia the Spaniards burned as demonic abominations. But in 1680, after eight decades of Spanish domination, the people of the pueblos drove the Spanish out of the country.

It is a big leap to equate road-ripping with the pueblo revolt, but in its own way the attempt to restore a damaged and desecrated wilderness is a meaningful ritual that seeks to reestablish the correct order of the world. Our connection with our surroundings is truly the key element, and that connection is more than doing the right conservation-restoration thing, more than saving little pieces of the natural world for the future. We are less than human if we do not do those things. Freeman House, in "More Than Numbers," takes us to the heart of the matter when he describes people who work to save or restore parts of the former world as experiencing "the rewards of an ever-deepening relationship to the places where they live ... a growing knowledge that humans are capable of reunion with the life systems that support them." Everyone once lived such lives of involvement as casually as they performed life functions.

Today the great majority of North Americans are literally removed from contact with and knowledge of the natural world. Most can't tell moose scat from bird seed, are ignorant of wild plants, trees, animals, even seasonal changes beyond the most flamboyant leaf color. For them the outdoor world is reduced to a view shed, that rectangle shaped by the car windshield. What we are truly involved with in our time is driving—guiding the vehicle, reading signs, watching alertly for danger, glancing at the strangers whizzing past in the opposite direction, seeking out eateries and bathrooms, all enlivened by the sense of achievement that comes with going somewhere, making a journey. We are in an adventure. But these adventures have as their price dependency, ignorance, diminished senses, truncated pleasure, crushed animals, and ecological ruination. Those who believe the natural world is dispensable may find themselves less than necessary and eventually tossed aside.

In this country the Lincoln Highway separated us from nature. The Lincoln was the brainchild of Carl G. Fisher, a man whose extraordinarily fertile imagination changed this country. He was a bicycle and auto racer, yachtsman, balloonist, salesman, and inventor; head of Prest-O-Lite carbide headlights for cars; creator of the Indianapolis Speedway. In 1912 he had the idea for a cross-continent road from New York to San Francisco, which he called the Coast-to-Coast [crushed] Rock Highway. Auto manufacturers (except Henry Ford) chipped in money to get the project off the ground; they were wild for the road. By 1919 it was possible to drive across the continent on disjointed segments of the Lincoln Highway. Drivers were utterly involved, as many primitive miles demanded they proceed with all four claws out and gears in grandma. The Lincoln Highway later became US 30, then parts were swallowed up by I-80 in the 1960s. Readers of this book can take joy in occasional sightings of bypassed sections, grass and brush thrusting up through the broken macadam. Should the automobile suddenly cease to exist, nature would reclaim all roads. In the meantime, it is dedicated human labor and struggle, without the thrill of sport, brilliant lycra road-ripping costumes, or coverage in glossy outdoor mags, that save us from ourselves.

How can we help? As these essayists show us, we can talk to others, from friends to apparent enemies, about the need for scratching out roads. We can write letters and campaign against horrific television ads for ORVs and muscle trucks shown trashing wilderness and wetlands.

When officials are up for election, we can ask where they stand on roadless issues and vote accordingly. We can get involved with local and regional anti-road groups, finding the ones who really do something in the field instead of putting all their effort and money into brochures. We can encourage our states to adopt regulatory laws and air patrols to catch vehicle spoilers in off-limits country. And in rural areas we can keep an eye on how our counties manage gravel roads. In my part of Wyoming I was taken aback last year when the county declared most of its hundreds of miles of gravel roads permissible travel routes for ORVs until I realized the move would keep many of the vehicles off fragile lands. And perhaps we can encourage colonies of irascible bees around wetlands to save them from mud-boggers.

Introduction

M any thoughtful people believe that the fate of the earth depends
on keeping nature unpaved," wrote Ted Conover in the June
2003 *National Geographic*. The writers in this unique collection of stories—some of our finest—are first and foremost among those believers. From Rosalie Edge, a feisty conservation activist in the 1930s, to
Peter Matthiessen, the well-known author of *The Snow Leopard*, they
lay claim that roads are a route to nature's destruction.

"What's wrong with roads?" you may wonder. "We drive on them
every day, to the store, to work, to take our kids to school. We depend
on them." True. Yet the roads and their impacts so eloquently and
provocatively described in this collection of essays are the "other"
roads, the black sheep of the roads family: wildland roads. All roads
have impacts, paved or otherwise, but they are not all created equal.
While even some wildland roads are important—either for resource
management, or for taking leisurely drives to see bright fall colors, or
for getting to our favorite fishing, hiking, or hunting spots—there are
thousands of miles of unnecessary and ecologically damaging wildland roads that pose significant dangers to public safety, that erode
into streams where the sediments dirty our drinking water and ruin
our fisheries, and that give off-road vehicles the way to intrude deep
into natural areas.

Most roads through wildlands are public land roads, cutting
through Forest Service, Bureau of Land Management, National
Refuge, and National Park Service lands. But wildland roads also
impact private lands that still remain undeveloped—especially in the
East, where much less land has been set aside for public use—and that

1

provide some of the last critical habitats for imperiled fish and wildlife.

The majority of public land roads—more than 440,000 miles—wind through Forest Service land alone. (By comparison, the U.S. interstate system, often called the largest public works project in the world, runs 43,000 miles.) The other major public land management agencies combined control approximately 100,000 miles of roads. And so we can use roads on Forest Service land, as some of these essayists do, as a focused example of "what's wrong with roads."

On Forest Service lands, only about 6 percent are paved and maintained for regular travel by passenger cars. The other 94 percent are dirt roads, some with little or no maintenance, many of which were supposed to be only temporary for logging operations—dead ends in the forest that are literally "roads to nowhere." And these roads are costly to maintain—the Forest Service reports a $10 billion backlog in forest road maintenance—as well as costly to the environment. Finally, the Forest Service estimates that more than a third of its total road miles, about 180,000 miles, are not necessary to meet forest transportation needs.

The political and social landscape of roads is beginning to change, although slowly. While the Forest Service is decreasing its road-building and starting to remove some unnecessary and dangerous roads, there are, to paraphrase Robert Frost, miles to go before we sleep. For example, the Gifford Pinchot National Forest in Washington is actively restoring wildlands, with 42 miles of road removed in 1999 and 72 miles the next year. This is progress, but it's barely 2.5 percent of the approximately 4,300 miles of roads on the Gifford Pinchot.

And so the twenty-eight writers in *A Road Runs Through It* call us with their stories to consider "the state of the road" and then to respond to it. While there are other fine, more academically oriented ecological books about roads, this collection tells stories. One of the authors, William Kittredge, has written, "We need to inhabit stories that will encourage us toward acts of the imagination, which in turn will drive us to the arts of empathy, for each other and the world. We need stories that will tell us what kind of action to take."

Alongside original stories written exclusively for this collection that "encourage us toward acts of the imagination" are others reprinted from magazines like *Smithsonian* and *Audubon*, and still others written for *The Road-RIPorter*, the quarterly publication of Wildlands CPR. Based in Missoula, Montana, Wildlands CPR is a small national conservation organization working since 1994 to decrease the number of public land roads and to revive natural areas by promoting road removal and limiting motorized recreation. Wildlands CPR is working especially hard to bring road removal to communities near or adjacent to Forest Service land, encouraging opportunities for the high-skilled, high-paying jobs such restoration requires. As a member of Wildlands CPR's staff, I have had the pleasure of collecting the stories for the essay section of *The Road-RIPorter* while also experiencing firsthand many of the impacts the writers describe, both the tragedies of mass road failure and the rewards of full watershed restoration.

What's wrong with roads? Part One, "Why Roads?" digs right into this question, offering the broader philosophical reasoning behind roads and our passion for driving on them. Often we seem to drive only to get to the next place, becoming visitors wanting to move on again and again. This is not a contemporary phenomenon. Even early in the twentieth century, roads ran deep in the American psyche and in the development of our public lands. In 1936, for example, alarmed by the proliferation of roads on newly designated public lands, Rosalie Edge, one of the writers in Part One, wrote a passionate pamphlet titled "Roads and More Roads in the National Parks and National Forests." Contemporary writer Stephanie Mills both playfully and seriously considers roads in her essay, "It's Delightful, It's De-Lovely, It's De-Roaded," encouraging us to imagine walking in a world without roads. Mary Sojourner, crouched at the edge of the Turtle Mountain Wilderness in Arizona, ponders the question of whether more is better when it comes to roads. Unable to walk farther because of a bad back, she is later offered a ride to see a hidden redstone arch. Choosing to make peace with the fact the she can't have it all—both motorized access and a road-free experience—the way to her answer, she writes, "is perfectly clear."

The second part, "Where the Deer and the Antelope Can't Play," highlights some of the more dramatic examples of why roads are harmful to wildlife. Not only do roads split wildlife habitat into smaller and smaller pieces, but the increasing number of vehicles means increasing numbers of roadkill as well. Derrick Jensen deals with snakes on the road with a baseball bat—to gently move them off the road or, humanely, to kill them as they writhe with broken backs after being car-struck. Barry Lopez, in "Apologia," stops his car south of the Snake River in Idaho to palm two stilled nighthawks, one in each hand. His actions draw the attention of a farmer, who steps off his tractor and approaches Lopez. He imagines disdain in the farmer's eyes for such a seemingly useless act, but instead the farmer is fascinated and asks to take one of the nighthawks to show his wife. "She's never seen anything like this," the farmer says. "Not close."

"Got Roads?" is the subject of the third part of the book. Enough is enough, say these writers in essays that explore the escalating "road densities" on our public lands, some as high as 30 miles of road per square mile of land. (Imagine a square inch with 30 inches of lines within its borders.) Summoning us to consider an aerial view of forest roads cutting hillsides from top to bottom in concentric rings, these writers question building even one more mile. Stephen Lyons drives a confusing pattern of road after road in Idaho with Dwight, an old logger who, even with years of experience in the Idaho backwoods, doesn't recognize where he is any longer. Guy Hand pleads to protect a California meadow from two-track roads that are "nothing more than a pot-holed portal for bad ideas."

Part Four, "Much Ado About Access," examines the link between roads and motorized recreation. The impacts of roads continue, with the increasing numbers of people who desire to drive through public land on dirt bikes, all-terrain vehicles (ATVs), snowmobiles, and swamp buggies. When citizens call for road removal and restoration, it is sometimes motorized recreationists who insist that their access rights are being denied. The writers in Part Four challenge that "right to access" firmly and passionately. Ed Abbey implores, "What does accessibility mean? Is there any spot on earth that men have not proved accessible by the simplest means—feet and legs and heart?"

While the first four parts paint a disturbing national picture of road after road and the growing number of off-road vehicles on (and off) them, the fifth, "Ripped, Restored, Revived," glimmers with hope. There is a growing movement not only to stop building new roads but also to remove unnecessary ones and to restore the land to its natural state. This part is bolstered by stories from the field, from T. H. Watkins's "road-killers" on the Clearwater National Forest in Idaho to Freeman House's salmon restoration projects in Oregon. Watershed restoration is important not only for the land but for nearby communities as well, because of the local, sustainable, family-wage jobs it creates.

As a companion to restoring roaded lands to a roadless or near-roadless condition, the final part, "In Defense of Wild Places," exudes strong preservation values. Here the writers ask us to consider conserving the base of our existence, the natural world. With noted sportsman and author Ted Kerasote leading off, the writers in Part Six articulately argue that preserving what we have—roadless and lightly roaded lands—is a key to preserving ourselves as an integral part of the wild world. Pepper Trail concurs in his essay, "Miles . . . from Nowhere," giving us the startling fact that the lower forty-eight's most remote spot is only 20.3 miles from a road. And you will not want to miss how Phil Condon concludes Part Six, and the book, as he writes with searingly honest passion for the wild.

What's wrong with roads? My two sons ask me the same question. And the answers, as portrayed by the writers in this book, are many, from habitat destruction to roadkill to the loss of quiet, wild places.

As the inheritors of our successes and failures, it's fitting to conclude this introduction to *A Road Runs Through It* by considering future generations of hikers, backpackers, and wildlife. I think of Pepper Trail who writes, "It is my fervent hope that when the time comes, it will still be possible for my son and me to take *his* twelve-year-old for a walk into an unknown, uncontrolled, and uncontrolling place: wilderness, miles from nowhere."

Maybe, with a little luck and a lot of hard work, that place will be even more than 20 miles from a road.

Thomas R. Petersen
Missoula, Montana

Part One: Why Roads?

"*We go ahead and drive the car, wondering what all these other people are doing on the road, why the traffic is so dense. Shouldn't they be at work or in school or something? We're streaming down the highway, part of the momentum.*"

—Tom Lyon, "Momentum"

The essays in Part One set the philosophical stage for the entire book, asking, in a variety of ways, "Why Roads?" Although we know the answer for our city, state, and interstate roads (though they, too, have their ecological impacts, they are needed to get us to work, to school, to visit friends and family), our wildland roads pose a conundrum: yes, we need some of them, but do we need (or even want) to drive everywhere?

It's Delightful,
It's De-Lovely,
It's De-Roaded

Stephanie Mills

E ven though my conscious mind knows uncomfortably much about the sterilizing effects of fragmentation on the land, my eyes want to see animals. When I drive along the county roads and state highways, things trick my wishful eyes into seeing badgers or wolverines. Rain-darkened stumps in the fields are, for a tantalizing second, black bears. Black plastic garbage bags and white plastic grocery bags hung up in roadside shrubs or tree branches appear to be great birds—ravens, snowy owls, big fierce animals. Then manmade reality reasserts itself and the passing terrain viewed at fifty or sixty miles an hour resumes its aspect of ecological poverty. Foolish of me to expect to roam the countryside in my automobile and encounter a complete ecosystem, to mistake a flapping shred of refuse for a wild thing. When I do see animals from the road they're either cows or corpses—bloated flyblown coons, possums, skunks, and deer, suffering the indignity of public mutilation. These pathetic remains shout shame and reproach. All kinds of roads want rescinding.

Long before the ubiquitous two-tracks and asphalt ribbons, railroads did plenty to slice and dice the wilderness. In my neck of the former woods, logging trains sizzled like lit fuses through doomed pineries. And across the prairies, iron horses served as shooting platforms for the bison massacre. My mind's eye sees The Road as an immense circular saw cleaving a linear track across the land, chewing up any living thing that crosses its path. This image holds as true in rural areas and small towns as in old-growth forests.

Just as a logging road leads to the exploitation of timber, the introduction of exotic plants and animals, and the wastage of soils and aquifers, so, for instance, paving the road over the Himalayan passes into Ladakh ("Little Tibet") allowed strategic military installations, the prostitution of traditional culture, and the introduction of alien communities and values. In both instances, the road leads to a whole-sale disruption of a climax community's equilibrium.

In effect, all roads do lead to Rome. Like all megatechnology, the technology of the road tends to confer most of its advantages on the powerful. Roads allow human populations both to concentrate and to disperse in the most ecologically damaging ways. By accommodating wheels and permitting greater speed, by diminishing the need for sensitivity to the terrain and attention to the journey, a road serves the charioteer or legionary far better than the ambling pilgrim. Roads are the premier technology of empire, of centralization and homogenization (or, as they say in the World Trade Organization, "harmonization"); they are the literal avenues of conquest and colonialism. The trade and transport of goods and the enslavement of beasts of burden follow the military uses of roads as night follows day.

While the Roman construction of roads was meant to facilitate the movement of governors and legions, commerce inevitably ensued. In our time, Old Ike, the military man, gave us the interstate highway system for national defense. For some reason, said defense came to involve a great deal of heavy truck traffic. These rumbling conveyances reverberate in the deep past. The archaic (and still used) bullock cart, integral to the emerging technology of roads, helped initiate a quantum shift in the relation of humanity to more-than-human nature: the fateful shift from communion to commodification. And it is not just the plants and animals that are reduced by this change.

Road-RIPorter readers don't need persuading that roads in wildlands have ever and always been monstrously destructive of ecological integrity. However, the delusion that driving into a wildland in some gross sport utility vehicle or barging in on a stinking noisy ORV constitutes an experience of Nature is similarly destructive of human integrity. It's a kind of self-infantilization and self-diminution. We expropriate a power that wrecks the landscape and imagine that to be freedom: rendering ourselves blind, deaf, and numb to the richness of the natural world by the intoxications of internal combustion.

I must confess to understanding the appeal. There are times when cruising down a county road in my little Toyota with the tape deck playing at top volume provides the movie-style exhilaration of a magic carpet ride lard butt, miscellaneous engine and exhaust noises notwithstanding.

I don't recall ever having been advised that seeing the USA in my Chevrolet was going to fracture the landscape, wreck the atmosphere, change the climate, and slaughter the four-footed multitudes. Which is not an excuse or plea of innocence. I, too, have croaked a few furry and feathered pedestrians in my driving career.

Considering that I was almost roadkill myself, you'd think there'd be no love lost between me and motor vehicles. Even now I'm experiencing twinges in the right leg that got all smashed up in that head-on collision twenty years ago. Ordinarily I'm blissfully bipedal, thanks to modern orthopedics' ability to put Humpty Dumpty back together again. Unlike the smeared squirrels, smashed skunks, and eviscerated coons that come to woe on the pavement, we humans sometimes get second chances. And the mission of Wildlands CPR is for humans to give second chances to the land itself, to create the conditions that will allow the edges to knit themselves back together again.

Perhaps roads are by now such a given of our experience that we can no more appraise them than fish can water. But try this thought-experiment: Imagine not just forests without roads, but a whole earth without roads (which I will not refer to as "arteries" of transportation because that connotes a vital, organic means of circulation). A world without roads, mind you, but not without traces, tracks, pathways, trails, and waterways. At those scales we're down to capillary gauge and the circulatory analogy begins to fit. These more delicate and dignified routes of human travel are permeable to the body of the earth and suitable to its unhurrying time. The wayfarer is enveloped by the world she moves through—both taxed and feasted.

Freed from roads, life loathes straight lines, moves to efface them. Enshrined and revered in the Basilica of All Beings is the Primordial Pavement-Prying Pickax, a symbol of the work that returned the world to flourishing. The trees grow back and overshadow the weeds. The odds are evened up between humans and the animals. Martian astronomers speculate wildly about the inexorable disappearance of earth's "canals" and its spreading mantle of green. Snowshoeing along a trail through a beech-maple forest, the wayfarer offers prayers of gratitude to ancestors who, with words, incantations, and vigils slew the metal-hearted monsters, and who with seedlings and hoedads did away with their spoor.

Roads and More Roads in the National Parks and National Forests

Rosalie Edge (March 1936)

INTRODUCTION

B uild a road!" Apparently this is the first idea that occurs to those who formulate projects for the unemployed. In consequence, a superfluity of four-width boulevards, with the verdure cut back for many feet on either side, goes slashing into our countrysides, without regard for the destruction of vegetation, and, too often without consideration of whether the road is needed at all. The motoring public always travels by the new road, and those who dwell along such highways, and have chosen their homes from a preference for seclusion, find themselves parked beside arteries of ceaseless traffic. No provision is made for pedestrians, and a man takes his life in his hands if he ventures on foot to call on his next-door neighbor. The city dweller is forced to go far afield if he is to see aught besides asphalt, or to breathe air not polluted with carbon monoxide gas.

The work of relief employment is not based primarily, as it should be, on the usefulness and desirability of a project; such aims are (of necessity it would seem) too often subordinated to the imperative need to put to work immediately thousands of men registered for relief through one agency or another. Vast sums are appropriated for work relief, and to use this money justly and usefully is a problem indeed. As a nation, we have adjusted our ethics to the porkbarrel; and each state, each county, city, and village, loudly and insistently demands a share of the spoils.

A project which is useful, or only mildly harmful, in one county is too often repeated merely to allay jealousy in another county, where the same project may be positively detrimental. Mosquito control may be quoted as one example. The dwellers in the thickly populated suburban districts of Long Island demand that mosquitoes be controlled on the surrounding great areas of salt marsh. Thousands of dollars are appropriated for this work, and armies of [Civilian Conservation Corps] CCC men begin to dig ditches in every direction. Then, as soon as it becomes known that Long Island townships have much money to spend on mosquito control, an outcry arises from upland communities, insisting that their mosquitoes also be destroyed. The situation in the uplands is entirely different from that of the seaside; in one the marshes are salt and in the other they are fresh. The various species of mosquitoes are not the same. While the mosquitoes of the salt marsh easily fly twenty-five miles, or more, the fresh marsh mosquito does not travel more than a mile away from its breeding place. What do county officials or project makers care for such elementary facts? Freshwater marshes, miles distant from any town, are drained without regard to their importance as breeding places of valuable birds and furbearers. Thus, in order to grasp at the money, which they see passed so easily from hand to hand, do the upland communities destroy sources of recreation and profit on which they might rely year by year.

So it is with roads. Through the medium of road-building, money may be buttered evenly over the whole country. There is a fixed idea in the American mind, inherited from a pioneer ancestry which suffered from having no roads at all, that any additional road must be good and that one cannot have too much of a good thing. Consequently, there have already been built with federal funds more roads than can possibly be kept in repair by state and local communities—roads parallel, roads crisscross, roads elevated, roads depressed, roads circular, and roads in the shape of four-leaf clovers; a madness of roads, too many of which will be left untended to fall into disrepair and disrepute.

ROADS IN THE NATIONAL PARKS

Turning to government-owned lands, we find that work relief has entered our National Parks and Forests in force. Each one of these has its CCC camps; and road-building is again the chief employment of the hundreds of men thus introduced into the wilderness. Can anyone suppose that a wilderness and a CCC camp can exist side by side? And can a wilderness contain a highway?

It is conceded that the National Parks must have roads. The Parks are recreational and educational centers for all the people, and admirably do they fulfill these functions. On the other hand, no one who knows the National Parks is so naive as to believe them to be wilderness areas. They have within their borders great hotels and acres of well-equipped camps. The crowds that visit them are splendidly handled; but the management of thousands of visitors makes it necessary to have offices and living quarters for a large personnel, besides stores, parking houses, docks, corrals, and garages; all of which encroach upon the wilderness. Virgin timber has been felled to build hotels, and valuable trees are cut each year for firewood. In the past, grazing has injured both the forests and meadows, and logging operations have been extensive within the Park boundaries. Some primitive areas, however, still exist in almost all the Parks. These should be guarded as the nation's greatest treasure; and no roads should be permitted to deface their beauty.

The Park Service is eager to prevent repetition of the vandalism that has ruined Park areas in the past, but great pressure is brought to bear by commercial interests that press to have new areas opened in order to obtain new concessions. In addition, there is thrust upon the Park Superintendents the necessity to employ CCC men, whether or not their services are needed, and the wilderness goes down before these conquerors. The support of the public at large must be added to the efforts of the Park Service in order to save the most beautiful of the wild places. The situation is well told in an editorial from Glacial Drift, the organ of Glacier National Park, as follows:

> Let those who clamor for the opening of the last primitive valleys of the park . . . remember that the charm of many places rests in their solitude and inaccessibility. Let those who consider accessibility and ease alone, weigh carefully which gives more enduring recollection, the dash over Logan Pass or the horseback or foot trip over Indian Pass, and learn that one appreciates in more lasting measure those things which one must gain through the expenditure of effort. Let those who urge more roads bear in mind that the marring of countryside does not end with the construction of a broad, two-lane, highway, absolutely safe when driven at a sane speed commensurate with the full enjoyment of a National Park, but that even the gentlest curves must be eliminated, the width ever increased, each

reopening a wound to leave a more gaping scar; with no more turns with delightful surprises beyond, for there are to be no turns; only greater speed and safety, though we may well note the irony of the latter in mountainous regions where improvement always has resulted in more fatalities. Let us recall the hundreds who dash daily over Logan Pass, without so much as a stop, or the great number who, like the camper from the Atlantic seaboard, boasted he had just been in three National Parks on that day and would be in Mt. Rainier on the morrow!

In the Parks we find hotels and other buildings in a style according, as much as possible, with the surroundings—how shocked we should be to find a skyscraper in a National Park! We need to develop roads that shall be suited to Park purposes and not to bring into their solitudes the great boulevards that are appropriate only where the population is densely crowded. Engineers are not trained in esthetic values; and when producing a triumph of their profession they give small heed to the beauty of the flora, or the interest of the other features of the landscape on which they lay their heavy hands. In the Yellowstone Park a road was last summer, quite needlessly, carried over a thermal spring. What is one less hot spring to a road engineer? The Yellowstone Park has many hot springs—but now it has one less. A road, suitable for the transport of great loads, is not needed in the Parks; but around the campfires any evening one may hear the boast: "We drove all the way up without changing gear," or "We never dropped below forty." Our Parks should not be desecrated for the whims of such drivers; obstacles might well be put in the way of fast driving in order to induce the tourists to contemplate the wonders of the forests and mountains spread out before them. Why cut away the crest of each rise, leaving ugly cuts with sides so steep that they cannot support plant life? A continuous easy grade is not essential for driving which is almost entirely recreational, and much primitive beauty is lost through exalting every valley and bringing every mountain low. Even the wilderness not traversed by roads is not safe from the despoiler. High up on Ptarmigan Pass in Glacier Park we met a tractor widening a so-called trail to the width of a wagon road, and watched the CCC men stoop and pick out small stones with their hands. They were making a Rotten Row of a trail across what is still happily a great wilderness of virgin forest.

Last summer we stood at the top of Logan Pass and watched the cars come sweeping to the summit. They might pause for five minutes in the great parking place, decorated with landscaped beds of shrubs bordered with stone copings, which belittle what was once one of the most glorious points of the Rocky Mountains. Many people did not leave their cars, others stepped down for a few minutes to look, and to wonder that such height could be reached without a heated engine. A ranger invited and even pleaded with the sightseers to go with him on a short walk to see the secluded wonder of Hidden Lake. "You can have no idea standing here," he said, "what a wonderful thing it is to go there . . . a very little way." While he spoke, his voice was drowned in the whirr of the self-starters. The little group of nature-lovers who followed him discovered the loveliness of the lake, and saw besides Rosy Finches and White-tailed Ptarmigan. They did not miss the company of the motorists who were by that time far in the valley below, rushing on in their enjoyment of perpetual motion.

For roads more appropriate to the National Parks, we offer two suggestions which we believe to be practical:

1. *One-way roads.* One-way roads could be narrow and so more easily follow the grade and contour of the land. Roads, roughly paralleled, leading in opposite directions, might be separated by a strip of woodland, as has been done in some of the parkways around great cities, preserving the illusion of wilderness and reducing the great scars that wide roads make on mountainsides. The cost might be increased but the project would have the advantage of providing work for an additional number of men. With no danger from cars coming in the opposite direction, it would not be necessary for a driver to see so far ahead as on a two-way road, and trees and shrubs could be permitted to grow close on either side. At convenient intervals the road should be widened so that a car may draw aside and stop to permit the occupants to enjoy the distant view or the nearby beauty. It is often argued that roads in the National Parks are needed for the aged and for those unable to take the horse and foot trails—but is it, indeed, fair to these people to be forced to drive along roads so wide that the flowers and shrubs and even the trees are too far distant to the right and left to be enjoyed, and which are lined on both sides with further bare spaces? What chance has anyone to identify a bird? May not a car sometimes

be permitted to saunter, to linger, and even to pause? We believe one-way roads would increase enjoyment, and ensure greater safety.

2. *Preventive landscaping.* We recommend that the landscape garden-ers, who do what they can to patch and cover up the wounds made by the engineers, precede, as well as follow, the road-builders. The groundcover might often be put aside, and replaced after the road is completed, or used elsewhere. Last September we traversed the road that crosses the Great Smoky Mountains from Cherokee, North Car-olina, to Gatlinburg, Tennessee. Two years ago this was a fine road, and adequately graded for all recreational purposes. Now, further smoothed out and straightened by CCC labor, the raw, steeply cut sides are artificial and ugly to a degree. The summit, like that of Logan Pass, is laid out in the manner of suburbs and cemeteries. This cicatrice across the heart of the loveliest of forests is a sin against Nature. The CCC men were heaping and burning fifteen- and twenty-foot-high rhododendrons, which had been roughly uprooted, with no regard to their value. The ground cover of small, woodsy wild things had been dug under. In some places landscaping had veiled the raw earth but with man-made art. We hope that this amelioration of unsightliness may be continued, but no art can replace Nature's treas-ures; these must be saved before they are ground beneath the road-makers' ruthless heel. Such destruction of native grasses, plants, and shrubs along our roads may be observed in every state.

ROADS IN THE NATIONAL FORESTS

The Forest Service has fallen prey to two commercial groups, the lum-bermen and the stockmen. Its policy is controlled by these two inter-ests, each of which maintains a powerful lobby in Washington. By the skillful use of misleading terms, the nation is kept in ignorance of the shameful exploitation of the National Forests. The whole problem of management of the Forests, of which the construction of roads is only a part, is obscured by undue accent on the fact that, while the Parks are for recreation, the Forests are for "use." But the Forest Service reserves to itself the interpretation of the word *use*, and narrows the usefulness of the Forests to the cutting of timber and the grazing of cattle, forgetting, or willfully subordinating, other uses of greater importance that are also the function of the National Forests.

. . . There is no justification for cutting wonderful tracts of virgin forests, the last of their kind, for such "use" as lumber, box shocks, or pulpwood. The few remaining stands of Sequoias, and stands of Douglas Fir, Sitka Spruce, Incense Cedar, and Sugar Pine, in which the trees reach 200, or even 300 feet in height, are wonders of creation which, living, have an esthetic and educational importance far transcending their commercial value. May we not make outdoor museums of the last remaining treasures of our once magnificent forests, as we put in museums, without apology, rare and beautiful examples of useful man-made articles? But, day by day, roads are advancing further into valleys which should be sacred to the nation as the galleries that hold its most valued art treasures. The lumberman walks softly behind the road-maker, computing the profit to be gained from trees which were already old when Columbus discovered America, and which cannot be replaced in a thousand years.

CCC camps are established in hundreds of the National Forests and the Forests are being honeycombed with roads. Roads in the Forests, if not surfaced with asphalt, are called "truck trails." The word *trail* presents to the mind a picture of a narrow woodland path wending its way beneath the trees. Actually, the so-called trail is a graded swath, usually following a stream up a narrow valley, over which may be transported machinery to cut huge trees, well described as "forest giants." When the railway is reached, one section of such a tree makes a load for a flatcar. Surely *trail* is a misnomer for a road wide enough for the motor truck, or the teams of many horses, that are necessary to draw it from the depth of the forest to the highway. . . .

. . . There would be no profit to the lumberman if the roads were not built at the expense of the nation. Until the public restrains the Forest Service from giving to a small group the forests that belong to all, every taxpayer contributes to the profit of the lumberman. The truck trails now being built, rapidly and secretly, up every exquisite valley in the Olympic National Forest in Washington testify to the unholy alliance between the timber interests and the Forest Service.

The roads that are eating into the heart of valleys are often wrongly declared to be for "fire protection." The only real fire protection is eternal vigilance, maintained from fire towers and other points of vantage, and from airplanes. Roads are, in themselves, the greatest of fire hazards, for man follows roads, and fire follows man. Tinder, leaves, and deadwood dry out along the roads, and the moist groundcover of moss and small plants dies, and dries back from the open spaces that have admitted the sun and wind. Time is the important element in fighting a fire. Firefighters from concentration camps, who come with cumbersome equipment long distances by roads, often do not reach a fire as quickly, nor extinguish it as quickly, as can fewer men, stationed at short intervals, with the simple tools that they can carry along a good but narrow trail. . . .

. . . Above all, the Forests should be preserved for the recreation of those whose need impels them to withdraw from time to time from conventional life. A mechanized world has crowded its citizens into densely populated cities. The tempo of life is speeded beyond man's capacity for endurance. The vital energy of man, whether of his body, his intellect, or his emotions, is consumed in his unceasing activity, and too close contact with the activity of others. When creative force is exhausted, some mode of recreation must be found. Recreation is a first necessity for the cure of maladjustments resulting from overstimulation. Some seek relief through a change in occupation, others in idleness; those who have few resources in themselves find diversion in crowds, others peace in solitude. The Psalmist said, "I will lift up mine eyes unto the hills from whence cometh my help," and we are sure that the hills of his vision were forested! Julian Huxley says, "There are many people to whom the sight of wild animals, living in untouched surroundings, is *profoundly stirring*, and indeed one of the most valuable things of life." When the meaning of the peace and solitude of the forests, the meaning of the beauty and sane-living of wild creatures, comes to be better understood, the National Forests may yet offer a higher service to the people.

To all such benefits roads are inimical. A minimum of roads may be permitted in the National Forests for the use of travelers, for the taking of timber rightfully cut, and for honest-to-God fire protection. Only trails belong to the deep forests; a road into a wild region is the prelude to its destruction, its forests, its scenery, and its wildlife. An increase of roads in the National Forests spells the doom of the last of the great timber.

In New York, a little wilderness is left in the Adirondacks. From this rises Whiteface, once a challenge to the hardy, offering a reward of wild loveliness to him who should climb its summit. Now a wide motor road binds Whiteface as with a rope, and holds it enslaved to anyone who has an hour in which to drive to its summit. When, in the autumn of 1935, Governor Lehman opened this road, headlines in the newspapers hailed the occasion as one of conservation. Conservation of what? We do not know—certainly not conservation of the forest primeval. A bill is now before the New York State legislature authorizing an elevator and shaft from the end of the highway to the peak of the mountain. This bill provides for a shelter house for the use of the public, for another house at which food and refreshments may be sold, and for devices (a merry-go-'round perhaps?) for the entertainment of visitors.

In Maine a highway now reaches to the foot of Katahdin, and the freedom of that mountain is threatened. A skyline road has brought low the pride of the Blue Ridge in Shenandoah Park, and another skyline is carving deep along the summit of the Great Smokies. Roads and more roads are dividing, shrinking, and destroying the remnants of the wilderness.

Little Vermont has set an example to the nation. She was tempted with millions of relief employment money to build a skyline drive along the crest of her Green Mountains. She refused to sell their beauty, and is preserving them inviolate. May we not hope that this example of courage, wisdom, and sound Yankee common sense will be followed by other states, and by the federal departments that act for us as custodians of the National Parks and National Forests?

Momentum

Tom Lyon

I 've been thinking a lot about why road construction is innocent until proven guilty—why we on the minority side have to struggle so hard even to get a hearing. We never got one on the Final Environmental Impact Statement that the Utah Department of Transportation prepared for Logan Canyon, Utah. It was an unbelievably bad document, full of false assumptions and misused or faulty statistics. It sailed through, as such things do. Then the Forest Service dismissed our 187-page appeal with a page-and-a-half bureaucratic slap, the back of the hand. But why? Why is it so easy for them and so hard for us? Why do the "Indians" always lose?

I remember sitting at the big table with Utah Department of Transportation and Forest Service representatives in the early days of the Logan Canyon controversy. UDOT, the Forest Service, and the federal highway people had convened an "interdisciplinary team" that included a few environmentalists. We would all present our different views and arrive at a consensus. But no such thing happened. We could not see why a faster, straighter road should be built, and they could not see why we preferred a winding, slower one. It was as if the two sides spoke absolutely unrelated languages. The momentum, however, was theirs, and after a number of meetings they dissolved the ID team, sent us letters of thanks, and went ahead with the project the way they wanted it.

You can see the same onrushing impetus operating in other parts of our strange life. A woman in Iowa gives birth to seven babies, to general approval. (Hardly anyone sees population growth as the real, hurtful thing it is.) The economy grows daily, to general approval (what gloomy faces we will see if it should ever *not* grow). NAFTA goes through; GATT goes through. Full steam ahead. You and I get a raise and we not only don't refuse it, we think it could have been more. We know better, rationally; we know this can't go on. What if everybody in the world lived like this? But we take the money. We go ahead and drive the car, wondering what all these other people are doing on the road, why the traffic is so dense. Shouldn't they be at work or in school or something? We're streaming down the highway, part of the momentum.

What we don't often see is that momentum makes us stupid. It shuts off awareness of the real, related, interdependent world. Keeps us within our metallic shells. Keeps us going straight and fast on the road we have built. This is truly a massive mental and spiritual disorder. We straighten, simplify, and speed up—the classic linear mentality, the classic mistake. This is what the Logan Canyon project is: an accurate expression of who we think we are and what we think the world is. What makes our situation so difficult now is that we haven't just made a technical mistake, we have become identified with our construction. The straight, fast road and the salary increase, etc., become crucial to our always accumulating identity. We are dedicated to safeguarding and expanding this identity above all, and our tight allegiance keeps us from seeing, from knowing in any deep way, what we're doing. The new, fast, straight road in Logan Canyon is like such roads anywhere, a symptom of our not seeing the world.

Speaking from the state of identity, we call our impacts "side effects," a revealing phrase. In Logan Canyon, there will be "side effects" on Logan River, on Beaver Creek, on trees, birds, flowers, snails, snakes, worms, deer, elk, and on and on. In reality, these are not "side" beings, however; the world doesn't work in parts. What a strong and sad disease it is that we don't see this.

It's fortunate that along with the ego-mind, the identity-builder, evolution provided a capacity for wider, relational awareness. This is where we touch the world of source, where we see the tree in its own right, feel its bark, feel into the life that stands there flowing upward and downward, feel compassion for it. This is where we don't just leave the tree alone, we honor it as a fellow vessel of sacred life. In relational awareness, we get a bit of perspective on this fierce little identity thing. We see the goodness of a winding, slow road and the greater beauty of a roadless canyon. We don't feel in such a hurry. We have stepped aside from the clanking, whirring machinery for a time. This kind of seeing doesn't translate well into bottom-line language— it doesn't carry across the big table very well. But when we are alive this way, aren't we more likely to do the right thing?

Not for Me

Mary Sojourner

I am in the throat of the Turtle Mountain Wilderness, crouched at the base of a basalt cliff, studying a delicate braid of tracks in the sand at the bottom of the narrow wash below me.

I will never make it into the heart of the Turtles. I am fifty-eight, a big woman, and one of my spinal discs is flatter than it should be—too many switchbacks and midnight city concrete, too many rapids run, too much, and never enough, boulder-hopping.

The truck is parked where the roads end. If I stand up, I'll see the windshield catching last Mohave light. Lace agate glitters and glows on the pale earth, white chalcedony roses, puddles of mineral cream. To the east, just beyond a portal that opens like a deep breath in the black rock, lies the unisex bathroom of a gang of coyotes. At the edge of a tidy deposit of scat is one scarlet flower, its blossoms like bells, bells holding light. I imagine how the flower seems to burn, as I imagine what lies west, in a streambed through which water must pour—I see the pebble curves that tell me eddies have swirled here—twice a year, once, seen only by what lives here. I would love to see that, flash floods no wider than my arm, thunder chaos of brittlebush, chalcedony, and scat.

And I am grateful to see what lies around me. Now. Here. A mile from the truck, a mile that took me an hour to cross, down into little arroyos, picking my way between fire-rock boulders, stopping to pick up a shard of crystal, an agate rose. I knew better than to bend over and I did it anyway. I'll pay for it later with fire in my back. How could I not touch this lover, this fierce Mohave earth softened by winter light? How could I not, as I once lay in the perfect arms of the per-

24

fect lover who perfectly would leave, breathe in the miracle of being here, being here, only now.

The Buddhists tell us joy lies in limitation. We Americans are taught the opposite. You deserve it all. More is better. Go for it all. I move away from the cliff and look up at the ragged cobalt mountains. I want to go up, into the high saddle, into what leads into mystery, up where I can look out and see forever. I want more. I want it all.

I cannot have it. My back holds me here. Some roads are closed to me forever. I consider that I have become the person the road-greedy claim to fight for. But what about the handicapped? What about the elderly?

On my slow way to this cliff, this wash, where light seems to catch on every facet of twig and stone, and shadows pour like blue lava, I walked across roads that went back to earth beneath my boots. Closed. Closed. I touched the signs. I whispered, "Thank you."

I leave nothing at the base of the cliff except gratitude, and make my careful way back to the truck. My friend, my road-buddy who loves road and roadless equally, emerges from the shadows. He is grinning. I look at his face and know I look in a mirror.

"How was it?" he asks.

"Very very good."

"Yeah."

We walk in silence. Later he will tell me how he traversed rock he might more prudently have avoided, and how that led him, heart in his throat, to a hidden arch in a saddle and the sight of the southern Mohave rolling in waves of mountains and desert, sunset and blue mist, to the far curve of the earth. I will tell him about coyote housekeeping and bells of light and how enough is enough, and never enough. But, for now, our silence is sweet earth without roads.

We camp in an abandoned mining claim. There is the requisite rusting bedspring, coils of wire, shattered Colt 45 bottles glittering like fool's agate. My friend cooks, linguine with garlic and capers. I spread out my sleeping bag and stretch. My back throbs. Fire shoots down one leg.

"Trying to sleep is going to be lovely," I say.

He laughs. "Would you have it any other way?"

I turn on my back, pull my legs up to my chest. Nothing releases. I look up into moonless sky, Orion striding eternally young and strong, across the eastern sky.

"You mean?" I ask.

"Doing it the easy way. I don't know, maybe driving up to the arch."

I twist left, right. Slowly. I keep my eyes open. I look. The mountaintops I will never see up close lie like *sumi* brushstrokes against the stars. I don't answer my friend. I don't have to. The way into the answer is perfectly clear.

Roadbed

Janisse Ray

People wonder why I'd make such a fuss about a road. It's only a couple miles of Georgia dirt, after all, and bad dirt at that. The clay gets slick as pig grease in wet weather. In dry, the road's so worn and dusty that after a car passes, some of the road rises like a congregation of drifters and wanders over to the house where I live. The house most people would bulldoze and hire a contractor to rebuild: it's full of holes. Haggard molecules of road dust crawl into the house through its cracks and holes.

I'm always dusting the road off the tables and shelves, and blowing it off rows of books and off the seashells and fossils and turtle backs we collect as if we run a museum instead of a farm. Still it gathers in little dust ponds, and I blow and sweep and haul the road back out where it belongs. I am constantly shooing it out of the house, old dirty nuisance.

And the way the road grips and shakes the GMC when I drive the half mile to the highway is enough to alienate a person. The truck is thirty-three years old and the old road is hard on it. Flakes of rust shake loose until they rain down and pepper the cab. Entire chunks of the truck are missing, and I know where they are. A rust-hound could find me anywhere.

That damn road is like a sad vagrant, the way it follows me wherever I go and insinuates itself in my life. It drifts all over my things, and settles everywhere.

When a scrubbed man wearing slacks and a pressed collared shirt that looked bought in some Atlanta department store twenty years prior showed up at the farm, waving a piece of paper in his hand like a little white truce flag, I could have offered him a cool glass of water. I could have apologized for not having a pitcher of sweet tea chilling in the Frigidaire (disrespecting the memory of all my mothers and grandmothers). At least I could have flung wide the screen door squealing on its dusty hinges and listened to what the man had to say.

But the man hadn't come to see me. I didn't own a foot of the land that interested him, along the road—not even an inch—and my signature on his paper was as worthless as a ticket to last week's movie. No, he needed my Uncle Percy, heir to everything closest to my grandmother's heart. So the man pulled up under the old rotting water oak in the front yard, the one that dangled its dangerous weak limbs over Uncle Percy's double-wide trailer, regularly and suddenly dropping them on the flat metal sheeting of Uncle Percy's roof, or into the dirt beneath where no grass would grow, where the oak's spoon-shaped leaves composted year after year against the metal skirting. The old tree had almost lived out its lifespan, same as Uncle Percy. I could not bear to think about him cutting it, because water oaks will cry themselves to death if you cut them. They weep and weep. You have to talk to them beforehand, someone told me, and make them understand what's happening so you don't have to watch them crying for days as they die.

Uncle Percy's mother was my grandmother. I would come to occupy Grandmama's house, which can hardly be described without the adjective *old*. The day the well-dressed man showed up, Uncle Percy was sitting on the steps of his mobile home. I would watch the man get out and stand under that guileless water oak's upraised and weakening limbs, holding the paper smooth and protected from the wind. I should have warned the man. I saw everything from my front porch, behind the azaleas that had grown taller than my head, taller than Grandmama would have permitted. Or should the man have warned me?

I never learned everything there was to know about my grandmother, Beulah, although she wasn't complicated. But I don't think she would ever have signed that paper.

We have roads because we need to move. Day-to-day movement is necessary for all foraging organisms. Unlike clams or oysters, humans don't live in flowing water that will bring nutrients to us. Nor do many thousands of species. Even plants move their roots in a search for water, and their leaves in a search for light. In fact, a species' ability to move in large degree determines the fitness of that species to survive. Animals move in order to forage for food and other nutrients, find water or shelter, or use seasonal environments (elk move down out of the mountains in the winter, for example). Sometimes animals move to accommodate life stages, as the flatwoods salamander migrates to lowlands for breeding, and some species migrate to birthplaces. On a grander scale, species move to expand ranges, colonize new environments, and to adjust to climate disruption.

For humans, roads make movement easier.

The man, who had just arrived by the road, would have greeted Uncle Percy as if he'd known him all his life. Because he had. They had been raised together as boys, closest neighbors; had attended the same country school and the same Baptist church; had been made to chop cotton, dip turpentine, and slop hogs. Except Uncle Percy graduated at sixteen and joined the air force, and the neighbor boy grew up and married and moved off and worked for some corporation up in Atlanta, where he raised his children. When he retired, he and his wife came back to the little community in south Georgia where they'd been raised, and they fixed up the old house. They insulated it and bricked it until you'd never know what it had been, where they'd come from. In general, they made it exceedingly livable, and they drove a Cadillac, and they did all the country things that people miss when they go away and give the best years of their lives to the city.

In a way it was the Cadillac that caused all the trouble.

Uncle Percy had come home after the air force and had not left. He worked parts counter at the auto parts store in town and then worked night shift for more than thirty years at Amoco, a factory eighteen miles west in Hazlehurst that manufactured the plastic fabric used in upholstery. Uncle Percy was never disagreeable. He attempted at all personal cost to keep the peace, to fit in, to do his job and not create a ruckus, to do what was expected of him and what he was told to do, and to be well liked. Every Sunday morning he was teaching Sunday school, and then church service, as if he waited all week for the opportunity to return to the same seat in the same pew in the same church he had sat in all his life.

The neighbor decided to run for county commissioner, now that he had come back to his backwards little county with ideas about progress, and he was elected.

Now he had papers but they weren't church papers, nor was the man trying to get elected. Whatever it was, of course Uncle Percy would sign.

Maybe I too would have signed, had I driven a like-new Cadillac and been afraid that the corrugation of the road would loosen wires and bolts and rip welds apart. Had I worried about dust in my computer system, maybe I would have uncapped the pen lickety-split, before anybody could say "Jack Rabbit."

In the early 1800s, Wilson Baxley migrated to Appling County, Georgia, from North Carolina. The indigenous people, the Creeks, had been stripped of their landholdings in the coastal plains of Georgia, and had been herded south to Florida and west to Oklahoma. White settlers began to move in. They created roads along old trading routes and between settlements. The northern part of Appling County, Georgia, which is named Spring Branch Community, was settled in the mid-1800s by the Baxleys, the Branches, the Carters, and the Moodys. My people.

At first Hilton Baxley Road was a two-path road, wide enough for a team of oxen. Then it was wide enough for a car. Then two cars. Then a tractor and a car. Or a school bus and a car.

When my mother was raised on the family farm, starting in 1939, she walked on Hilton Baxley Road to school, to church, and to Little Ten Mile Creek, where her brothers swam. When I was a girl in the late 1960s, the bridge down the lane from Grandmama's farmhouse was still wooden, and without guardrails, a rattling affair of loose beams and boards through which the meandering brook could be seen.

As a girl I spent most Saturdays at my grandmother's house. Gnarled and sapsucker-pocked crabapple trees grew out by the road, from which we gathered sharply sweet pomes. Few cars passed. After the letter carrier arrived, and left, I could retrieve the mail. Sometimes Uncle Bill drove his cows along the road, from one pasture to another, and sometimes a cow and her heifer got out of a downed fence, and unable to reenter, came bawling along the road. I walked from my grandmother's house to the creek many a hot summer day.

As an adult, I came to despise roads. They meant fragmentation of the native landscapes I loved, death to the fauna. They meant mortality to our already numbered black bears and panthers and indigo snakes. In our national forests, roads were bulldozed into beautiful forests, and next the forests were destroyed. Salamanders trying to cross roads on rainy nights, migrating to ponds to breed, were smashed.

We seemed to have gone crazy for roads. In the twenty years of my adult life, I have seen roads forced through salt marshes, through neighborhoods, through forests, through coastlines, through prairie and scrub. I've seen roads made into highways, and highways into superhighways.

How can I hate roads? They are the way we pass through this world, the way we visit each other, the way we connect places. They are the formula by which my beloved comes home to me, the opportunity that takes my son away. They are romantic boulevards to other lives, other possibilities. They are the way we enter the world of humans.

In the natural history of roads, human passage evolved from path to trail to trace to way to lane to road, but at some point the meaning of the word road changed. As long as humans perambulated, we had no need for a thoroughfare wider than our swinging arms. As long as we rode horses, we had no need for roads wider than a team, and sometimes a lane for wagons to pass. Roads connected people to one another, threads through wilderness. Then, road was a verb meaning "to join." Now it connotes "divide." In our past hundred years of life in this country, since the Model T was created in 1908 following invention of the automobile in Europe, our roads ever widened until they became great swaths piercing landscapes. The widest road I have ever seen was in Los Angeles, about twenty-four lanes, each wide enough for a tractor trailer, twelve going one way and twelve the other. Dividing everybody from everybody. Each person in his or her own car, divided.

The United States contains almost four million miles of roads. Added together, these roads and roadsides make up more than 1 percent of the country, an area equal to the combined area of all our national parks. But the area affected by the noise, pollution, animal deaths, and other ecological impacts linked to roads is much larger: 22 percent by one estimate.

New highways everywhere (check out Mississippi) are unnecessarily destructive of life. On the worst-built roads, two directions of traffic are separated by a wide, ecological dead zone of median, devoid of trees in case of accident; and the shoulders are at least a hundred feet wide, planted with high-maintenance grass. The roadways cut a swath seemingly one-eighth of a mile wide through the countryside.

What I love is movement on the smallest of scales. I love footpaths and trails and little boats on rivers.

When I moved into my grandmother's farmhouse, however, I fell in love with the beautiful red road that ran alongside my home, despite the extra housework it caused me and the extra hassles when it wasn't in such good condition. Daily I watched the road and what traveled upon it. Lanita walked in the evenings, the Morris boy whizzed by on his four-wheeler, a cottonmouth made a sandy wiggle, a raccoon left paw prints in the ditch-dirt.

Appling is a poor county and doesn't have a lot of money to pave every road within its borders. But if you get elected county commissioner, you get to name one road you'd like paved, and that road doesn't have to be the worst road there is. It doesn't have to be washed out or corrugated or closed because of a faulty bridge, and it doesn't have to be well populated. You can live on a pretty good road with only four or five other houses on it, and if you're county commissioner, you get to butter your own bread.

And if you talk nice enough, everybody will sign the papers you need signed. Except my mother. She wouldn't sign. She had come to own the house along the road where I lived, and although my uncle Percy signed, my mother wouldn't. Like me, she didn't want the road paved. So we wrote letters to the neighbors and to the editor of the paper that said, "A paved road is not progress." We took the case to court and my shy, angelic mother had to stand in front of a brusque judge and tell him why she opposed the road-paving. The county left a check for us at the probate judge's office, thinking we wanted money for our little strip of land, but we let the check lie. We didn't want money. We wanted to preserve the old-growth longleaf pines lining the road, and the rural character of the farm, and the peace and sanctity of the countryside. I couldn't imagine covering that wonderful old dusty omnipotent dirt—my great-grandparents had walked on it, do you understand that?—with asphalt. "When I turn off the highway, coming home, I hope it always will be onto a cool, tree-shaded, clean road made of Georgia clay and sand," I wrote. We met with the road department and saved the old-growth longleafs.

I have become increasingly bitter about the ignorance of the federal Department of Transportation, state road departments, and county road supervisors. I am convinced that a road-building lobby as organized and destructive as the development lobby is driving the manic road-building going on in our nation. Most roads are wasteful. Most are unnecessary. Dare me to say it: all are contrary to environmental ethics, and all are enemies of wild America.

The judge arbitrated for pavement.

Let me tell you some things about roads you might not have known. The road itself takes away wildlife habitat. In 1979 a scientist named C. R. Ferris

determined that in Maine each kilometer (.62 mile) of I-95 built displaced
130 pairs of breeding birds, which translated into 62,400 pairs of breeding
birds along the almost 300 miles (480 kilometers) of I-95 in the state. For a
roadway that is 33 yards wide, each kilometer of length deletes 750 acres of
active or potential wildlife habitat.

Loss of land is passive fragmentation of wildness. The automobiles that
both cause and accompany roads are an active form of fragmentation.

- *In 1974 more than 146,000 deer were killed on U.S. highways.*
- *In a study that lasted four and a half years in the mid-1970s, 13,000*
  snakes were counted dead from highway collisions on a 2.9-mile section
  of U.S. Highway 441 that bisects Paynes Prairie, a state preserve in
  Florida. The reptiles, which totaled about 1.3 tons, were killed while
  crossing the road or while sunning on the pavement.
- *On a single day—February 22, 2000—ninety roadkilled turtles were*
  collected on a one-third-mile stretch of U.S. Highway 27 in Leon
  County, Florida, by biologist Matthew Aresco of Florida State Univer-
  sity. The road bisects Lake Jackson.
- *Seventy-five black bears were killed on Florida roads in 1997.*

One spring I left the Georgia farm and went off to Mississippi to
teach, and before we came home in June, Mama told me over the
telephone that work had begun on the road. She said it didn't look too
bad. We arrived after dark, understanding even before we turned off
the four-lane U.S. Highway 1 onto Hilton Baxley Road that perhaps
we would no longer recognize our territory, and that as beings loyal
to nascent locales, who peregrinate with maps and pictures of our biological homes within us, that for a time we would be profoundly confused and even lost—although we would use other sensibilities, like
rationality, to drive directly the half mile to the farmhouse, and know
it to be home.

Next morning by light of day, we examined the road. What had
been a narrow country dirt lane had been widened to a ninety-foot
strip. The trees along the shoulders of the road, unable to run away,
had been severed at their bases and stacked like old tin on the ground,
and their roots had been gouged from the earth, as if they had never
been. The underbrush had been scraped away and even the trees that
grew in the demilitarized zone had been denuded of limbs that grew
into the easement, sheared limb from body. Vegetative matter, bushes
and ferns and branches, had been pushed by heavy machinery into
gnarly flanks waiting to be burned.

There was no need to be so horrified. I was not looking at dead bodies. Vegetation, although living matter, has no nerves, or brains to register pain.

That first morning as I jogged along the road, I saw details of the destruction. How a young tulip poplar, not three feet high, had been pushed over by the dozer but had not died. How ferns, once ensconced in a woody glade, were green arrows skyward. How the branch of the creek had been obliterated—earth pushed into it, the run erased, so that water, dammed at the culvert, backed up and formed a soggy bottom. Stakes, flagged with hot-pink plastic ribbon, marked the edge of the right-of-way. And by golly, the dozer was making that easement clean, right to the line.

Later, when I faced the workers, I said I'd noticed the stream had been destroyed, and who had decided not to use silt-fences? and that I was calling the Army Corps of Engineers and Altamaha River-keeper. And I did.

We can shout and scream and beg and plead and pray out loud and until they kill us, or force lye down our throats, no one can take this right away. So. They can stuff their asphalt and concrete down my throat, but that leaves my hands free and I can write. They forgot to tie my hands. They forgot to secede from the democracy and make this a dictatorship. They forgot to anoint themselves kings and behand me, or behead me. Beyond that, I could only honor the dead. And the about-to-die. I could document.

That evening I prepared my canvas shoulder bag for action: notebook, pen, tape measure, camera. I clomped the half mile to the intersection of Hilton Baxley and U.S. 1, where the trees had been stacked lengthwise into orderly piles. I could at least say good-bye to the trees and officially mourn them.

First I tried to name the species. You wouldn't want to die in a battle somewhere and go unidentified, not honored. Where base height would have been, I measured diameters. A slash pine, 71 inches. Slash pine, 52 inches. Slash pine, 72 inches. Another, 49 inches. Water oak, 49 inches. 39 inches. Cedars. Pecans. Red maples, wild cherries. I measured dozens and dozens of trees, hugging them. Thus I made my way along the road, crazy with my grief. When I had progressed beyond the bulldozers, I measured standing trees trapped within the boundary of pink tape. Each I hugged, saying good-bye.

I wasn't scientific. I was crazed. My notes are the notes of a person grief-stricken and distraught, a person determined that the destruction of land for roads doesn't go unnoticed, unnamed, and unprotested.

The paving has not yet begun. Perhaps before the road crews arrive, one of these months, the price of gasoline will have skyrocketed, and our country will begin to come to terms with its obsession with fossil fuel and its mania to consume. We've known for a long time that fossil fuel supplies are finite. We've known not to get too dependent on them, nor to fall too deeply in love with shiny and fast Cadillacs. We've been told this: one day we'll pull up to the gas pump and nothing—not a drop—will come out. Now scientists are telling us that fossil fuels won't run out all at once, as we've imagined; they'll run out slowly. Global production of petroleum will peak—this event is called Peak Oil—and then fossil fuels will begin a long slide out of our lives and even later, out of our memories. After Peak Oil, petroleum will get harder to find, what is found will be less available to us Americans, and it will be of poorer quality. We will then have to restructure every aspect of capitalistic American life.

We know that oil production *will* peak—indeed may be peaking as I write this, if predictions are correct (around 2005)—because we saw U.S. oil production peak in 1970. Now, a few decades later, our country produces only a quarter of the oil it uses and imports the rest.

Paving the road by the farm is part of an American idea of progress that is quickly becoming outdated, losing its context and its potency. Paving makes possible more traffic, faster traffic, more comfortable traffic—hence requiring more fossil fuels. What do I need to say to my neighbor so that he sees the futility in this? What can I say that will ignite him to be thinking beyond petroleum?

Come in, my neighbor, my countryman. You have come walking the red road through moonlight to my door. Let's rinse the dust off the glasses and pour a noggin of moonshine, to toast our ancestors who also sat together almost in prophecy of this night, they who still walk the roadbed invisible in their suits. While we can, before we too join them walking there, let's talk.

Part Two: Where the Deer and the Antelope Can't Play

"*I carry each one away from the tarmac into a cover of grass or brush out of decency, I think. And worry. Who are these animals, their lights gone out? What journeys have fallen apart here?*"

—Barry Lopez, "Apologia"

In Part Two we travel from examining why we have roads in the first place to one of the more egregious examples of how roads, paved and otherwise, can result in ecological damage: roadkill. As the human population increases, so does the number of vehicles, with exploding numbers of roadkill the result. The Humane Society estimates that one million animals are killed on our roads every day.

But the last two essays of the section offer hope: fewer roads, and connected passages between wild landscapes, can allow freer movement for elk, deer and other wildlife; and fewer animals stilled by the roadside.

Apologia

Barry Lopez

A few miles east of home in the Cascades I slow down and pull over for two raccoons, sprawled still as stones in the road. I carry them to the side and lay them in sun-shot, windblown grass in the barrow ditch. In eastern Oregon, along U.S. 20, black-tailed jackrabbits lie like welts of sod—three, four, then a fifth. By the bridge over Jordan Creek, just shy of the Idaho border, in the drainage of the Owyhee River, a crumpled adolescent porcupine leers up almost maniacally over its blood-flecked teeth. I carry each one away from the tarmac into a cover of grass or brush out of decency, I think. And worry. Who are these animals, their lights gone out? What journeys have fallen apart here?

I do not stop to remove each dark blister from the road. I wince before the recently dead, feel my lips tighten, see something else, a fence post, in the spontaneous aversion of my eyes, and pull over. I imagine white silk threads of life still vibrating inside them, even if the body's husk is stretched out for yards, stuck like oiled muslin to the road. The energy that held them erect leaves like a bullet; but the memory of that energy fades slowly from the wrinkled cornea, the bloodless fur.

The raccoons and, later, a red fox carry like sacks of wet gravel and sand. Each animal is like a solitary child's shoe in the road.

Once a man asked, Why do you bother? You never know, I said. The ones you give some semblance of burial, to whom you offer an apology, may have been like seers in a parallel culture. It is an act of respect, a technique of awareness.

In Idaho I hit a young sage sparrow—*thwack* against the right fender in the very split second I see it. Its companion rises a foot higher from the same spot, slow as smoke, and sails off clean into the desert. I rest the walloped bird in my left hand, my right thumb pressed to its chest. I feel for the wail of the heart. Its eyes glisten like rain on crystal. Nothing but warmth. I shut the tiny eyelids and lay it beside a clump of bunchgrass. Beyond a barbed-wire fence the over-grazed range is littered with cow flops. The road curves away to the south. I nod before I go, a ridiculous gesture, out of simple grief.

I pass four spotted skunks. The swirling air is acrid with the rupture of each life.

· · · · ·

Darkness rises in the valleys of Idaho. East of Grand View, south of the Snake River, nighthawks swoop the road for gnats, silent on the wing as owls. On a descending curve I see two of them lying soft as clouds in the road. I turn around and come back. The sudden slowing down and my K-turn at the bottom of the hill draw the attention of a man who steps away from a tractor, a dozen yards from where the birds lie. I can tell by his step, the suspicious tilt of his head, that he is wary, vaguely proprietary. Offended, or irritated, he may throw the birds back into the road when I leave. So I wait, subdued like a peni-tent, a body in each hand.

He speaks first, a low voice, a deep murmur weighted with awe. He has been watching these flocks feeding just above the road for several evenings. He calls them whippoorwills. He gestures for a carcass. How odd, yes, the way they concentrate their hunting right on the road, I say. He runs a finger down the smooth arc of the belly and remarks on the small whiskered bill. He pulls one long wing out straight, but not roughly. He marvels. He glances at my car, baffled by this out-of-state courtesy. Two dozen nighthawks career past, back and forth at arm's length, feeding at our height and lower. He asks if I would mind—as though I owned it—if he took the bird up to the house to show his wife. "She's never seen anything like this." He's fas-cinated. "Not close."

I trust, later, he will put it in the fields, not throw the body in the trash, a whirligig.

· · · · ·

North of Pinedale in western Wyoming on U.S. 189, below the Gros Ventre Range, I see a big doe from a great distance, the low rays of first light gleaming in her tawny reddish hair. She rests askew, like a crushed tree. I drag her to the shoulder, then down a long slope by the petals of her ears. A gunnysack of plaster mud, ears cold as rain gutters. All of her doesn't come. I climb back up for the missing leg. The stain of her is darker than the black asphalt. The stains go north and off to the south as far as I can see.

On an afternoon trafficless, quiet as a cloister, headed across South Pass in the Wind River Range, I swerve violently but hit an animal, and then try to wrestle the gravel-spewing skid in a straight line along the lip of an embankment. I know even as I struggle for control the irony of this: I could pitch off here to my own death, easily. The bird is dead somewhere in the road behind me. Only a few seconds and I am safely back on the road, nauseated, light-headed.

It is hard to distinguish among younger gulls. I turn this one around slowly in my hands. It could be a western gull, a mew gull, a California gull. I do not remember well enough the bill markings, the color of the legs. I have no doubt about the vertebrae shattered beneath the seamless white of its ropy neck.

East of Lusk, Wyoming, in Nebraska, I stop for a badger. I squat on the macadam to admire the long claws, the perfect set of its teeth in the broken jaw, the ramulose shading of its fur—how it differs slightly, as does every badger's, from the drawings and pictures in the field guides. A car drifts toward us over the prairie, coming on in the other lane, a white 1962 Chevrolet station wagon. The driver slows to pass. In the bright sunlight I can't see his face, only an arm and the gesture of his thick left hand. It opens in a kind of shrug, hangs briefly in limp sadness, then extends itself in supplication. Gone past, it curls into itself against the car door and is still.

Farther on in western Nebraska I pick up the small bodies of mice and birds. While I wait to retrieve these creatures I do not meet the eyes of passing drivers. Whoever they are, I feel anger toward them, in spite of the sparrow and the gull I myself have killed. We treat the attrition of lives on the road like the attrition of lives in war: horrifying, unavoidable, justified. Accepting the slaughter leaves people momentarily fractious, embarrassed. South of Broken Bow, at dawn, I cannot avoid an immature barn swallow. It hangs by its head, motionless in the slats of the grill.

I stop for a rabbit on Nebraska 806 and find, only a few feet away, a garter snake. What else have I missed, too small, too narrow? What has gone under or past me while I stared at mountains, hay meadows, fencerows, the beryl surface of rivers? In Wyoming I could not help but see pronghorn antelope swollen big as barrels by the side of the road, their legs splayed rigidly aloft. For animals that large people will stop. But how many have this habit of clearing the road of smaller creatures, people who would remove the ones I miss? I do not imagine I am alone. As much sorrow as the man's hand conveyed in Nebraska, it meant gratitude too for burying the dead.

Still, I do not wish to meet anyone's eyes.

· · · · ·

In southwestern Iowa, outside Clarinda, I haul a deer into high grass out of sight of the road and begin to examine it. It is still whole, but the destruction is breathtaking. The skull, I soon discover, is fractured in four places; the jaw, hanging by shreds of mandibular muscle, is broken at the symphysis, beneath the incisors. The pelvis is crushed, the left hind leg unsocketed. All but two ribs are dislocated along the vertebral column, which is complexly fractured. The intestines have been driven forward into the chest. The heart and lungs have ruptured the chest wall at the base of the neck. The signature of a tractor-trailer truck: 80,000 pounds at 65 mph.

In front of a motel room in Ottumwa I finger-scrape the dry stiff carcasses of bumblebees, wasps, and butterflies from the grill and headlight mountings, and I scrub with a wet cloth to soften and wipe away the nap of crumbles, the insects, the aerial plankton of spiders and mites. I am uneasy carrying so many of the dead. The carnage is so obvious.

In Illinois, west of Kankakee, two raccoons as young as the ones in Oregon. In Indiana another raccoon, a gray squirrel. When I make the left turn into the driveway at the house of a friend outside South Bend, it is evening, hot and muggy. I can hear cicadas in a lone elm. I'm glad to be here.

From the driveway entrance I look back down Indiana 23, toward Indiana 8, remembering the farm roads of Illinois and Iowa. I remember how beautiful it was in the limpid air to drive Nebraska 2 through the Sand Hills, to see how far at dusk the land was etched east and west of Wyoming 28. I remember the imposition of the Wind River Range in a hard, blue sky beneath white ranks of buttonhook clouds, windy hay fields on the Snake River Plain, the welcome of Russian olive trees and willows in creek bottoms. The transformation of the heart such beauty engenders is not enough tonight to let me shed the heavier memory, a catalog too morbid to write out, too vivid to ignore.

I stand in the driveway now, listening to the cicadas whirring in the dark tree. My hands grip the sill of the open window at the driver's side, and I lean down as if to speak to someone still sitting there. The weight I wish to fall I cannot fathom, a sorrow over the world's dark hunger.

A light comes on over the porch. I hear a dead bolt thrown, the shiver of a door pulled free. The words of atonement I pronounce are too inept to offer me release. Or forgiveness. My friend is floating across the tree-shadowed lawn. What is to be done with the desire for exculpation?

"Later than we thought you'd be," he says.

I do not want the lavabo. I wish to make amends.

"I made more stops than I thought I would," I answer.

"Well, bring in your things. And I can take whatever," he offers.

I anticipate, in the powerful antidote of our conversation, the reassurance of a human enterprise, the forgiving embrace of the rational. It waits within, beyond the slow tail-wagging of two dogs standing at the screen door.

From a Wonderland Road

Carolyn Duckworth

Sunset seems to have turned to twilight over northeastern Yellowstone. Then the clouds move east enough for a deep golden light to slant over the peaks, illuminating Specimen Ridge in the mid-distance for five more minutes. I swing the spotting scope up and away from Antelope Creek toward the nearest slopes of the ridge. In this contrasty light, I sometimes can discern a grizzly or two. Once I had in view two bears traversing the slope when one veered downhill at a run, pulled up in sagebrush, and came up shaking the life out of what was probably an elk calf. From that distance and in that light, I could see the small form pale and limp in the bear's jaws. The grizzly lowered its load to the ground and began to feed; the other bear cruised up and joined in.

Tonight, no wildlife drama in sight, I sit back into the twilight, feeling the wind, hearing the faint rush of the creek hidden in the décolleté of the valley. And enjoying the lack of traffic. I sit less than ten feet off one of Yellowstone's major roads, the road over Dunraven Pass, over which more than 4,000 cars pass on a busy summer day as they cross the flanks of Mount Washburn. The pass has been closed for two summers now while the road is reconstructed from the bed up—something not done since the early 1930s when the road was finally made fit for automobiles. It reopens in one month, and I've been coming up here at least once a week to enjoy the quiet for a little bit longer.

At the time of the park's establishment in 1872, European-American visitors rode their horses and drove their wagons over trails long established by the tribes who had been visiting and passing through Yellowstone for centuries.

Traversing the park, west to east, north to south, are old roads marked by parallel travois tracks. Routes from the Columbia Plateau and Great Basin to the Great Plains; routes into the park's heart of hydrothermal mysticism and origin stories; routes to the lakes and rivers where summers passed full of berries, fish, and meat.

Specimen Ridge, artistically lit in a midsummer sunset and blazing hot in a midsummer noon, forms the southern boundary of Lamar Valley. Its spine is littered with shattered petrified trees from volcanic eruptions 50 million years ago. On that ridge, two years ago, I hushed my hiking companions and swept my arms over the ground, pointing. We all slowed and shifted focus from the distant to the near, scanning the ground of this slight rise in the ridge, exposed to the south, which means it is warm and windswept of snow most of the year. It seemed like a good place to rest and chip chert for tools. Sure enough, we began seeing the chips and flakes; we even found a row of rocks that seemed placed in a perpendicular formation. More than likely arranged by human hands, however long ago. And as we continued our slow descent down the ridge, we realized we were walking parallel to another trail. Or were the two trails one? Perhaps a set of travois ruts laid down by hundreds of years of travel?

Now called the Bannock Trail, the ancient road that traverses northern Yellowstone west to east predates the Bannock's heavy use of it in the 1800s. The Bannock, like other tribes west of the park, increased their travel through Yellowstone after bison were wiped out near their homelands. They crossed Yellowstone on their way to the plains where buffalo could still be found. Early European-American explorers witnessed these travels and gave the tribe's name to the trail.

The Bannock Trail crosses the modern road system on Blacktail Plateau, northwest of Mount Washburn and Specimen Ridge. I can just barely pick it out as I stand on top of the hill overlooking the old trail. The travois twin-track winds down the hill in a more sinuous curve than that of the current road, which sends you down the hill in an S-curve. From the base of the hill, both tracks—the two-pole and the four-wheel—shoot straight west. I've never pulled a travois, but I can guess that after the speed of gravity pulling you down the hill, you'd run out for a few yards until the momentum slowed, and then proceed at the usual flatland pace. Today—and I know this from experience—that S-curve not only sends your car downhill but builds up a speed that you don't even notice once you are on the flat. And along you dash, 10, 15, 20 miles over the speed limit. I'm used to this now, and I downshift as I come off that curve so that I don't rocket west— and am passed by rental cars, diesel pickups with five-wheeler hitches, flatbed trucks hauling horses or ATVs, SUVs with local plates, and the occasional zippy RV. No one honks; after all, we are in a national park. Nor does anyone stop if they squash a ground squirrel or two. After all, they are running around all over the place.

This year during several days at peak summer season, I counted road-killed Uinta ground squirrels across the entire roaded section of Yellowstone's northern range. This was a relatively simple task: I learned to scan the road ahead for dark spots and small lumps on the pavement. Approaching one, I'd slow, note the mileage on the odometer, scribble it down along with "gs, eastbound" or "gs, west-bound" or "gs, center" in my field journal. (I do not recommend this for the novice; I have more than ten years of practice keeping field journal shorthand as I drive.) Because people have the potential to see elk, deer, bison, coyote, bear, and wolves along this road, it's relatively acceptable to cruise along at 35 mph instead of the posted 45 mph. (I pulled over whenever possible to let others pass safely; road rage in a tourist is nothing compared with that of a local late for anything.)

Ground squirrels are creatures of the grasslands; thus I would begin the Uinta roadkill search as I emerged from the volcanic cliffs along Lava Creek into the plateau's open landscape. One midday (peak Uinta activity), six squashed ground squirrels spotted the 4 miles from Wraith Falls in the west to the top of the S-curve. From there to Tower Junction—another 10 miles—the road passes through forest more than grassland and I neither saw nor heard live or dead ground squirrels. Surprisingly, I also saw few as I traveled the 20 plus miles of grassland along the Lamar River. I heard their alarm squawks as I drove by, but saw only two road-killed Uintas. Duly noting them in the field journal, I continued on until the last pullout in the Lamar Valley.

On each of these roadkill counting trips, the return yielded different results. A few more ground squirrels would have been killed by the time I retraced the route, and most of the squashed squirrels from the trip out were gone. Only a stain remained on the pavement. Ravens, magpies, and coyotes scavenge roadkills. One time I stopped in an animal jam created by people watching a coyote trying to yank a dead squirrel stuck to the pavement. Sometimes I had to slow as I approached a roadkill because I could see live ground squirrels in the road, eating their dead.

This stretch of Yellowstone road was a heavily used trail by prospectors, miners, and suppliers traveling from Mammoth Hot Springs to Cooke City, a busy mining hamlet in the 1800s. The old dirt roads of that time probably impacted wild animals very little, except perhaps to move elk and other wary creatures away from the route. When you read accounts or look at photographs of that era, it's clear that speedy travel was not possible.

Rotten roads were the norm well into the twentieth century. In Mary Shiver Culpin's *The History of the Construction of the Road System in YNP, 1872–1966*, she includes an old photograph of the Dunraven Pass road in 1912. The mountain slopes from the upper right corner down to the lower left corner of the photo, the road looks as if it were carved by an ice cream scoop, and a horse-drawn carriage travels the narrow one-way path rutted by previous carriages.

Yellowstone roads remained the domain of horses and wheeled carts and coaches until 1915, when the first motorized vehicle was allowed in the park. The following year, more than 3,000 automobiles entered the park. By 1920, 13,000 cars and buses were bumping their way around Yellowstone. Today, more than one million cars travel Yellowstone's roads from May until October.

On July 3 this year, my Dunraven visit came at noon—considered peak travel time on the peak weekend of the year. I counted cars for thirty minutes. Fifteen vehicles passed me as I sat on a rock listening to the creek and watching Parnassian butterflies nectar the blooming stonecrop. The following evening, July 4, ten cars passed in a half hour. Scenery, getting from point A to point B, two trailheads for a popular hike, and wildlife-watching comprise the attractions of this road. The latter becomes a major incentive at sunrise and sunset when you are most likely to see grizzlies and wolves.

Amazingly, this road, so famous for its bear-viewing and increasingly for its wolf-viewing, does not extract a huge toll in roadkills of any large mammals. Of the 310 miles of paved roads in Yellowstone, it has the second lowest roadkill rate of any section: one animal per 10 miles per year. During the 1990s, no grizzlies were killed on a road that passes directly through one of their major habitat areas.

In contrast, a 17-mile stretch of U.S. 191 on the west side is the roadkill corridor of Yellowstone. It is the only road in the park with a legal speed limit of 55 mph; the actual speed is closer to 75 mph. It is also the only road on which semi-tractor trailers and other heavy commercial vehicles can legally pass through the park. During the 1990s this stretch of road claimed 461 large mammals at a rate of more than 2 animals per mile per year.

The major roadkill studies of the 1990s focused on large mammals, from beaver to bison. Even the Dunraven Road study, which surveyed one tenth of the park's road system, counted only the big animals. I wonder about ground squirrels, marmots, magpies, and ravens. How many of these smaller animals are killed each year while crossing the roads, scavenging roadkills, and going about their wildlife business? I especially wonder what we might have found out had anyone counted the Uinta and marmot mortality on Dunraven Road before the road reconstruction so we could compare the mortality afterward—when, despite what the environmental assessment assures, vehicles will no doubt be traveling faster than 35 mph. The new road will be wider, less curvy, and safer for higher speeds than the old road, which often stripped cars of their hubcaps or dislodged tailpipes with its deep potholes and high frost heaves.

The first time I came up Dunraven this summer, ground squirrels danced giddily close to the pavement, crossed daringly close to my approach, and chattered back and forth. They were several generations removed from the last ground squirrels to experience 4,000 cars per day traffic. How many generations will be squished before their ancestors' caution is relearned?

People—from visitors to scientists to park managers to media—pay more attention to the megafauna mortality on Yellowstone's roads. Mourning was visible in June 2003 when a female grizzly was hit and killed. She had been seen every spring and summer for years, traveling an old trail parallel to the modern road between Norris and Mammoth Hot Springs, her two cubs following her. In April she would be seen at Roaring Mountain, a hill bare of vegetation but full of heat and steam. Or she'd be with her cubs in Norris Geyser Basin, where elk and bison had died over the winter, providing her family with food. Eventually she'd head north toward Mammoth Hot Springs, causing massive bear jams wherever she emerged into view. Thousands of people saw her each year; for many people it was the first and only grizzly they'd see. Bear 264. Midsummer two years ago, a Gardiner motel marquee spelled out the news: "Bear 264, we will miss you." She had been hit one evening by a car, the driver swearing he wasn't going over the speed limit and that she had just "run out of nowhere."

The death of grizzly 264 shocked many people not only because she was so well-known, but because grizzlies are seldom roadkill statistics in Yellowstone. Of an annual average of 85 large mammals killed by vehicles in Yellowstone, grizzlies comprise less than 1 percent. Grizzlies are one of three threatened species in Yellowstone, so one's death is notable scientifically and is factored into a complex formula for determining the health of the grizzly population in greater Yellowstone. Thus, when 264 was struck and killed by a vehicle in 2003, her loss reverberated through the ecological community. Another grizzly died in 2004 on the road from West Yellowstone into the park. The year 2005 began with yet another grizzly hitting the pavement, this time along infamous U.S. 191. A photograph of this bear—a huge male, bloody and lifeless—circulated among park employees and was considered for a new poster campaign to alert visitors to the problem of roadkills.

Most roadkills occur at dusk and at night in Yellowstone, no different than in other places. The difference is that this is a national park, the first national park in the world, and it set a precedent in its emphasis on individual vehicular transportation.

The precedent began in the first years of the park, when a succession of superintendents begged the U.S. Congress for money to improve foot and horse trails for more comfortable wagon roads. They emphasized visitor safety and comfort first, accessibility to the park's scenic and thermal wonders second. In the early years of the National Park Service, established in 1916, Stephen T. Mather and Horace Albright set the standards for automobile roads, emphasizing the importance of designing and maintaining park roads that impacted the landscape as little as possible. Their forward-looking point of view was maintained somewhat after the 1920s when the federal Bureau for Public Roads took over park road construction and maintenance.

Roads built in the 1920s and 1930s finally changed a tour through Yellowstone from a bone-jarring, tire-maiming ordeal to a pleasant automobile tour. They remained the literal basis of Yellowstone's road system until the late twentieth century when deterioration of the roadbeds was so thorough that only reconstruction could repair them. Thus, today's visitors receive fluorescent orange or green sheets of paper tucked in their park newspaper as they pass through an entrance gate; the colorful paper details road construction delays throughout the park and nearby public lands. The alert is paid for by federal highway funds, which also pay for additional rangers to staff barricades and explain the schedule intricacies at nearby visitor centers, and pay for the road construction itself. Millions of dollars pour into Yellowstone each year for this massive project. This highway money is included when federal officials proclaim that Yellowstone's budget has increased each year during the current administration and that its maintenance backlog is being reduced. Yet employees still live in trailers toxic with black mold, and people in wheelchairs must enter some visitor centers through the back door.

But the roads will be improved and maintained. Thanks to the daily oversight and determination of park employees, these roads are being rebuilt as sensitively as possible given the constraints and requirements of federal highway projects. Unfortunately, they can do nothing about decisions such as the new Dunraven Road that will welcome vehicles up to 30 feet long but won't be safe for bicycles. Nor can they change the fact that improved roads equal increased speeds equal increased roadkills of all animals in Yellowstone.

During July 2005, I drove the park's roads more than usual. Half the trips were to count road-killed Uintas on my way to enjoy the quiet on Dunraven Road. Visiting friends provided another reason to venture onto the peak-season busy roads, which I usually drive only to get to trailheads. They were staying at Lake Hotel, in the southern part of the park. I joined them for dinner several nights, showed them hidden hot springs, gave them numerous tips on where to go to see which animals, and shared their excitement when they viewed from the road three black bears and one bull moose all in one location. I also advised them about hiking trails to get away from the roads, a major goal of theirs. They climbed Avalanche Peak, walked back to Lone Star Geyser, and explored the rims of the Grand Canyon of the Yellowstone. I couldn't join them, not this year—several foot problems laid me off of hiking. Instead I listened to their stories, imagined the views and smells and sounds, and knew that Dunraven's quiet this year was especially welcomed and will be sorely missed when the barricades come down and 4,000 cars a day pass by.

Transfixed by the Headlights of the Hurtling Machine

Derrick Jensen

W hen I'm on the road, I always carry a baseball bat in the back of my truck to use each time I see a snake. If the snake is sunning herself, I stop the truck and use the bat to shoo her to safety. Sometimes, if the snake is especially sluggish, I loop her over the bat and carry her out of traffic. If she's already dead I don't use the bat at all, but carry her to my truck, then take her to some quiet spot where she can decompose with dignity.

But most often when I stop I have to use the bat not to save the snake but kill her. Too many times I've seen them live and writhing with broken backs, flattened vertebrae, even crushed heads.

I hate cars, and what they do. I do not so much mind killing, if there is a purpose; if, for example, I'm going to eat what I kill. But I despise this incidental killing that comes each time a soft and living body happens to be in our way. Such a killing is without purpose, and often even without awareness. I have driven through swarms of mating mayflies, and have seen a windshield turn red blotch by blotch as it strikes engorged mosquitoes.

I once saw a migration of salamanders destroyed by heavy traffic in a late evening rain. I leapt from my car and ran to carry as many as I could from one side of the road to the other, but for every one I grabbed there were fifty who made it not much farther than the first white line.

A couple of years ago someone dropped off a huge white rabbit near my home. Knowing the cruelty of abandoning pets into the wild and the stupidity of introducing exotics did not lessen my enjoyment of watching him cavort with the local cottontails a third his size. But

51

I often worried. If at one hundred yards I could easily pick him out from among the jumbled rocks that were his home, how much more easily would he be seen by coyotes or hawks? Each time I saw him I was surprised anew at his capacity to live in the wild.

I needn't have worried about predators. One day I walked to get my mail, and saw him dead and stiff in the center of the road. I was saddened, and as I carried him away to where he could at last be eaten by coyotes, I considered my shock of recognition at his death. I had been, as I believe happens constantly in our culture—in our time of the final grinding away at what shreds of ecological integrity still remain intact—fearing precisely the wrong thing. I had been fearing a natural death.

But in one way or another, most of us living today—human and nonhuman alike—will not die the natural death that has been the birthright of every being since life began. Instead we will find ourselves struck down—like the rabbit, like the snakes, like the cat whose skull I had to crush after his spine was severed by the shiny fender of a speeding car—incidental victims of the modern, industrial, mechanical economy.

This is no less true for the starving billions of humans than it is for the salmon incidentally ground up in the turbines of dams, and no less true for those who die of chemically induced cancers than it is for the mayflies I killed by the thousands, blithely driving from one place to another.

All of us today stand as if transfixed by the headlights of the hurtling machine that inevitably will destroy us and all others in its path. Oh, we move slightly to the left or slightly to the right, but I think, as I carefully place the rabbit in a tufted hollow at the base of a tree, that even to the last, most of us have no idea what it is that's killing us.

Keeping the Hunt Wild

Scott Stouder

M ike Duffy had been elk hunting since daylight. It was two hours after dark when he hung his rain jacket outside the tent, parted the canvas flap, and stepped into the lantern light. His hair was plastered to his forehead and his eyes seemed as wild as the land outside, but a smile stretched across his bearded face.

I handed him the hot drink that had been sitting next to the woodstove for almost an hour. "So where did you kill the bull?"

As of this night, Mike had listened for fifteen years to others tell their stories of killing elk without a story of his own. This night, in Oregon's Eagle Cap Wilderness, with rain pounding the tent roof, he would finally tell his story.

"He's a long way up the mountain," he answered wearily as he stripped his soaked clothes, donned dry shirt and pants, and paused to take a sip from the cup. "Near the top of the divide, about a half mile down in a steep canyon."

We would spend the next few hours reliving his hunt and the next few days packing and caring for elk meat. That's the best of wilderness elk hunting. The worst is that it's surrounded by myths. Below are three of the most common.

Not everyone owns a horse or a healthy body, and only elitists can enjoy roadless areas.

This is a half-truth (the first half). Considering that 93 percent of the United States is already inundated with more than 4 million miles of roads, carving roads and human amenities into our last bit of unspoiled land certainly won't endear more of us to the wonders of nature. As for elitism? I'll put my twenty-year-old, $900 horse and worn fifty-something legs up against a $25,000 SUV or $50,000 motorhome any day.

We have to manage land, or wildlife and fish populations won't be healthy.

This weary assertion appeals to many who generally have little ecological experience. Certainly our mauled, multiple-use lands need a helping hand, but wildlife in wildlands seldom benefits from motorized intrusion or heavy-handed management techniques. The land, as well as its fish and wildlife, evolved just fine for several million years without being slapped into line by chainsaws, helicopters, herbicides, or hatcheries. It's only been in the last few centuries that humans have created the super-ecosystemic alteration powers that have devastated salmon runs, poked holes in our protective ozone canopy, drained wetlands, and altered the earth's web of life. Wildlife, given a complete home, can manage just fine without human interference.

Without roads the public is locked out.

This is my personal favorite. I've yet to see a locked gate or a "Stay Out" sign in unroaded public land—wilderness or otherwise. The only lands on which I've seen gates and signs are roaded, privately owned lands.

Today, over three hundred eighty-five thousand miles of roads crisscross our national forests. That's enough to stretch around the globe three times and almost nine times the length of America's interstate highway system. Worse, we can't afford to maintain this giant motorized web. The maintenance backlog alone on the Forest Service road system exceeds, as this is written, $10 billion.

Perhaps more threatening than traditional road-building, off-road vehicle (ORV) use is continuing to escalate on public lands. Industry figures put current ORV sales at about 2,000 vehicles a day. Add those numbers to the estimated 5 million snowmobiles, all-terrain vehicles, and off-road motorcycles already out there and the question becomes: Why build roads if we can drive across the land without them?

In the spring of 2005, the Bush administration abolished the protection of our last roadless public lands with the rollback of the 2001 Roadless Rule. Since that dark day, there is no effective, comprehensive national policy addressing the cumulative threats of development and industrialized recreation to our public lands.

However, there is a policy that was designed by Congress to protect our public lands from being consumed by our own greed. It's called the 1964 Wilderness Act. But with the hardening of America's political climate since the early 1980s, congressional wilderness designation has been deemed too radical for our last roadless areas.

It is not, of course. Of the more than 2.25 billion acres in the United States (including Alaska), only 104 million wilderness acres exist. That's a paltry 4.5 percent of our national landmass. We are hardly wallowing in wilderness.

. . . . .

After Mike finished his drink and his story I stepped outside of the tent. The night air reminded me of other times and other wilderness hunts.

For a quarter of a century my father, brother, uncle, and I hunted elk and deer in Idaho's Frank Church River of No Return Wilderness. One morning I left camp before daylight and walked up a steep trail to a point we called Fire Knob. As the first light spread across the land, I found myself surrounded by elk. They were skylined above me, their long necks silhouetted against the light blue of the predawn sky. Thinly screened by trees, I shrunk behind a windfall as two cow elk took tentative steps toward me and stopped. The day's first sun hit the tops of the pine trees. The air slowed. The world yawned. Then the primal scream of a bull jolted the mountain awake.

He bugled from the heavy timber on top warning the cows not to wander. But they, and the wind, continued to drift downhill. Frozen, I was suspended half crouched and half standing while the bull battered a hapless pine sapling. My feet tingled toward numbness and my legs began to tremble as minutes crawled by. But my focus was riveted to a sunlit opening the bull had to cross to retrieve his wandering harem. He did.

The herd bolted at the shot, but the bull lay where he had fallen. As I walked up to him, the liquid brown eyes glazed to black glass. After leaning my rifle against a tree, I knelt on the ground beside him. Fresh green strips of tree bark clung to the thick base of his mahogany rack. The warm morning air reeked of pine resin, elk, and fresh earth. I reached down and touched him, and the years I'd spent wandering and hunting in wildland flooded my consciousness like a tide.

Images of other elk I'd hunted, horses I've loved, and the faces of family and friends with whom I'd shared the wilderness blurred my emotions. I knelt beside the dead elk with my eyes closed until my only tangible thought was simple gratitude for being a free person on this earth. I stood up, shrugged out of my pack, and pulled my hunting knife from its sheath. Its familiar heft and the pragmatic need of caring for the meat helped settle my emotions.

But this elk—this being—was more than a piece of meat and I wasn't able to render him to components quite yet. I looked at his teeth. Some were missing. All were worn down from winters of stripping aspen bark and scraping bunchgrass from snow-covered hillsides. He was connected to these mountains. Here was his place. As I looked out over the rolling spruce-and-pine carpet that buckled and broke into ridges and canyons, I knew for certain that he knew this land with more detail and intimacy than I could understand.

I call the hill "Fire Knob" because a wildfire swept over it years ago. Today it's covered with mixed bunchgrass meadows and clumps of jackpine. The knob is really just a hump west of The Long Ridge and The Meadow. It's just a little north—actually an extension—of The Brushpatch. Those names identify places where I'd spent my Septembers for more than twenty years. They're geographical blurbs on mental maps that exist on no paper. But they do exist.

The elk, deer, and grouse who live on Fire Knob know where it is. The moose and elk who spend summer days deep in The Brushpatch know every trail leading to The Meadow where they feed at night. The wolves, cougars, and black bears know every ridge, trail, and creek that bind the land and its intricate web of life together. Human hunters have mentally woven the drainages and ridges together into personal treasures they revisit each autumn.

The animals know these places because it's their home. Humans know them because the Wilderness Act forces us to travel slowly and watch the land.

But it might have been different.

In the early 1980s, soon after the 2.2 million acres of Idaho's Frank Church Wilderness (named after the Idaho senator who sponsored the federal legislation) was classified under the 1964 Wilderness Act, an Idaho state legislator introduced the idea of paving a highway into it.

"Why would some politician want a road up here?" my uncle asked one night after I told him the political history of the place while we watched the sun fade from the spire-topped spruce trees that ringed The Meadow.

The question was legitimate. I answered it the only way I could.

"Because he's never seen a bull elk ghost through the mist of a spruce bog in The Brushpatch or heard wolves howl from The Long Ridge. He's never watched a cow and calf moose drift from the trees and feed at the edge of The Meadow at sunset. And he's never hung on to his homeward-bound horse miles from camp on a moonless night in wildland and reveled in the pure joy of being alive."

I thought about those words as I sat on Fire Knob and looked across the land the Indians called "No Return." I thought about what I'd feel when I rode out of this wilderness and drove home through waves of vehicle traffic and passed supermarkets with the hunt wrapped in cellophane. I thought about what I'd hear after the silence, what I'd eat after the elk's heart, and where I'd sleep after nights with stars.

I also thought about what I would say to those who would trade a hard day with a pack string for an hour's ride on a cushioned seat. The threat of a road into the heart of wilderness may seem unrealistic to some, but wild places will exist only so long as free people work to protect them. Today others are working to weaken that protection. The senator who introduced the idea of the road over Fire Knob and across The Long Ridge still stalks wilderness inside the Beltway. And he hasn't changed. He doesn't know about Fire Knob, he's never even walked out The Long Ridge. But that's the whole point. To truly know and love land you have to walk under its trees, lie down in its moss, and sit beside one who calls it home. When you watch the light die in the eyes of an old elk and look across his timbered canyons and ridges through tears you can't define, you realize it's easier to destroy something you don't understand than to kill something you love.

These old memories, and Mike's new ones, flowed through my mind later that night as I lay in my sleeping bag listening to rain on the canvas roof and dry pine crackling in the stove.

"Are you worried about packing the meat out tomorrow?" I asked.

"No. We have plenty of time," Mike answered in the darkness.

That's right, I thought. We do have time. Time to pack the elk out. Time to reflect on the absolute privilege of being a hunter and a free person on this earth. And time to be thankful that somebody before us had the foresight to preserve a small space in the world as wilderness.

Only Connect

David Quammen

This essay is a period piece, reflecting one view of the Wildlands Project in its early days. Since its first publication in December 1993, the green canoe and the red one have paddled many miles.

The man in the green canoe is Dave Foreman, former Goldwater Republican, former hellion, former Marine OCS candidate, former farrier, former Washington lobbyist, former monkey-wrencher, co-founder of Earth First!, and widely regarded as this country's most influential radical conservationist during those years when Reagan administration resource policies cast their dank shadow over the American landscape. His canoe is a Penobscot, riding low with a ten-day supply of provisions. He dips a paddle. He snaps the tab on a beer. He savors the sight of a great blue heron as it takes wing from the riverbank and cranks upward across a pale August sky. "GBH," he says quietly, for the benefit of those gazing elsewhere. Foreman is a protean man with a durable set of principles, a mild private demeanor and a wild public image, a sense of humor. He's also a survivor. Within recent years, he has survived a poisonous spider bite, an FBI raid, a conspiracy indictment, a trial, and hepatitis. Today he's an amiable middle-aged guy in a slouchy camo hat, cruising downriver with binoculars and a bird book. From a crooked pole jammed amid his canoe cargo flies a Jolly Roger bandanna, apt symbol for a piss-and-vinegar insurrectionist who knows the wisdom of not always taking himself seriously. Foreman's not in retirement, God forbid, but he is on vacation.

The river is flat as a griddle, and broad—a green shallow slick of brown water flowing between soft grayish bluffs. It's the Missouri, graceful and solitary here in Lewis-and-Clark country just below Fort Benton, Montana. Ancient cottonwoods, snaggy and unpruned, stand in groves along the bottomland. Pelicans rest in the backwaters. A few Herefords graze on the banks; they stop chewing, at leisurely intervals, and lift up their muzzles to gape. Foreman speaks in low tones across the water, conducting a desultory conversation with a man in another canoe, a red one, some yards away.

The man in the red canoe is Dr. Michael Soulé. Whereas Foreman is bulky, beer-bellied, strong, and could pass for a blacktop contractor, Soulé is lean and slight, with a small professorial beard and the hands of an orthodontist. He's not a stuffy man, far from it, but he chooses his words thoughtfully—even the jokey ones. Out here on the river, he wears a life jacket and sunscreen and soggy sneakers and a straw cowboy hat, beneath which he vaguely resembles the comedian George Carlin cast against type for a western. Among average Americans, who don't read the technical journals of ecology or population genetics or that discipline now known as conservation biology, Soulé's name is not so familiar as Foreman's. But he's eminent within his field, which is the scientific study and preservation of biological diversity. He was the first president of the Society for Conservation Biology, after its founding in 1985. He was the organizer of crucial conferences, the editor of landmark books, the author or coauthor of important papers that continue to serve as load-bearing walls for the whole edifice of conservation-biology theory. He helped to define the concept of minimum viable population, for instance, and to develop a method of assessing the various sorts of jeopardy faced by severely endangered species. His reputation is global, though limited mainly to that global community of field biologists, theoreticians, and resource managers who concern themselves with the abstruse scientific aspects of conservation.

Soulé's canoe is an Oscoda, and it appears to have traveled fewer river miles, taken fewer scratches and thumps than Foreman's. There's no Jolly Roger. But it's carrying its share of the food and the equipment and the beer.

From the put-in at Fort Benton, Foreman and Soulé and their party intend to cover 150 miles—among the wooded islands and past the old ferry landings, through the White Cliffs area, through the Missouri Breaks, all of which is officially Wild and Scenic—to a takeout near the western end of Fort Peck Reservoir. Fort Peck is where this majestically sleepy river turns into a comatose man-made lake. The canoeists could be there in less than a week, if they lean on their paddles, but they aren't in a hurry. Their purpose, so far as I in my nosiness can deduce, is threefold: (1) to enjoy some late-summer peace and some remote landscape; (2) to get to know each other better; (3) to discuss a vastly ambitious, provocative, and visionary new enterprise in which Foreman and Soulé have allied themselves. Their name for that enterprise is the Wildlands Project.

At the heart of the Wildlands Project is the notion of connectivity. This notion proposes that, for scientific reasons, wildlife reserves and parks and wilderness areas and other parcels of wild landscape should be left connected (or be reconnected by ecological restoration) to each other in a geographical network. Connectivity isn't generally the case in late-twentieth-century America, and less so with every passing year. Instead we have its antithesis, fragmentation, as our forests and prairies and wetlands and natural deserts are inexorably chopped into pieces, leaving discrete and far-flung fragments to stand insularized in an ocean of human impact. The fragments carry names such as Glacier National Park, the Bob Marshall Wilderness, the Little Belt Mountains, the Big Belts, the Crazies, the Bridgers, the Tobacco Roots, the Greater Yellowstone Ecosystem—to cite just one regional set of examples. The bold hope and the quite serious plan of the Wildlands Project is eventually to link those fragments, and other sets, back together.

I've extracted an invitation to share part of this river journey and discussion. As the canoe flotilla moves downstream, I skitter between Foreman and Soulé in a kayak, the craft of choice for gadflies. It's a nifty mode of travel, allowing me to dart in and out of conversations, though it leaves others to carry the baggage and fly the flag.

· · · · ·

Four years ago at a small conclave of Earth First! activists geared toward spiritual reinvigoration and tactical brainstorming, I heard Dave Foreman tell the troops: "Go out and talk to a white pine. Go out on a moonlit night and try to *connect* with the soul of a 200-year-old white pine."

Earth First! is now part of his past, his own sense of tactics has evolved, and his "try to connect" message presently carries a different meaning. The new meaning is more geographical than spiritual, more scientific than mystic. We've got to connect the last fragments of wild landscape to one another, he argues. We've got to link them, by way of corridors that allow fauna and flora to pass back and forth, if we hope to stop the deadly trend of species being lost from those fragments through a process that some scientists call ecosystem decay.

This argument has a distinguished pedigree, as Dave Foreman is well aware. He knows that it comes straight out of a branch of science called island biogeography, which involves much more than islands. As a studious nonscientist who pores through the scientific literature, Foreman knows that island biogeography grew to prominence during the 1960s and 1970s, became the preferred theoretical framework for many ecologists and population biologists, and served as one of the chief sources for the ideas of conservation biology. He knows that ecosystem decay is the process whereby a patch of habitat—if it's too small and too thoroughly insularized—loses species as though spontaneously, the way a lump of uranium loses neutrons. For instance: The Bridger Mountains, once they were insularized, lost their population of grizzly bears. The Crazy Mountains, once insularized, lost their grizzlies. The Greater Yellowstone Ecosystem, a much larger area, retains a grizzly population to the present—but even that population may eventually be lost. Each loss of this sort can result from subtle causes involving only the mischances of demography, genetics, and environmental fluctuation, whether or not the species is protected from hunting. Those subtle causes have been elucidated over the past thirty years in the journals of theoretical biology. The whole subject of ecosystem decay, and of its relation to the sizes and patterns of parks and reserves, has been pondered exhaustively by the experts while remaining completely obscure to almost everyone else. Foreman is an exception. During his gradual metamorphosis from eco-radical firebrand to conservation-biology wonk, he has read all about it—from the early works, such as Robert MacArthur and Edward O. Wilson's *The Theory of Island Biogeography*, to the later papers of Michael Soulé.

The MacArthur-Wilson theory, as interpreted latterly by conservation biologists, implies that a habitat patch can retain its full complement of species *if* it continues to receive immigrants (wandering individuals) from other patches. How can such immigration be fostered? One possible way is with habitat corridors. Those corridors may be narrow, encompassing no great amount of area, but as long as they provide travel routes for restless animals and dispersing plant seeds, they can accomplish a disproportional measure of good. So says one school of thought, anyway. An opposing school notes that the same corridors might have negative consequences that outweigh any positive ones, such as facilitating the spread of diseases, fires, or other forms of catastrophe that might wipe out a population of creatures. And whether the corridors would be cost-effective, in terms of the financial and political capital required to establish them, is also a much-argued question. Although the anticorridorists include some respected scientists (such as Daniel Simberloff, a brilliantly argumentative ecologist who has served on the board of The Nature Conservancy), Michael Soulé's own research and reflection have landed him in the procorridor school.

The potential role of corridors for preventing ecosystem decay was suggested as early as 1975. In the years since, there has been a great deal of theoretical refinement and debate, though not much field-testing or application. "Conservation biology, as long as it's talked about in abstract terms, remains just that," Foreman tells me. He means: It remains emptily abstract. "What we've got to do is make it real."

I ask Michael Soulé how he came to be involved in the project. His answer surprises me slightly. "I wrote to Dave and I said, 'What's the next step?' Because conservation had come to a dead end. Nobody had any vision. And the obvious thing was connectivity."

Foreman himself was surprised. He showed Soulé's letter to one of his current coconspirators and crowed, "Look, somebody *agrees* with us."

. . . . .

In a ninety-page document that serves as both manifesto and blueprint, Foreman and Soulé and a few other collaborators have offered a short "Mission Statement" describing the essence of their enterprise. "The mission of The Wildlands Project is to help protect and restore the ecological richness and native biodiversity of North America through the establishment of a connected system of reserves." Healing the landscape, they say, will entail "reconnecting its parts so that vital flows can be renewed." From there they continue in more exuberant language. "Our vision is simple: we live for the day when Grizzlies in Chihuahua have an unbroken connection to Grizzlies in Alaska; when Gray Wolf populations are continuous from New Mexico to Greenland; when vast unbroken forests and flowing plains again thrive and support pre-Columbian populations of plants and animals; when humans dwell with respect, harmony, and affection for the land; when we come to live no longer as strangers and aliens on this continent." Apart from the idealism of that vision, which is admirable, the crucial content lies in the words *unbroken, continuous,* and *connection.*

What it brings to my mind, besides theories of island biogeography, is a certain famous passage from E. M. Forster's novel *Howards End.* Forster's heroine, Margaret Schlegel, was pondering what she might say that could vivify the soul of her obdurate, mean, myopic, business-obsessed, yet righteous and well-intending future husband. At the moment, it didn't seem to her a difficult question. "Only connect! That was the whole of her sermon. Only connect the prose and the passion, and both will be exalted, and human love will be seen at its height. Live in fragments no longer." But the man, Henry Wilcox, was incapable of comprehending her and incapable of making vital connections, either between the two sides of his own nature or between himself and another human—at least until his life had been shattered to still smaller and meaner fragments.

Foreman has given me a copy of this document—not *Howards End,* no, but the Wildlands manifesto—and I carry it in my drybag as we float the river. I've read the mission statement, and Foreman's own introductory note, and a wise essay by Soulé on the theme of incremental consensus-building and long-term patience; and I've looked over the maps. These maps represent specific but tentative proposals from working groups allied to the Wildlands Project in various regions—a hypothetical sketch of reserves and connecting corridors for the southern Appalachians, another for the Adirondacks, another for Florida, still another for the northern Rockies. I've closely examined that last map, the one covering those fragments of wild landscape with which I happen to be personally familiar. I've seen the large dark ovals, indicating park-and-wilderness aggregations as they already exist, and the gray swaths drawn to represent corridors, or proposed corridors, passing fluidly down the page like runnels of chokecherry syrup. I've traced those runnels against the map of Montana in my head, and the fact isn't lost on me that they flow over the Little Belt Mountains and the Crazies and the Big Belts and the Bridgers and the few tiny towns in between, crossing small county roads and ranches and two different stretches of interstate highway, presenting the dreamlike ideal of a restored biogeographic connection between the Glacier Park complex and Greater Yellowstone. How will that dream be realized? How will the landscape be transformed? How will the highways be transcended? My first impression of this grand design had been that it's scientifically sound, ethically compelling, and politically impossible.

Now I paddle over and put that reaction to Foreman. Isn't his project hopelessly unrealistic? Does it have any practical viability in the real world of congressional turf battles and economic stress? Will it ever be tolerable to the hardworking, vote-casting folks who are already desperately concerned for their prerogatives to continue cutting timber or pasturing cows or driving their dirt bikes into the backcountry?

"I'm sort of a practical guy," Foreman tells me. Yes, it's an audacious proposal, he agrees, and he doesn't expect quick victories, but he does hope to turn that proposal into the focal point of the debate over how we should—and *can*—preserve biodiversity on this continent. "I think it's *very* practical." There's a parallel here, I realize, with the guerrilla-theater radicalism of Earth First! Foreman himself, the old stage-stomping, fist-waving agitator, always understood clearly (as many of his followers didn't) that the real usefulness of Earth First! was to move one flank of the debate out to extremity, not because extremity itself would ever triumph but because the middle-ground position would thereby also be pulled in that direction.

"Our job is not to operate within the bounds of political reality," he tells me now, as the river carries us sweetly along. "Our job is to change political reality."

· · · · ·

We camp beneath an old crabbed cottonwood on the right bank and, after dinner, after dark, the discussion continues. Foreman smokes a cigar, partly to keep the mosquitoes away, partly because he likes the taste, partly no doubt because he finds cigars appealingly retrograde. Soulé and I content ourselves with chocolate-chip cookies. Somewhere across the river, coyotes hoot. I sit on an ammo box, listening carefully to what Foreman and Soulé say about conservation biology, the science of jeopardized populations, and politics, the art of the possible.

Just how much *is* possible? I wonder. The Wildlands manifesto proposes a three-category schema of ecosystem conservation, consist-

ing of core reserves (which would be strictly managed for the protection of biological diversity), buffer zones (multiple-use lands surrounding the core reserves, which would constitute at least marginal
habitat, insulating the reserves from intensive land uses as practiced
on the terrain beyond), and corridors (for that crucial connectivity).
One step toward realization of the schema might be to establish a
Wildlands Recovery Corps as a new branch of the Forest Service.
This corps of restoration ecologists and landscape engineers would
focus on the potential corridor lands, instituting soil-stabilization
measures to mitigate erosion, closing unneeded roads, doing whatever possible to nurse back native vegetation and faunal diversity. The
notion of just such a Wildlands Recovery Corps has already been
included within one bill introduced in Congress. But that bill has
gone nowhere. Judged in biological terms, the WRC in particular and
the Wildlands Project in general make excellent sense. The big problem is that too many local people—ranchers, timber-industry workers, off-road-vehicle enthusiasts, inveterate government-haters, and
salt-of-the-earth xenophobes, as well as most of the region's congressional delegates—seem to find the very notion of federally mandated
landscape reconnection so loathsome and scary.

From my ammo-box chair, I ask Soulé: Won't the Wildlands proposal, with its breathtaking scope, exacerbate the polarity that already
makes America's conservation debate seem like a class war?

"I know your question was rhetorical," Soulé answers politely. "But
the same could be said of the Emancipation Proclamation. Doesn't it
exacerbate polarity? Yes it does. Anytime you extend liberty to another
group, it exacerbates polarity. Even if the new group are animals."

And so on. Skeptical questions, thoughtful answers, no sense of
easy resolution. The mosquitoes continue feeding until late.

· · · · ·

At the end of the second day, exhausted and eager to make camp, we
come to a fork in the channel. The river map tells us that this is
Boggs Island, about forty miles downstream from Fort Benton. It's
public land, nicely forested, and it may be our last decent chance
today for a campsite. A question arises: Which side of the island
should we scout? The question is deemed unanswerable and so,
before I know it, Foreman's green canoe has cruised off down the
right channel, Soulé's red canoe has disappeared to the left. The

whole party splits. Not foreseeing that it makes any difference, I
swing my kayak to the right and follow Foreman.

The island is big. The bank along our channel is steep, with no
convenient inlet for beaching boats or unloading gear. Foreman and
I climb up and find a campsite, passable though not ideal. The undergrowth is thick. Someone complains about poison ivy. Someone else
notes that maybe Soulé and his group have found something better.
Do we have a plan to rendezvous and confer? We don't. The island is
too wide and brush-choked to cross on foot, and Soulé doesn't answer
our shouts. So I volunteer to paddle back upstream in the kayak, drop
around into the other channel, and find him.

Paddling against this gentle current is like climbing a rope, hand
over hand, stroke after stroke. I get almost to the nose of the island
before fast shallow water stops me. There I pull my kayak up the bank
and begin dragging it overland toward the other channel. This proves
more difficult than I expected: heavy thicket, no trail, deadfalls, this-
tles and thorns, a forty-pound boat with a propensity for snagging
itself on branches, and I'm in a pair of neoprene mukluks. Finally I
stumble out to the other channel and set off on the current again. I
paddle down the length of the island, finding Soulé and his group at
the very bottom. They haven't spotted a campsite, no, though they
have enjoyed watching a beaver. Okay, I say, can they pull their canoes
upstream along that side for a few hundred yards, to where Foreman
is waiting? Not hardly, they say, and call my attention to the fact that
the bank is impossibly brushy and steep. Then can they *paddle* these
barges upstream? Not hardly. So I set off alone, upstream again, to
complete my circumnavigation of the island and report back to Foreman. Before long I meet his group, aboard their canoes and floating
down. Now I'm getting dizzy. In the interval, they have made a decision: On grounds of poison ivy or fractured communications or some
other ineffable factor, Boggs Island is not the place.

At the bottom of the island, we all finally reunite. Soulé's group
agrees: no stopping here. It'll be better to go on and, in what remains
of daylight, find a spot somewhere downstream. They all paddle away.

I linger behind, adrift on the slow water. My arms are tired and I
feel slightly perplexed, contemplating both the small chore of choosing a campsite and the huge challenge of persuading America to
accept Wildlands.

The Wildlands Project has great merit. But it will never succeed and probably shouldn't, I suspect, if the effort to realize it becomes an us-versus-them political battle, since us-versus-them is just another form of fragmentation. It can only succeed through patient persuasion, as Soulé warned in his wise essay; it will also require a system of positive incentives for the folks who would be directly affected, and a large measure of (the one thing that Earth First! considered anathema) compromise. Drawing corridors on a map is easy. The hard connections to make are those between aggrieved humans on one side of an issue and aggrieved humans on the other side.

Within a few minutes, Foreman and Soulé have pulled far out ahead and all I can see are dots on the water, one greenish, the other red. I wish them good luck. It's a long, long way to Fort Peck.

Part Three: Got Roads?

> "*The access roads planned for Blue Creek and Eightmile totaled 265 miles, far more than enough to undercut all of these steep mountainsides and bring down a whole rare world into the creeks.*"
> —Peter Matthiessen, "The High Country"

From the broad philosophical view of roads in Part One, to the focused view of a specific impact in Part Two, we broaden out our view again. The writers in Part Three say that maybe enough is enough, in essays that explore the astounding number of roads and their cumulative impacts on our public lands. Road after road cuts through our forests and deserts, some of them abandoned after logging operations were complete. Some logging and mining companies *still* want to build roads on public land, even through land sacred to Native Americans. From California to Georgia to far northern Alaska, roads are slicing through ancient forests, red-rock deserts, pristine streams, and fragile tundra; they are slicing through the heart of our wildlands, leaving scarred, damaged and denuded landscapes in their wake.

The High Country
Peter Matthiessen

Coming up from Pecwan, on the Klamath River, to Low Gap, we could see across the whole wild reach of upper Blue Creek and its forks to the remote High Siskiyous, where we were going. There are no roads into Blue Creek, only rough car tracks for the loggers, and on this dry summer afternoon, the truck raised a long column of hot dust as it descended the raw eroding zigzag scars down the steep mountain-side. Where the trees were stripped off, the sumps, torn earth, and lit-tered deadwood evoked the desolate, blasted hills of war, and the effect was especially depressing where the defoliant called 2,4,5-T had been used by the Simpson Timber Company to "inhibit" broadleaf growth in favor of the conifers; in these seared areas, there was no life of any kind, no birds or flowers or berries, and the streams were poisoned. "Some people make the mistake of boiling their camp water to purify it—that just concentrates the poison," John Trull said, glaring out the window. Trull, a big man with a boyish grin, had been a logger and a cat skinner for many years, but as a woodsman and an Indian—though he looks white, he has Cherokee blood and is married to a Yurok woman—he was troubled by the scope of the destruction. . . .

. . . Where the track descended toward Blue Creek, Dick Myers, Trull's stepson, saw a young black bear in a thicket, but otherwise the summer trees were still. We parked the truck where the cat track ended, in alders by the stream. Five miles downstream from this place, Blue Creek joins the Klamath River, which flows north and west perhaps fifteen miles to the Pacific. Until the great logging boom came to this part of far northern California after World War II, lower Blue Creek was forested by great coast redwoods; the few that remain stand like mourners for the many that are gone. Having logged out the redwoods, Simpson Timber was now seeking access to the old-stand Douglas fir and other valuable timber trees in the inner reaches of Blue Creek and its eastern forks, which lie entirely within the Six Rivers National Forest. For a variety of excellent reasons, the Indians and the environmentalists, the scientists and fishermen, were trying to stop it. Even those local people like John Trull whose livelihood depended on the lumber industry had strong mixed feelings about the imminent destruction of Blue Creek, which is one of the last clear streams and wildernesses in the country.

In recent years, Blue Creek has become a symbol for the fight to save the Siskiyous, which rise seven thousand feet and more above the Klamath. One group of isolated peaks and rocks, traditionally approached through the ascent of the forks of Blue Creek, is a sacred "High Country" for the Indians—the Yurok; the Karuk, farther upriver to the east; the Tolowa, of the northern coast and southern Oregon; and occasionally the Hupa from the Trinity River, which flows into the Klamath at Weitchpec. *Yurok*, or "downriver people," seems to be a Karuk ("up to the east" or "upriver people") term for these small, scattered bands of the lower Klamath, from Bluff Creek to Requa, at the river's mouth, and a short distance north and south along the sea. Though all tribes of the region are now quite similar in customs and beliefs, they are very different in origin; the indigenous Karuk are of Hokan linguistic stock, the more recent Hupa and Tolowa are Athapaskans from the Canadian Northwest, and the Yurok are Algonkin, a small western offshoot of those woodland tribes that once occupied almost all of eastern North America.

In addition to its traditional role in Indian life, Blue Creek is a superb spawning stream for both steelhead and salmon—one of the finest in the Siskiyous, which are the most productive watershed in California—and the people knew that logging would hasten the end of the dying salmon fishery so crucial to both whites and Indians in the depressed economy of this region. As Dick Myers says, "Poor logging practices make these creeks run too fast in winter and spring so that they dry up much too soon during the summer. It spoils the rivers, and it spoils the fishing." Botanically, these mountains are one of the most varied regions on the continent, and a reservoir of rare animals and relict plants such as the Brewer's spruce, whose closest relation is found in northeast Asia. For all these reasons, very suddenly this little-known wilderness has become one of the most controversial in the country.

The traditional way into the High Country is one of a network of old Indian paths known to the Indians of the lower Klamath as Thklamah, meaning "ladder" or "steps" (the stepping-stones for ascent into the sky world); the term is transcribed by sentimental bureaucrats as the "Golden Stairs." This path begins just above the confluence of Blue Creek with its Crescent City Fork and climbs the ridge between those streams in a northerly direction to a point off to the east of a huge dark boulder. Perhaps one hundred feet in height, the boulder is poised on the bare saddle of a rocky ridge as if it had descended from the sky. This is Ha-ay-klok, Rock Set upon a Rock, known as Medicine Rock in the nineteenth century and now called Doctor Rock. It was and is an important site for medicine training, of which healing is only one part, practiced mostly by women; the men who went to the High Country to "make medicine" were on a vision quest, in pursuit of spiritual power. In recent decades, with the demoralization and acculturation of the tribes that the logging boom served to accelerate, Doctor Rock and other sacred sites have been little visited except by hunters. Dick Myers, who had never visited the High Country, was delighted to be going by the Steps, in case the fight to save Blue Creek was lost. "Nine tenths of the people have never been to Doctor Rock," he said, "and the rest of 'em went up most of the way by truck."

We shouldered our packs and forged across the torrent, hip-deep and still swift and cold here in early July, to the wooded bench or "flat" on the far side, where we headed upstream. On the east bank, Slide Creek comes swiftly down from Blue Creek Mountain. The huge dead trees that choke its mouth are not the consequence of wasteful logging practice but of the frequent slides that give this creek its name. Natural landslides are common in this region, where the most recent uplifting of two million years ago did not turn the old rivers from their courses but only deepened them, so that the steep mountainsides may fall away even without excessive rain or snow. The soil itself, shot through with intrusions of the beautiful weak slaty jade called serpentine, is poor and shallow, and those slopes that are marginally stable when bound up by forest roots collapse quickly in the first rainfall and erosion that follows road-building and the removal of the trees. This is the main reason why environmentalists insist that the Siskiyous should not be logged at all. This situation is worsened by the winter and spring floods that undercut the slopes, causing whole tracts to fall away into the torrent. The Christmas flood of 1964 scoured all rivers in the region and changed the whole appearance of Blue Creek, washing out the forest banks and leaving broad gravel bars that emerge in summer.

According to Forest Service personnel, the Siskiyous, with no ranches and few visitors, is the only wild region left in California to which restoration of the grizzly has been considered. (The creature is now officially extinct in California.) Blue Creek is still a haunt of the fierce wolverine, one of California's rarest mammals, and also of its scarce mustelid cousins, the marten and the arboreal fisher. An uncommon creature of these streams called the sewelel, or mountain beaver, is considered a "pest" by foresters, who would like to eliminate it. The shy cougar comes and goes, and the rare spotted owl frequents the stands of old-growth timber near the creeks.

It was just this primordial forest of immense fir and cedar, concentrated on the shady and well-watered deposits of good soil nearest the streams, that was most coveted by Simpson Timber Company and the sawmills of the coast, which were fighting hard against all efforts to have it protected by the National Wilderness Act, passed by Congress in 1964. As in the Olympic National Forest in Washington, where Simpson and the Forest Service had a special understanding, the industry counted on assistance from this cumbersome and conservative bureaucracy, which tended to oppose the protection of national forest land in favor of commercial possibilities, even where—as in the Siskiyous—other values far outweigh the worth of what will almost certainly be a single "crop" of timber; once that crop has been harvested, this fragile region may not recover for a thousand years.

Both sides of lower Nic-Wich lay on a Simpson holding that penetrated the national forest from the west, and the access road that came down through the national forest from Lonesome Ridge was the only lumber road in the Blue Creek drainage east of the Crescent City Fork. In this lower stretch, at least, Nic-Wich was ruined. The ugly detritus of deadwood and shale pitched all the way down from the clear-cuts high above gave a vivid idea of what Blue Creek would look like if the Forest Service management plan were carried out. Much of the land slope in these dark V-shaped canyons lies at a sixty- to seventy-degree angle—as steep as the steepest staircase, as anyone will learn who cares to try it, either up or down—and a Forest Service study acknowledges that 83 percent of the land area in the Blue Creek Management Unit and the contiguous Eightmile Unit to the north is "moderately unstable or worse." In one region of the Siskiyous, another study shows, the soil loss from new clear-cuts may reach twenty-two tons per acre every year, most of which descends to spoil the streams. (Both of these studies are considered optimistic by outside observers.) Since productivity may be reduced 80 percent with the loss of just one inch of the thin topsoil, and since in the Coast Range thousands of years may be required for a new topsoil to form, the prospects for reforestation here are dismal. Yet despite accumulating warnings (many from its own personnel or from experts hired under Forest Service contract) that the High Siskiyous are too steep, fragile, and unstable to support intensive logging—that owing to the loss of soil, it would not in fact be possible to observe the agency's own legal obligation to manage its forests with a perpetual and sustained yield, and that the inevitable "mismanagement" would therefore be illegal—the Forest Service has held stubbornly to plans to sell 929 million board feet of timber out of Blue Creek alone. The access roads planned for Blue Creek and Eightmile totaled 265 miles, far more than enough to undercut all of these steep mountainsides and bring down a whole rare world into the creeks.

Everywhere else in the Northwest the result of logging (and eroding logging roads) has been the extensive siltation of the waters, the muddying of the clear gravel beds used by the salmon species and the beautiful anadromous rainbow trout that are called "steelhead." The fish must cover their fertilized eggs with stream gravel to protect them, and the gravel must be clean and porous so that cold water providing crucial oxygen can circulate at the constant temperature necessary for embryo development. Logging drastically increases erosion and sedimentation that may smother the gravel beds, and in addition, the clearing of the land, by increasing sunlight, raises the temperature of the water to a degree that may prove fatal to the young. In many places, logjams resulting from erosion slides or wasteful cutting can prevent access to a spawning stream for years.

The sudden and drastic decline in the Klamath fisheries is precisely coincidental with the advent of heavy logging in the region. Already, all commercial fishing has been stopped in the Klamath delta, between the coastal highway bridge and the mouth of the river, which is the traditional gillnetting grounds of the Yurok Indians at Requa. (The Yurok, like the Puyallup-Nisqually and many other coastal peoples from northern California to British Columbia, have been blamed increasingly for fisheries depletion caused by dams, logging, and industrial pollution; where no Indians are handy, sea lions and cormorants will do. When I was in south Alaska's Kenai Peninsula in 1957, the depletion of the salmon fisheries by overfishing was being blamed on the greed of the Kodiak bears.) And so a renewable resource that provides many jobs, not only in commercial fishing but in the tourist-attracting sports fishery as well, may be wiped out by a self-devouring industry that will devastate the mountainsides before moving on.

Since it is generally agreed that artificial reforestation of this region, with a sustained yield, is unrealistic, and since the Klamath sports and commercial fisheries, though much depleted, are worth millions of dollars annually, one wonders at the willingness of the Forest Service to abet the destruction of a natural resource of such long-term benefit to many in order to further the short-term profits of a few. And this is true not only of Blue Creek but throughout the whole Siskiyou wilderness, which is presently threatened with irretrievable destruction despite the warnings of geologists, foresters, biologists, and anthropologists alike that the potential loss, not only to the Indians but to the whole nation, far exceeds the value of its wood.

In recent years, the excuse that has been trotted out for the proposed "multiple-use management" of the Siskiyous is the alleged loss of jobs in the timber and sawmill industries in Humboldt and Del Norte Counties caused by government expropriation of coastal forests for Redwood National Park. But the decline of the vast private timber reserves started more than twenty years ago in Humboldt County, long before Redwood National Park came into being. As early as 1952, when the lumber boom had just begun, Humboldt County farm adviser W. D. Pine predicted that unless the lumber companies brought their wasteful practices under control, the county would suffer the same boom and bust that had occurred in other timber regions, forcing the companies to intensify their operations here in northern California.

Despite strenuous public propaganda to the contrary (one thinks of all those phony ads in which happy deer and chipmunks gambol merrily among the noble stumps of managed forests), there was no serious attempt at sustained yield. Overcutting, waste, and the wholesale export of unmilled logs to other countries, in particular Japan, accompanied the scare campaigns that threatened America with a lumber shortage, as the companies proceeded with the rapid despoliation of this great conifer forest that is widely regarded as the finest in the world. Increasingly, as private holdings dwindled, and the sawmills replaced the precious redwoods with former "weed trees" such as Douglas fir and hemlocks, pines, and cedars, the industry sought leases on the national forest lands that lay just inland from the private holdings. That part of lower Blue Creek that lay west of the national forest was already logged, and so was its once beautiful West Fork; the west bank of the Crescent City Fork was under lease and going fast. But its eastern slope was still intact, and so were upper Blue Creek and the whole East Fork, which together constitute the heart of the Blue Creek drainage.

Old paths along lower Blue Creek were overgrown or washed out by the floods. In the woodland heat, we probed and backtracked for a time before giving up and returning toward the river. "I ain't never been lost," John Trull remarked, "but I sure as hell been confused for about five days." On small sand traces of the gravel bars and on the soft earth of the flats above, the scats and prints of deer and bear and porcupine were common, and everywhere was the sweet scent of wild azalea; in this primeval place, the introduced blackberries so bountiful these days along the Klamath were nowhere to be seen. Rufous hummingbirds came to fire-colored columbine along the stream edge, bright water poured among the rocks, and the white wing patches of mergansers flashed between high silent walls of the great evergreens upriver. Where steep bluffs or slides prevented progress on the rocks, we forded and forded again, feeling for footholds in deep swirling pools in the swift torrent. Dick sang and whooped in mock alarm. "Just so's you don't get excited, that's the main thing!" he called out, and gave me a big grin.

"I'm pretty young," Dick Myers said (he was in his thirties), "but I can still remember when even the lower part of Blue Crick was still blue, a pretty, pretty blue." And above Bear Pen Flat, where the scars made by the loggers faded from view, Blue Creek was still beautiful, still blue. It is a swift cold stream—a small river, really—perhaps thirty feet across and four feet deep in its strong channels even at this dry time of the year, with a bright sparkle in the breeze that in fair weather comes up the Klamath from the sea each afternoon.

John Trull, skipping from rock to rock with his old fly rod, was fishing for our supper, and Dick Myers winked at me, then grinned in the direction of his stepfather. "Come on, Grandfather!" he yelled, to cheer him on. As we moved north, John worked the eddies for the eighteen-inch rainbows that he recalled from other days, but the stream was full of early summer hatches, and the trout were sated, and in the fresh afternoon wind, it was hard to see the fly in the dancing water.

Now the sun was gone behind the steep green walls to the west, and the air was cool. By the time we reached the point of rivers where the Crescent City Fork came foaming down under steep bluffs to join Blue Creek in a broad pool, we had forded Blue Creek six or eight times and were soaked and tired. Twilight had come, and we made camp quickly in a grove of hemlock and white cedars—the Port Orford cedar, one of the loveliest of the big timber trees in the old forests. A mature cedar may be worth six thousand dollars, John Trull said, but the species was threatened by a root fungus that is spread through the forest by logging machinery that is not hosed clean. The breeze had died, and while John and I cut sword fern and evergreen boughs to sleep on, mixing in fresh pungent branches of pepperwood (California bay or laurel, alias Oregon myrtle) to keep off the mosquitoes, Dick took the rod down to the pool, returning shortly with some small, fat trout for supper.

Soon we lay down and the fire died, and through the black needles over our heads shone the cold stars of the wilderness. I stared straight up for a long time in great contentment. I had wanted to come to Blue Creek for three years—I was here at last.

As the traditional approach into the High Country, the Steps are considered to be sacred ground, and at daybreak the next morning, Dick Myers purified himself in the cold river. The air was dank and gray in the ocean fog that fills the Klamath basin every night, and because we were making a pilgrimage to Doctor Rock, we burned tobacco in ceremonial purification to alert the mountain spirits of our coming and ask for their assistance on the journey. Then we set off into the forest, tracing the lines of moss-covered rocks that were lifted aside by travelers of other days, pushing through the salal and huckleberry that had overgrown the trail where the fall of a huge tree let in light. Among hoary firs, dead still and heavy in their decades of thickened bark, the huge rhododendrons in pink-lavender blossom looked light and fragile.

At a fork in the path, the old Blue Creek Trail headed off toward the east; here rotting Forest Service markers (dating back at least to

1943, when this trail was last brushed out, says Jimmy Skunk) had been clawed down by bears. We followed the north fork, uphill, through forest too huge and dark for brush and wildflowers; for the most part, the old trail was still plain. Here and there were the flat rocks used as ceremonial resting places by people climbing up the Steps. Higher, there were hollow "pitch trees," in the trunks of which fires were built in time of snow; and the shadows of old camps could be discerned in the oak hollows, where people came to collect acorns for winter. Acorns and salmon were the basis of the Indian diet, although other foods were also plentiful. (The driving energy of the great fish as they fought the river without taking food inspired the fasting aspirants who sought power in the High Country.) The white cedar and madrone and tanoak on these lower slopes were the largest I had ever seen, and even my friends were astonished by a heavy tree that rose from its bed of spiny fruits—a gigantic golden chinquapin, which these days is usually seen as a shrubby bush.

Bear scat was everywhere along the path, and John Trull, in the lead as usual, found the big scrape and dropping of a cougar. The cougar persists in the High Siskiyous, though it is not so common as it was. In the 1930s a Yurok friend traveled on horseback with her family from Cedar Camp Spring, near Summit Valley, across the ridges to Doctor Rock; she told me that cougar screams at night had given the party a lot of trouble with the horses and that she herself had seen a cougar cross the path.

Increasingly as we ascended, the sky appeared among the treetops and the trail thickened with brush, so dense in places that we just pushed through, feeling for emptiness with our boots. And so we were astonished, perhaps two hours above the forks, to hear a human voice not far uphill. Whoever this might be had stopped to listen; we stopped, too, as the voice said, "Either that is men or that is bears." Then an old Indian parted the huckleberry bushes; behind him stood a young white man in the green uniform of the Forest Service. Both sides stared, astounded by this meeting on a trail that had scarcely been traveled by anyone in thirty years. But after a moment we nodded, offered our names, grinned, and sat down; among Indians, it was not a situation where one merely nodded and went on.

Guided by the Indian, the Forest Service man was flagging the old trail with plastic streamers in preparation for the crews that would come in the late summer, when water is low and regrowth poor, to brush the trail; following directions given to them by James Stevens, they had made their way down from Peak 8 and Doctor Rock. To the Karuk man, Cliff Ferris, John Trull said, "Don't you remember me?" and Ferris, a weathered Indian in a black hat and canvas vest, squinted, grinned, jumped to his feet, and crossed the forest path to shake Trull's hand. They had known each other twenty-six years before, when both were loggers, and both had lived for the wild, hard-drinking Saturday nights on Second Street, down in Eureka, and especially the bar called the Golden Horn.

As early as the 1930s, some of the old trails across the High Country, made originally by Indians and later used by trappers and gold prospectors, evolved into a series of rough tracks and fire roads that emerged at the mouth of Bluff Creek on the Klamath. With the advent of intensive logging after World War II came a plan to consolidate this network with an all-weather road, but the Christmas flood of 1964 washed out most of the Bluff Creek section, and in 1965, the proposed road was rerouted. Using a timber-access road already in existence (the so-called Eyesee Road, north from Orleans), it would climb quickly onto the high ridges, then follow the ridge systems north to a point beyond Flint Valley, from where it would follow the old track west along the ridge between the Blue Creek drainage and Eightmile Creek. Passing Chimney Rock on its way to a point north of Peak 8, this track would meet the southbound section from Smith River, which departs Highway 199 about seven miles west of the village of Gasquet—hence the name Gasquet-Orleans Road, or G.O. Road.

In the late 1960s, Robert Irwin of the Forest Service's Gasquet Ranger District had reported to his superiors that the proposed route—and the east-west Chimney Rock section in particular— invaded the sacred High Country of the Indians, and he recommended that this area receive protection. The Irwin report was substantially ignored. In the Multiple-Use Plan issued in 1969, in the customary bureaucratic babble ("This site will be a management unit of the Travel Influence Zone"), the Forest Service conceded that certain ceremonial rocks should be protected from encroachment by the G.O. Road and that a "V.I.S. interpretive display" (whatever that is) would be posted at a suitable "overlook." Subsequently it was proposed by the supervisor of Six Rivers National Forest that "core zones" of forty-five acres around each sacred site would be quite adequate; how this magical figure was arrived at was not explained. The

Forest Service also offered to erect nice chain-link fences, presumably to protect the sites from "multiple use." But interpretive displays, V.I.S. or otherwise, were scarcely needed by people who had used the place for centuries, and since silence and solitude and a clear unbroken view in all directions were essential to receiving the spiritual power of the High Country, the Indians' idea of encroachment differed widely from that of the Forest Service, which intended to run its road under the south side of Chimney Rock and on across the north side of Peak 8; this route was only three miles north of Ha-ay-klok, which was to become the "Doctor Rock Recreation Area, Zone 7-11A Recreation Area, Primitive Experience."

When I asked Dick Myers if the spiritual leaders of the tribes had continued the traditional use of Doctor Rock, he shrugged his shoulders. He had heard that a few people still went up there, among them a Karuk medicine man named Charlie Thom. A group of younger Karuk, guided by Thom, were doing their best to mend the tattered remnants of the ancient way and had made medicine in recent years at Chimney Rock; Dick was impressed by this because the Karuk had suffered much more than the Yurok in the white-man wars, their surviving elders were now very few, and almost all Karuk ceremonial equipment and regalia have disappeared through theft and loss and fires.

But as for the Yurok "spiritual leaders," he looked doubtful. "A lot of people going 'round these days calling themselves 'spiritual leaders' that wouldn't know the first thing to do at Doctor Rock. Nobody gives a damn what they call themselves, it's only when they get into *believing* it and make themselves spokesmen for us with the Forest Service that people say, 'Hey, wait a minute, who is *that* guy? He has no authority.' Because Indians know just who you really are. And the Forest Service uses people like that, that's where they get their excuse for doing what they were going to do anyway; they pretend they're acting in good faith, listening to them old Indians, but of course they're not."

One of the "old Indians" he referred to would tell me later, "The Indians had power—no more now. They used to train for it. Now they sleep all night instead—they never make it. Nobody ever done nothin' for Chimney Rock, Doctor Rock—nobody said a word. Now everybody kickin' about it, but what do they know about it? They never seen a Indian doctor. I know the songs, lots of Indians songs for a doctor, but I ain't a doctor. Them Karuks that say they been usin'

Chimney Rock to make medicine, they must be liars; anyway, they got their own rocks, over east in the Marble Mountains."

On the basis of such testimony, proponents of the G.O. Road claimed that the Indians no longer used this sacred area, and it is true that its use is much diminished. In the century of disintegration that followed the wars with the white man in the 1860s, most of the people had lost the way into the High Country, and apart from a few hunters in autumn, there were only a handful of Indians who still went there on a power quest or to make medicine. Much of the medicine that was made (particularly at Ah-Kah, or Bad Place) was dedicated to good luck in gambling, success in murder, and other unspiritual pursuits. One man told me that he had gone up there by the "Golden Stairs" in 1928 with a friend who wished to make medicine to ensure victory in a footrace from San Francisco to Grants Pass, Oregon. However, it has always been true that only a few "high" people, the aspirant Indian doctors and/or priests, were supposed to go there, and that those who did go were not to speak of it, even when the High Country was threatened—hence the criticism of the Karuk Charlie Thom when he testified that he and other Indians still used Chimney Rock for spiritual purposes. Also, the Indians, resigned to being ignored, had failed to speak up until the High Country was invaded, by which time the G.O. Road was substantially complete. In 1975, when I first visited the Klamath region, the highway section through Flint Valley had already been started; by the time I returned, in 1976, the last unpaved stretch was the old east-west track known as the Chimney Rock section, which would not only provide automobile access to the sacred rocks but would lay open the upper Blue Creek drainage to the huge yellow earthmoving machines, and the cable rigs and logging trucks and shrieking saws.

The construction of the Flint Valley section was already well started when it was discovered by two off-season hikers on the day after Thanksgiving, 1974. They alerted the public, and a suit was brought by the Sierra Club on the grounds that no environmental impact statement had appeared. The impact statement came out at last in May 1975, but court appeals delayed the completion of this Flint Valley section until June 1976, when the U.S. district court ruled that the Forest Service might proceed. However, the court took pains to comment that the geological and other surveys conducted for the impact statement had been inadequate, and that on ethnographic grounds (the unconstitutional infringement of Indian religious rights) there was clear basis for another suit. There was also evidence, it said, that the Forest Service had manipulated and suppressed pertinent data. One report (ordered destroyed by a Forest Service officer) clearly supported the Sierra Club's position that the G.O. Road would cause massive landslides and destruction of the watersheds. Another estimated that proposed road-building and logging in the Siskiyous would increase sedimentation in its streams by 1,500 percent.

Though the Sierra Club had no more funds to bring another suit, the Siskiyou Mountains Resource Council was now formed to organize growing public support for the protection of this wilderness, for which the last rampart in a losing battle was the all-important unpaved section of the G.O. Road. In November 1977 there appeared a new environmental impact statement devoted entirely to the problems raised by the Chimney Rock section and weighing the arguments of alternative routes. In this ponderous document of five hundred pages—ostensibly an objective review and summation of conflicting opinions, expert and otherwise—an anthropological survey that the Forest Service had contracted, paid for, and previously approved and that rejected the proposed route across the High Country, was sharply attacked by regional Forest Service archeologist Donald Miller, who lacked any firsthand ethnographic experience of the region. On the basis of a very suspect paper (which has caused Miller to be publicly criticized by colleagues), the Forest Service determined that the already immense expense of the proliferating and voluminous impact statements should be increased still further by a whole new ethnographic survey from which the only anthropologists with significant field experience of the region's Indians and the High Country were to be excluded. Needless to say, all three of these authorities— Arnold R. Pilling, Thomas Buckley, William Bright—had issued strong statements against the G.O. Road.

By this time, a coalition of environmental organizations (the Siskiyou Mountains Resource Council, the Sierra Club, National Audubon Society, Friends of the Earth, and many others), realizing that the High Siskiyous would be spoiled forever by the completion of the G.O. Road, had made common cause with the Indians, scientists, fishermen, and an increasing number of concerned citizens who wondered why their taxes should be squandered on a twenty-five-million-dollar highway between two small and remote villages, crossing a ridge system that is hot and dry in summer (there are no lakes, and the streams lie far down in the steep ravines) and extremely foggy, cold, and wet for the rest of the year. Despite all the Forest Service rhetoric about "multiple use" (known locally as "multiple abuse"), the G.O. Road had no serious purpose besides expediting swift, free access to the Six Rivers National Forest for the lumber corporations, which were being presented with a "glorified logging road" at the taxpayers' expense. Even that old Indian who was offering the Forest Service the kind of testimony it wished to hear had no illusions about the G.O. Road. "All the Forest Service wants that G.O. Road for is haulin' logs out; I know that. They don't think I know that, but I do."

Unless an alternate route was adopted, the Chimney Rock section—the weak central link in this heavy chain across the mountains—would determine the fate not only of the High Country but of Blue Creek. Defenders of the area thought that wilderness designation was the only real protection for the Siskiyous, and they hoped to achieve this in the course of a new series of roadless area public hearings (known as RARE II).[1]

A Yurok medicine man, Clavin Rube (whom I had visited with Craig Carpenter in 1976), objected to the wilderness designation because it suggested federal ownership of Yurok territory and would require that the true owners take out permits to walk on their own land; the U.S. government treaty of October 6, 1851, with the "Pohlik or lower Klamath Indians," designed to eliminate Indian title to these lands, was never ratified by the U.S. Senate or signed into law by the president of the United States. Rube also objected to the term "wilderness" for a home country that Indians perceive not as "wild" but natural, complete, a perfect place under the dominion of higher powers, a "good place," full of strength and beauty, where Indians may go to be restored. No Indian would quarrel with either of these points (or with the idea of entrusting jurisdiction of the High Country to responsible Indian authorities), but they won't matter much if the towering rocks and clear silences of the High Country are reduced to chain-link fences, car horns, nonbiodegradable litter baskets, and V.I.S. interpretive displays, with forty-five-acre "recreation" areas for the Indians.

---

[1] The right of the federal government to limit exploitation of disputed land while its wilderness survey was in progress was contested in court by a Denver "legal foundation" led by James G. Watt, who later became Secretary of the Interior.

In Eureka, I had paid a call on Joseph Harn, the supervisor of Six Rivers National Forest. In the waiting room outside his office the publications were two neat, unread issues of *Forest Industries* and the *Sierra Club Bulletin*, as if he sought to bring these two into peaceful balance; and in fact Joe Harn turned out to be a hearty, open, friendly man with a big sunburn and an old-fashioned mustache, who would make a terrific small-town politician. Perhaps this is why he was chosen for this job, which had changed hands several times in the last few years as the plot thickened.

Rather skillfully, Harn implied that environmentalists were just another "special interest group," like the lumber interests, against which the American people and their national forests must be defended. "If nobody's happy, we must be doing *something* right," he told me with a laugh, and I got the idea that he says this pretty often. It was certainly true that nobody was happy, but what the Forest Service was doing right was very much a matter of dispute. Joe Harn, like all Forest Service people, was courteous and friendly in the face of some hard questioning, having been trained to be politic and "nice" to everyone. But this eagerness to please becomes quite dangerous when, as inevitably happens, the district supervisors and rangers are courted by the local establishment, which does not include environmentalists or Indians. In a sawmill economy, it is led by the big lumbermen, with whom foresters share a "management" mentality that tends to abhor the concept of unmanaged wilderness.

"No one used to care what the Forest Service did," Harn complained. "That's when there was plenty of timber, and forests were just for public recreation. If we said, 'Let us show you what we're doing here,' people would say, 'Don't bother us, we're going fishing.' All they wanted to do was recreate. Now it's different. Some say we try too hard to please Big Lumber, and some say we try too hard to please Environment. But what we're here for is to find just the right balance, to do what's best for everybody." And few people would seriously deny that the Forest Service does the best it can; whether or not that best is good enough is another matter (interested parties on both sides of any national forest issue are apt to think of the Forest Service as wishy-washy). In regard to the G.O. Road, Harn made the point that no one had spoken out against it "originally," which of course was true; but it was also true that in the remote area, a great deal of the "improvement" of old roads was done before the public at large knew what was going on, and even now both ends of the G.O. Road, terminating on the public highways, had been left not only unfinished but unmarked, leaving the public as ignorant as ever about what was going on back in the mountains.

Next day I talked a little while with Joseph Winter, staff archeologist for Six Rivers, whose predecessor, Jerry Wylie, courageously opposed the construction of the G.O. Road before his transfer. Winter acknowledged that the Indian "leaders" who have been most cooperative with the Forest Service might not be the true spokesmen for their people, but said that he wished to work with any who expressed interest, in order that "Native Americans would feel included in the process." It was because of Karuk protest, he pointed out, that plans had been canceled for the Red Cap Bridge across the Klamath near Orleans, which would have destroyed a traditional site for the White Deerskin Dance. This was certainly commendable, and the more reason to wonder why the Forest Service was persisting in its plan to build a highway through the heart of the sacred High Country.

To complete the picture on the G.O. Road, I rang up Richard Reid, the Western Timber Association's "public relations forester," who does the talking for the big lumber corporations. Reid pointed out that 25 percent of "stumpage" fees (fees for trees sold while still standing) received by the Forest Service went for schools and highways of local counties; in other words, the taxpayers were compensated for the failure of corporations to reinvest in these beleaguered counties where they made their money. (Louisiana-Pacific had publicly revealed that its local profits were reinvested in the Southeast and Texas.) "It's in the best interest of everybody to complete the G.O. Road," Reid concluded, pointing out that to leave the road unfinished would be so wasteful. That was certainly true, but there was much more at stake than the waste of money; one might just as well say that it is wasteful for an alcoholic to abandon his unfinished bottle. Since the G.O. Road was a rotten idea in the first place, didn't it make sense to cut our losses? "I'm afraid I'd have to disagree with you on that," said Reid, whose title had recently been changed to "information officer."

. . . . .

The ridge climbed steeply once again, emerging from cool, early morning forest into the hot scrub of the upper slopes. Here the trail lost itself in montane chaparral of oak, manzanita, chinquapin; the sharp, stiff, thorny leaves of canyon live oak scratched our bare arms and the open holes in my old jeans. We fought our way uphill through these coarse thickets, stopping every little way to gasp for breath.

The sun was high, the red rocks glared, the air was still. "Got to take it one step at a time," Dick sang out cheerfully. But John, who was still moving in his quick, urgent gait ("Got to move like that— that's the way I go best"), was stopping more and more often, and he showed the strain. He and Dick were halfway through their water, which in summer is scarce in the High Siskiyous—one of the many reasons why few people will ever go there just to "recreate"—and I wondered if we would find any at the summit. Last September, I recalled, there had been water in a rank meadow pool between Doctor Rock and Peak 8, but autumn rains start early in the Siskiyous, and there had been rain before my visit.

Meanwhile, the Steps were growing steeper, the brush fields thicker, the day hotter—the great heat of the day would come in midafternoon. We had pushed uphill eight or nine miles and perhaps four thousand feet, and still there was no sign of our destination. But now small cairns built by pilgrims of other days began to mark the trace, and finally I saw Doctor Rock itself, a dark monument on its bare saddle, toward the west. After eight and a half hours of hard climbing, we had reached the ridge, yet the ridge seemed to be leading us away from Doctor Rock.

"Come on," John said. "I got to see what in the hell we come all the way up *here* for." We were footsore and staggering in the heat, and when we came upon a small warm pool in a rank meadow, blue-flecked with violets and blue-eyed grass, we sank down and rolled out of our packs. The pool was shallow, rather warm, and teeming with dragonflies and torpid salamanders—"water dogs" Trull called them in disgust. (Salamanders are sok, or "poison reptiles," to the Indians, and those in alpine ponds are particularly feared, since their stare can detect an evil heart or unclean being.) But I, for one, was glad to see the water and I drank heavily, after which we lay flat out in the long grass. An hour later we were ready to go on, leaving our gear behind in the small meadow, but our legs felt weak, and we soon found that we had to climb still higher. On a wooded slope, at a cold spring in the rocks, we drank again, then headed west, crossing a beautiful meadow guarded by a great monolithic granite and climbing once more to a bare ridge of red peridotite and windworn cedars. Before us lay the gaunt face of Peak 8, but Doctor Rock stood on the far side of a deep wooded gully, a steep descent and another climb away.

We could not believe it; we had imagined ourselves right on top of it, and still we were far off. And I remembered how, the year before, approaching Doctor Rock from the other direction in broad daylight, we had also had strange trouble drawing near, and how a medicine woman had said that the resistance of the place had come about because we had not been correct in our preparations. Perhaps John and I should have bathed this morning in the cold water of Blue Creek; perhaps we should have paid respect at the ceremonial places and not just flung ourselves down anywhere along the trail.

It was late now, and our strength was gone. We talked about going on, but we could not move. On this high place of incense cedars and knobcone pine, we saw a place were deer had gathered and where a fool grouse had been dusting. To the west, the ridges fell away to the Pacific; to the east, beyond Chimney Rock, lay the horizon of the Marble Mountains. Last year, from just west of Doctor Rock, I had seen the snow cone of Mount Shasta, eighty miles away, and now John spoke about "the line of power" used by the old Indians that ran east and west from Mount Shasta to Red Mountain and included Chimney Rock and Doctor Rock; this "line of power" was part of the sacred solitude and silence. Seeking power, the aspirants would sit in a near-trance, sometimes for days, on ledges or "seats" constructed on the sides of the high rocks; usually the seats faced toward the east, to meet the Creator in the rising sun.

For a long time we sat among the cedars, gazing out over the silence of the High Country. This was the sixth of July, and still there was a frost of snow on the Marble Mountains. Tomorrow, because we were traveling light and had little food, we would have to return to our camp at Blue Creek, then head downriver to Bear Pen Flat, to Slide Creek and the road on out over the mountains. And so we talked more about going on, but no one moved. I reasoned that I had already been to Doctor Rock, that the purpose of this trip had been to ascend the Steps; the others declared the intent to return another day. And still we sat there, though Doctor Rock was not much more than a hard mile away, and we had another three hours of good light. "This would be a pretty place to make our camp," John said. "Too windy for mosquitoes. But the old people say that you must never sleep up here on these high ridges. There is wind that comes that takes the man away, leaving just the skeleton."

Finally we turned and retraced our steps along the ridge and down through the pines to the beautiful meadow with the mighty granite, then on through the quiet shadowed wood where water flowed ice-cold from the stones and out again into a glade where the glistening beargrass—an extraordinary member of the lily family with tall stalks that bear round full heads of cream-white blossoms—was shimmering with summer light. And there were other lilies, too, and iris and lupine and blue vetch, yellow arnica and buttercups. Harebells, mountain penstemon, wild rose—at least fifty species of wildflowers in sight at once, the most various display I have ever seen. The ground rock of the Klamath Mountains, of which the Siskiyous are part, has changed little in the more than one hundred million years of its existence, though these high ridges did not rise until two or three million years ago, an uplift—and a steepening—that is still going on. Because these ancient hills include representative plants of four main botanical regions—the Pacific Northwest, California, the Cascades, and the Sierra Nevada—and because no icecap ever came to obliterate the older forms, the flora includes at least thirteen hundred species of vascular plants, including a few relicts of the Tertiary period, sixteen million years ago. The California Rare Plant Society—one of the many groups now fighting to save the Siskiyous—has identified thirty plants as "rare, very rare, or endangered" (the Forest Service refers to these as "a few sensitive species"); and there are a number of flowers and trees that are endemic to this region, including the Brewer's spruce and the Sadler oak. Seventeen of the twenty cone-bearing trees known to occur here are found in an area of one square mile, near Russian Peak; there are said to be more conifers (and lilies) in the Klamath Mountains than in any comparable region of the earth—cause enough, all by itself, to save such country.

Hermit thrushes sang on every side, robins and nuthatches, warblers and chickadees; a jackrabbit came and went away; I saw a skink of brilliant cobalt blue. At camp we made a quick hot fire of manzanita twigs and ate up the last of the food; we were not hungry, and John Trull was already lying down. Earlier a bear had dug a yellow jacket's hive out of the meadow, and we had heard one rummaging back in the bushes. Big bear piles were everywhere, no two alike because of the great range of bear diet, but we did not think we would be bothered. Though black bears are common here, they remain wild in the absence of "refuse areas" and litter baskets and carefully avoid the camps of human beings.

The night was cold, no mosquitoes came, and stars appeared among the silvertip firs and knobcone pines that kept their silent watch around the meadow. Two days before, a Hupa friend had told me about five young Hupa who were up here someplace by Doctor Rock, trying to make medicine; they had come without spiritual training or guidance, and everyone knew that what they were doing was very dangerous. "They never come up here by them Steps, or we'd have seen sign," Dick Myers said. "They had more sense than us, then," John Trull grunted.

Next day there were big thunderheads over the Klamath, not usual at this dry time of the year, and the day after that we were told by Aunt Queen James that she, too, had been aware of the big thunderheads and assumed they were there because "Dick had gone fooling around up at Doctor Rock." For the last sixty years, Aunt Queen has lived alone on the *rancheria* of her father-in-law, Segap, or Coyote, known to the white men of the time as "Coyote Jim." The rancheria lies where Tully Creek comes down on the south bank of the Klamath, facing the sacred mountain of Kay-wet, or Burrill Peak. The old lady was nearly-deaf and suffered cataracts but was still full of curiosity and humor; she was smiling now but became serious again. "You have to do right up in that place," she warned us. "You can't fool around or eat food or drink water. You can't sleep with your woman for a year before you go. You can't let those white people go up there. The white man, too, can be hurt if he doesn't do right; he can be dead."

"She means you can't go leaving sacred pipes and things up there that would not have been touched by righteous people in the old days," Dick whispered tactfully.

When the first environmental impact statement was in progress, Aunt Queen was interviewed by two Forest Service people in regard to the significance of the High Country. According to Dick's wife, Debbie Myers, who had been present, about two hours of tapes were made, yet Aunt Queen's testimony never appeared on the official record. Speaking against the intrusion of the G.O. Road, Aunt Queen had picked a spoon up off the table, turned it over, sniffed and inspected it, then put it down again before her, asking the Forest Service people,

"Why does the white man have to turn things over and upset things, change things, in trying to understand them; why doesn't he accept things as they are and leave the world alone?" Apparently, other testimony of this kind was also disregarded—in the words of a young Yurok lawyer, Abby Abinanti—"because it was inconsistent with what they wanted to find."

Long before dark in the endless summer evening, we were fast asleep, and we slept hard until first light. Even then, after ten hours' rest, it was difficult to bring John back to life. "Come on, Grandfather," Dick said in his gentle voice; it was important to leave before the sun was high in order to bushwhack down through that hard scrub to the cool forest on the ridge. We set off at daybreak, without breakfast, and once under way, we made good time, rounding the mountain and traversing the steep barren slopes that led down into thick undergrowth, pausing just once to gaze at the lovely sunrise worlds below. During the night, the ocean fogs had rolled into the Klamath gorge, pushing thick white tentacles into the canyons of Blue Creek, leaving the ridges all around like green islands in a sea of clouds; this silent world lay far below the rock where we sat perched like three unshaven angels. And seeing the white river flowing in from the white ocean, I understood much better the Yurok concept of the world as a kind of disc bisected by the Klamath, rising and falling minutely on the surrounding sea.

John Trull frowned and cleared his throat. "You're very close to heaven here," he muttered. He glared at us, as if daring us to laugh. Then he spoke about a time, up in the mountains, when he had found himself quite suddenly in a beautiful, strange place where he had never been before and yet which seemed somehow familiar, as if remembered from another life. He had walked along as if entranced, weeping and laughing simultaneously, as if on the point of remembering something that would bring him instantly and forever a profound understanding of the world, of life and death.

Bewildered and uncomfortable, he stopped speaking, and for a little while we sat in silence on the mountainside. But I had been to this place, too, and so had Dick. We were silent, not because we were embarrassed, as John thought, but because we were awed by John's precise description. "That's where I stop," Dick said at last. "Whoo-ee. That's where things get too wild for me." And it occurred to me that what John had described was the world that the aspirant Indians of other days who had come up these Steps into the High Country had wished to enter. In the words of Florence Shaughnessy, an old Indian lady down at Requa, where the Klamath rolls out between huge sand-bars, rocks, and cliffs into the sea, "You come upon a place you've never seen before, and it has awesome beauty, everything above you, below you, around you, is so pure. This is the beauty we call *merwerk-sergerh*, and pure person is also *merwerksergerh*."

John Trull was embarrassed by the suggestion that what he had had was a mystical experience; such experience, he had always thought, was strong evidence of a weak mind. Sighing, he stood up and set his pack, wondering aloud if his old shoes would get him home. He jerked his chin at the red shale and serpentine all around us, then at the stands of oak under Red Mountain; the hardwoods were a soft pale green in the dark pelage of the conifers. "Ain't really worth loggin' the few firs that grow big up this high—firs need good soil." He shrugged his pack into place and started down the mountainside toward the trees. Dick Myers nodded. "But they used up everything else, so they'll cut here anyway. They're even loggin' out the tanoaks now."

To the south lay the scarred slopes of Nickowitz Peak and Barren Butte and Lonesome Ridge, and from far off came the shriek of huge machinery, but in the deep valleys between, and as far as the eye could see off to the east, the only mark in all the landscape was the raw gash made by the deep cut-and-fill construction of the G.O. Road. "I'm sure against the G.O. Road," John Trull sighed, "but I might not be, I guess, if I was workin' on it."

To the west of us, Red Mountain, on the high ridge between the Crescent City and West Forks of Blue Creek, was already a dese-crated shrine; we had a full view of the cat-road network that zig-zagged back and forth across its eastern face, the blocky hard-edged scars of random clear-cuts that broke the flow of the whole landscape. This was what was planned for the whole drainage. On the far side of Red Mountain, mercifully hidden from our view, the West Fork of Blue Creek had been ruined—"a disaster area," says Tim McKay of the Northcoast Environmental Center, "a catastrophe, the epitome of bad logging practice—Simpson just trashed it." Most of the western prospect from the High Country today is what the Forest Service classifies as "Class C or Discordant Landscape." In the quiet words of Florence Shaughnessy, "It is just greed that is wrecking this country, just plain greed."

We moved rapidly downhill into Blue Creek, swinging easily along through the old forest and arriving at the river edge well before noon. At camp we made a scavenger's meal of what had been left behind—bran flakes, raw potato, chunks of jarred venison—and kept on going, pausing to swim in a deep hole at the first bend, fording, refording, and fording again, pausing to gather a mouthful of wild strawberries, going on.

· · · · ·

A few weeks later, coming south from Oregon, I had an impulse to return to Doctor Rock, and I stopped in the village of Gasquet to ask directions for the G.O. Road, which was as well hidden at its northern end as at its southern terminus at Orleans. At the South Fork Road, about seven miles west of Gasquet, there was a large dramatic sign: AUTHORIZED VEHICLES ONLY. EXTREME DANGER DUE TO SLIDING AND FLOODING. Until it arrived at Big Flat, about twelve miles from the highway, there was no indication that this became the G.O. Road, or even a clue that it led south to Orleans. And in fact, this road was in a chronic state of disrepair, owing to the unstable nature of the steep valley sides that were collapsing all around it. In many places, half the pavement had fallen into this South Fork of the beautiful Smith River (which, like Blue Creek, was one of the best spawning streams in California), and the truck eased precariously along a single narrow lane with sagging edges. Here reconstruction crews were building bridges over the river, to try their luck on the steep, unstable slopes on the far side. A great deal of good money thrown after bad shores this road up until the next flood year comes along, when mountain torrents will wash it out entirely.

In the hot, dry twilight of deep summer—it had been 105 degrees in Grants Pass, Oregon, when I passed through there at five that afternoon—I climbed slowly from Big Flat into the High Country. There were no other vehicles on this forlorn road, and an hour passed before Peak 8 and Doctor Rock came into view; seen from the north, the dark mass of Doctor Rock, where I would go the next day, was emblematic on the southern sky. I parked the truck on an old jeep track off the highway, on a bare point overlooking the Pacific where my small campfire would be no threat to these tinder forests, and made a quick supper before dark, along with the Pacific sunset, the sea clouds. Just as dark came an unearthly hum rising eerily over the wash of ocean wind in the stunted spruce beside the truck; a pair of sphinx moths, heavy-bodied, with proboscises like the bills of hummingbirds, whirred on their cyclone wings among pale yerba buena blossoms by the road. Then it was dark, and the sphinx moths fell silent as the earth came to rest. I stamped the fire out to the last spark. Except for the soft wind, there was no sound.

Last September, on my first approach to Doctor Rock, I was instructed by Indian friends from the Hupa reservation to burn ceremonial tobacco north of Flint Valley; on the second trip, with Trull and Myers, we did it at the foot of the "Golden Stairs." Early this morning, before setting out, I did it once again, facing east, then south and west and north, then gazing across Red Mountain to the Pacific. And as I finished, there came an insistent thump upon the earth. Startled, I turned to see an Indian, an older man with a thick walking stick, approaching me along the jeep track from the G.O. Road. The heavy old man, passing by without a glance, only grunted "Morning." I guessed he was making a pilgrimage to Doctor Rock, but I wanted to be sure; knowing I shouldn't, I asked where he was going. He whirled to squint hard at this white man who had no business here at daybreak. "What?" he demanded. "Oh, someplace over there." Not wishing to name a medicine place, he waved his stick toward the south and kept on going.

I let him go until he was out of sight, then started off myself, entering the forest and walking uphill to the trailhead where the path heads south under Peak 8. Last year, in a suggestion box placed at this point by the Forest Service, I had inserted the suggestion that the box be removed; this was Indian sacred ground, I said, and such touristic eyesores had no place here. And I was pleased to see that the box was gone—perhaps some bear looking for food and finding nothing but suggestions had knocked the damned thing away into the woods— and that the Forest Service had not "improved" the path, which was still a dim trace, heavily overgrown.

Though I went slowly through the chinquapin, eating a few huckleberries for my breakfast, I soon overtook the Indian, who was rolling slowly through the bushes like a bear. He whirled on me again and with his stick waved me ahead, but when I said I was in no hurry, he went on without a word. Perhaps my lack of haste had mollified him, for in a little while he paused to show me the big prints of a deer—"There's plenty of doe prints, but this here's a good buck"—

and another place where a human being had sat down. "Funny thing is, there's a sign of one man going this way, maybe two, but I can't find no sign coming back." On this dry ground, in this thick scrub, I was impressed that he had picked up any sign at all. It had not rained in several weeks, and of course, these tracks belonged to Cliff Ferris and the Forest Service man, who had been dropped off on the G.O. Road.

To my surprise the old man said that he had never been to Doctor Rock before, although he had once worked as a logger in Bluff Creek—was this the path? I nodded. We were now moving out of the forest again, onto the open west slope of Peak 8; last year in this place, at daybreak, I had surprised a sow bear with her cub. Ha-ay-klok, the Doctor Rock, awaited us on its bare ridge, taut and black in the sharp early light, and from below, the huge monolith called Ah-Kah, Bad Place, rose from its dark bed of giant firs. Ha-ay-klok and Ah-Kah are the only huge isolated granites in this landscape, the one high on its crescent on the sky, the other deep down in a ravine; one understands why the Indians perceived them as the Good Place and the Bad. And the man said shyly, "For us, this is like the white man's church, y'know. I been wantin' to come up here for a long time." When I said it was too bad he had run into me, that he must have planned to be here by himself, he nodded. His people used to come up here to hunt, he said, for there had always been a lot of game near Doctor Rock, but once his uncle had come up for something else. "I don't know what he was doin' here," he added quietly.

Slowly we crossed the bare serpentine slope and went down into the saddle between Peak 8 and Doctor Rock. There I turned off the path, telling him that I wished to see if the summer water was still good in that small pool below, where a swampy stream down from a cedar grove made a green meadow. He stopped and turned around to squint at me. "You better go up there by yourself," I said. The old man smiled and invited me to visit him at Requa. Giving me his name and directions to where he lived, he added, "You can't miss it." He went on up the ridge toward Doctor Rock, and I went down to the green meadow, all set about with bright, wild tiger lilies and lavender spiraea. A band-tailed pigeon crossed the evergreens, and the jays squalled. The pool was filmed with a light algae, but the springwater down from the cedar grove was cool and good, and the salamanders there seemed full of life; they did not hang around to stare but withdrew into the shadows of the water.

Editor's Note:

Matthiessen's original piece appeared in *Audubon* in January 1979, and was used thereafter as anti–G.O. Road literature in the campaign to save the High Country. It has been an up-and-down battle since then: "Ups" have included removing the "Golden Stairs" from the proposed trail system, and substantial protection for the Siskiyous in the 1980 California Wilderness Act. The "downs," however, were that the Blue Creek and Eightmile Units were excluded from the Wilderness Act, and at the time, the Forest Service was determined to complete the G.O. Road, even going ahead, in 1983, with the contracts with an Oregon construction firm to complete the road.

Litigation and injunctions delayed construction, and in 1990 Congress passed the Smith River National Recreation Area Act, which included language that formally closed the road corridor. In 1997 the Forest Service, in the name of "forest health," reopened this sacred area for salvage logging at Little Medicine Mountain (the area was burned the year before). There was a series of civil disobedience actions blocking the entrance road in an attempt to prevent further desecration. After a few weeks of protest, the civil disobedience was put down and Little Medicine Mountain was logged.

Court action was only one effort in resolving the G.O. Road controversy. Ultimately, the determination not to build the G.O. Road was administrative and legislative, by the Forest Service and Congress. It was not, in the end, a judicial decision. But the threat of litigation may have contributed to action by the other branches of government.

Across the Checkerboard with Dwight

Stephen J. Lyons

Blue falcons. That's what Dwight says we've been hearing all afternoon out on the beat-up logging roads above the northern Idaho
town of Clarkia. "They say they're extinct but they're all over this
country," he tells me. I hear what sounds like a flicker, but then I see a
contradictory flash of blue. Nothing in my bird guidebooks—old or
new—mentions blue falcons. "There's another one," Dwight says. I
follow his line of vision, but I see nothing but empty sky.

This country is a giant bowl of clear-cuts and second growth, and
soon-to-be third growth, the old growth of cedar and white pine
replaced by nursery-grown hemlock. Also present is a botanical stew
of dying native plants and aggressive, exotic forest invaders, like
meadow and orange hawkweed, a species that can produce 3,200
plants per square yard. Everywhere in various stages of decay are what
Dwight calls "black pine," a spindly little tree that he says was planted
by Roosevelt's Civilian Conservation Corps to combat erosion. "They
weren't supposed to live this long," Dwight grumbles, as if their death
couldn't come too soon. Any biological diversity that once existed has
been replaced with moonscapes and slash piles the size of stadiums.
"Panoramic" is a word to describe the clear-cuts we drive through. So
complete and final. And quiet. In just a decade Idaho has lost one million acres of roadless acres, or 11.4 acres per hour.

Sadly, I am no longer shocked by the devastation. Maybe this is
destruction fatigue. After twenty-five years out West, my heart has
been broken so many times that I've built up an immunity. It's a desperate and mostly failed attempt at self-protection. When did I cross
over? When did I stop believing in the permanence of landscape?

Maybe it was the stand of redwoods that disappeared overnight near Blue Lake, California, or the four-lane, paved road punched in through the old-growth country of the high Siskyous. Maybe it was in Colorado when the Animas River turned the color of mercury after a mine's tailings pond broke and dumped its poisons into the waters. Maybe it was after a tractor-trailer of chemicals crashed into the Little Salmon River and killed every single fish. Whatever it is, I am not proud of my reaction today. I should be outraged, but instead I am worn out.

Dwight is a different story. At sixty-eight, Dwight should by all rights be dead from all the dangerous woods work he's done, or at least retired, and I guess he is from logging, road-building, and all other forms of body-breaking labor that are common up here in the Idaho mountains. Skinny as a snow pole, a bag of protruding bones, Dwight doesn't have hardly a waist to hang his jeans on. He breathes from an inhaler every couple of hours. He has colitis, a congestive heart condition, and 20 percent heart efficiency, which almost led to his death this past spring when he got pneumonia. He looks ten years older than he actually is, but hears and sees perfectly and knows all the plants and trees and subtle contours within a hundred miles.

Speaking of snow poles: "You know Jim don't you?" Dwight asks. "One winter he stole a bunch of these snow poles. Good wood. But the Department of Transportation guys finally caught him in the spring when he used the poles for his garden fence."

Dwight always has some scheme in the works, like a warehouse-load of older model car and truck parts he traded a .30 gauge shotgun for—and that are sitting in his Elk River shop.

It's a good thing, too, about the automotive parts, because the starter on this pickup truck Dwight has me, my wife, Jan, his wife, Carol, and their black poodle, Lady, cramped into is quickly deteriorating. Every time he turns the key he expends another act of faith. The windshield is shattered, too, and with each bump the crack expands like a spider's web. We're 30 or so miles from any help, another 40 from a good auto repair shop, and 150 from the nearest emergency room. But Dwight has a spare starter under the seat, along with a loaded .357, and all kinds of stuff I can feel rolling underneath my butt every time he hits one of those Forest Service–dug Kelly humps—put in, Dwight complains, to keep the public out. This complaint leads to a lecture on the different philosophies of two Forest Service district supervisors: The district ranger in the St. Joe National Forest keeps the roads maintained because he wants people to enjoy the forest; the district ranger in the Clearwater National Forest is a mean so-and-so who wants to keep the taxpayers down below on the paved roads.

For no good reason, I have complete faith in Dwight's ability to navigate us safely through this maze of new and neglected skid roads. Maybe because he's so well prepared. Jacks, thermoses, come-alongs, chains, ropes, shovel, cooler, spare bullets, standard and metric wrenches all jostle around in the bed of the pick-up. "Hold onto Lady's leg so she won't fall out," Carol tells me, as we all bounce up and down like kids on a trampoline.

Storytelling keeps Dwight's mind in motion, and driving around this country ensures that his emotions stay sharp. "I was riding my three-wheeler down a road just the other day when here comes a Forest Service truck. This ranger, a young guy, said, 'Can't you read?' I said 'Yes.' 'Then why are you driving on this road?' I said, 'Because my taxes helped pay for this gravel, and I'm just using up my share.' He said, 'Don't get smart with me. I'll have you arrested. And what gives you the authority to drive on this road?' I reach down and pull out my .357 and answer, 'This gives me the authority.' Well, the guy drives off real fast, and I figure the sheriff is going to be waiting for me at my house when I get back to town. But he isn't."

Three days later, Dwight is on the same closed road, and meets the same guy in the truck. "This time he didn't even slow down or look at me," Dwight says.

I've heard this story before, from other people, on a similar theme: Native, hardworking Idahoan stands up to a cocky, disrespectful U.S. Forest Service employee, or some other federal authority figure bent on denying property and gun rights, who, when faced with the great western equalizer—a loaded gun—backs down and slinks away. In this part of Idaho, it's hard to find people who are not suspicious of anyone in a uniform.

Just after Dwight tells his story, he pulls the pickup over to the side of the road, jumps out, and, with an agility he shouldn't have, clambers up into a second-growth mess. He comes back with a bouquet of huckleberry plants torn out at the roots. "The Forest Service says this is illegal. I could get a fine for pulling off these branches. But they will allow 4,000 sheep to graze up here and eat everything down to the ground. Now, is that fair?" He has a point. He usually does. We stand around the bed of the pickup, delicately relieving the branches of the tiny berries, while he disappears to bring back armful upon armful of illegal plants.

We will climb the same steep hills from where the steam engines used to winch millions of board feet up the top of a hill known as "The Incline" in the early part of the century to waiting narrow-gauge trains. We will only get out of the truck to eat lunch, drink coffee from Dwight's battered thermos, pee, and pick huckleberries.

This trip was Dwight's idea, a birthday present to Jan, to show her how the roads connect up here and to teach us some of the history of how this country was opened up. She's known Dwight for more than a decade and constantly teases him, which he visibly enjoys. "Now, Dwight, is there any difference between a good story and a lie?" Most of Dwight's stories are true, or at least close enough to truth for telling, and all of them good ones. I don't know what to believe. "There's not a woman in Elk River over the age of sixty-five who wasn't a whore once," he declares at one point. Carol quickly reminds us that she's not quite sixty.

Dwight and Carol have been together forty-four years and married for forty-one. They belong to the Seventh-Day Adventist church. By the age of twenty, Carol had borne four children. Then she had another. They fed their children a diet of poached deer and elk that Dwight smuggled in the bottom of gasoline fuel drums past the Forest Service checkpoint at Clarkia. "They knew I was getting game, but they couldn't figure it out," he says.

Dwight has worked in the woods all his life, except for a stint in the Merchant Marines and four years serving in the Korean War after lying about his age—fifteen at the time. He built and maintained roads up and down this country, logged for himself and others, and worked for the Forest Service at a time when he says it was still an honorable profession. He can tear down and fix anything.

Carol cans all their food as she's done for four decades. This time of year—August and early September—she picks and sells huckleberries. Twenty dollars a gallon: washed and cleaned. Because the berries are unusually small this year, it takes her an hour to pick a quart. Her labor comes to $5 an hour. Carol does a lot of trading—huckleberries for corn, huckleberries to pay for the year's rent for Dwight's shop, huckleberries for quilt scraps—she cleans houses, and for a modest fee she transports folks in Elk River to the hospitals in Lewiston and Moscow—a hundred-mile round trip.

Dwight hates water. Instead he prefers coffee and Pepsi. He used to drink a half gallon of Canadian Mist a day. On his fiftieth birthday he drank his usual ration plus another fifth his boss gave him, then a fresh fifth of vodka at a friend's house. His buddies were all taking bets to see when Dwight would keel over. At 3 a.m. he was still drinking the vodka and telling stories. His companions had passed out.

"But that's not why I stopped drinking," he says. "I quit because I lost a whole week of my life, and I still don't know what I did that week. I had a job as a welder, and they say I went to work and did my job. But I don't remember it." The next week Dwight came home and said to Carol, "That's it. I quit."

He still has a drink now and then, Carol gently reminds him, like last year at the Lewiston rodeo. He quit smoking cigarettes last year, a habit he began at the age of ten. Wasn't hard, he boasts. "I say if you're going to do something, just do it."

At lunch while our wives are off talking, Dwight calls me over to the truck and shows me the .357 handgun. Then he reaches in his pocket and digs out four of his special "people bullets" that will "tear a big hole in a man. You never know what you'll find up here." He slips me the pistol, and for the first time in my life I hold a gun. It feels good, like a well-made tool. My initial impulse is to shoot it randomly into the woods, but I hand it back to Dwight.

"When did you fire this last?" I ask.

"Yesterday, at a rock 25 yards away."

"Did you hit it?"

"You bet."

· · · · ·

I brought a map of the Clearwater National Forest and Palouse Ranger District of the St. Joe National Forest to keep up with Dwight, but within an hour into the trip we have driven off the map. The map is useless anyway. In addition to its unwieldy size—4 feet by 4 feet—and the dozens of folds that are hard to negotiate with Lady tap dancing on my thighs with her sharp claws, there are too many colors. There are thirteen, many in earth shades of red and clay and brown, and each color represents a landowner. When I spread the map out, it looks like those early maps of Africa after the European powers carved it up. For a state like Idaho that complains about all the federal non-tax-paying lands—more than 70 percent of the state is federally owned—a map like this one shows a rather different version. Five of the owners are timber companies: Champion International, SAW Forest Products, Potlatch Corporation, Plum Creek Timber Company, and Bennett Tree Farms. One color will run into another, and sometimes a square-mile will have three or four colors competing for ownership. Even when the dominant color of the squares is dark green, signifying public lands, a patchwork of Plum Creek Timber Company pink intrudes.

The reason for the checkerboard appearance of this map, and most Forest Service maps in the West, is because of an act of Congress. The 1864 Northern Pacific Railroad Land Grant is perhaps the one document most responsible for the presence of private timber company holdings on America's public lands. In the 1995 book *Railroads and Clearcuts* by Derrick Jensen and George Draffan, the authors write, "In 1864, during the Civil War, the United States Congress created the Northern Pacific Railroad Company and empowered it to construct a rail line from Lake Superior to Puget Sound. To aid in the construction and maintenance of the railroad, Congress conditionally granted Northern Pacific nearly 40 million acres of land." At the time, this was 2 percent of the entire forty-eight states, almost the equivalent in area of present-day Washington State. The amount of right-of-way in the grant was not large, 200 feet on either side of the proposed tracks, and some ground for stations.

The largest portion of the grant was for construction and maintenance of the rail system: a band 40 miles wide through the states of Wisconsin, Minnesota, and Oregon; 80 miles wide through the territories of North Dakota, Montana, Idaho, and Washington. Land was granted in alternating square miles, and, as Jensen and Draffan write, "a 'checkerboard' pattern of ownership was created that is still visible on maps and landscapes of many Pacific Northwest forests."

Most of the day Dwight leads us through lands owned by one of the principal beneficiaries of the 1864 Northern Pacific Railroad Land Grant Act, Potlatch Corporation. We also pass briefly through Bureau of Land Management property at Hobo Pass, as well as a few miles of area labeled on the map in green as "Adjacent National Forest Lands," which looks a lot like the well-used Potlatch land. Millions of board feet have been harvested from these "working forests."

· · · · ·

"It must have quite a feat to build those donkey steam engine railroads up these steep Idaho hills to get at all these trees," I say as we inch along, sheer drop-offs out my window.

"It took a lot of dead men and a lot of will power," Dwight whispers. "The woods is the great killer of men." We stop along an abandoned watering stop for trains. Dwight points at a hill. "Imagine hauling a 30-pound saw, a gallon can of gasoline and oil, a saw kit, ax and hatchet and wedges, a maul, and your lunch pail up that bank in two feet of snow," he says solemnly. "Then you'll understand why there are so many drunken lumberjacks." We sit in the cab for awhile with the engine idling and no one speaking; incredibly, not even Dwight, who continues to stare up the hillside as if expecting the ghosts of broken loggers to come marching slowly down toward us, the sun glaring off their steel helmets and suspenders.

Dwight can't maintain the silence for long and soon launches into another story. When no one let the water out of the dam at the Elk Creek pond in April and Dwight's shop, with all those car parts, was flooded with spring runoff, he called the Idaho Department of Parks and Recreation and warned that if they didn't start letting some water out he was going to dynamite the dam and then they could figure out how to fix it. They let the water out. "Next spring if they don't let the water out, I'm going down there with a D-7 Cat."

The real reason his shop was flooded was because the town official, who has a key to the dam's lock, hates Dwight. This dates back to an incident years ago when they were logging together. The guy was a loader at the time, and Dwight was a logging truck driver. Each time his adversary loaded logs on Dwight's truck, he would tear off (purposely, Dwight maintains) the truck's mirrors.

"Finally, I says to him, 'If you don't stop hitting my mirrors I'm coming up there with my ax, and we'll straighten it out.' He laughs and takes some logs and tears my mirror off. I jumped into that cab with my ax and he took off and ran down the road. The big boss comes up and says 'What's going on up here?' I tell him, and he orders the guy to pay for my mirror, or he'll write him a pink slip on the spot. The guy pays for the mirror and we never had any more trouble." Until he got the key to the dam.

We drive on and Dwight becomes confused by all the new roads. "You have to come out here every couple of months because everything changes all the time," he grumbles, dodging another newly washed out portion of a logging road.

．．．．．

Little wonder Dwight is confused. The Clearwater National Forest has 4,558 miles of roads within its borders. To the north, in the Panhandle National Forest, are 8,312 miles of roads, or 10 miles of roads for every square mile of land, the highest density of roads of any national forest in the United States. Both figures are probably low. If one factored in "jammer roads," abandoned skid roads built in the 1950s and 1960s, the original figures might double. More than 440,000 miles of roads jigsaw through our public forests, or roughly ten times the entire U.S. interstate system. You could drive the quarter of a million miles to the moon and still have plenty of road left over.

．．．．．

Dwight finds his way around by searching for landmarks: Freezeout Ridge, Cornwall Peak, Grandmother Mountain and Grandfather Mountain, Elk Butte, Orphan Peak, and a new cell phone tower on the top of a nameless hill. But how can he still identify them when they are bare of trees? The lack of birds, deer, squirrels, and people is eerie.

We end our eight-hour day of driving at a cafe in Fernwood, Idaho. Dwight calls Fernwood, "Funnywood." In the men's room are two posters of women in bikinis, one straddling a Harley, and the other, right above the toilet, is standing on a beach, holding a wet beer bottle with droplets of water dripping down her tight abdomen. Radio news reports are filtering in that Princess Diana has been involved in a single car crash in Paris, but that she survived. No one pays any attention. In this isolated part of America, the idea of France is equivalent to the idea of Mars.

This will be our last trip together. In a year Dwight will be housebound, hooked up to a bottle of oxygen. In 2004, he will pass away. The huckleberries will be even smaller and less abundant. I will travel very little into the mountains in the coming year. I have excuses, plenty of them: my daughter's last year of high school; a commitment to drive less and use fewer resources; an undependable car; and a lack of time. Closer to the truth is that I want to preserve the image of wilderness that I first saw when I came out West twenty-five years ago. What we witnessed today is too much truth. Miles upon miles of clear-cuts with no end in sight. Silt-choked streams and rivers in muddy ruin. No animals or birds. An emptiness of landscape and still an insatiable consumption. We are never full.

Jan, who knows Dwight well, tells me he feels the weight of loss, too. After all, he's worked out here all his life. Many of his sentences begin, "I remember when ..." Dwight will see the destruction through to the end. He can't turn away. I can come and go from these mountains as I please. I am hardly privileged, though, or better than Dwight because I love grizzlies, wolves, and trees. Dwight loves them too, but on a more intimate level. He paid for his love with his health. I sign petitions and write letters.

Dwight had his favorite groves, but only a handful remain, like the stand of cedars and alder where we ate lunch. After hours of driving in deforested areas that were unnaturally hot, the tiny forest was a throwback: cool and shaded, and filled with birdsong and native plants. Somewhere in the distance we could hear water running. Dwight seemed at his happiest during lunch, commenting, "When you spend a day up here in the woods you just know there is a creator."

I often think of Dwight's comment about a creator, especially when I walk through a forest. For all the recent writings about nature I cannot recall a more eloquent statement. Now when I mourn the wildness we have lost, I cannot separate Dwight from that loss.

At the cafe, while we drink the worst coffee I have ever had, I tell Dwight that I once drove all the way to Montana without hitting pavement. He laughs. "Heck, I can drive to Canada without touching pavement. Have to cross a couple of highways, though." Then he tells me how he would do it: Avoid the lakes, stay to the east of Sandpoint, drop down into Libby, follow the Yaak River north, and you can cross the border at any number of places. No checkpoints, too, he says with a smile, like he's done this a hundred times. And I believe him, every word.

Two Ways of Being

Mary O'Brien

August 3, 2000

Gravel is chattering against the underside of our van, so we talk and laugh a little louder. We occasionally look out at the low vegetation and seemingly still, gray water as we pass by. It's cold, windy, and rainy out there, and it's been that way for three days. We grind north on another road for three miles, where it comes to an inexplicable end at a pile of shoved-up gravel.

Okay, time to get out. We put on our hats and rain jackets, pile out of the van, and are stunned into silence. A vast gravel plain surrounds us. To the north, Sheep Creek roars hard against a craggy, mist-shifting cliff. The wind is wild, the rain is wild, and this precipice, stream, and gravel outwash could be part of a dream sequence: jagged, turbulent, and blurred in gray.

This, I think to myself, is the profound difference between two ways of being human in North America's still-wild places. Being stunned into silence, awe, respect, and precaution by their wind, light, sounds, and untamed lives; or digging mines and oil wells into them, clear-cutting forests off them, building lodges and towns on top of them, and slamming roads, industrial recreation machines, and vans full of hyper executives and social tourists through them until the tatters of wildness slide by, noticed, if at all, out a window.

The water and vegetation we had been passing at 50 mph is North America's largest remaining Pacific Coast wetland: the Copper River Delta in Alaska. On a map, you can trace our road, a 52-mile gravel berm constricting the delta's sheet flows into culverts and streams between bridge pilings. Start at Cordova, just south of Prince William Sound, where on Good Friday 1989, at least 11 million gallons of oil destined for machines like our van hemorrhaged from the *Exxon Valdez* after having been piped 800 miles from Prudhoe Bay in the north. Head east across the outwash from Scott Glacier, a finger of the Chugach Mountains' vast ice blanket. Cross Alagnik Slough and its fecund marsh at the base of McKinley Peak. Bridge-hop onto and off Long Island, an oval chunk in Copper River's mouth. Start heading up the east bank of Copper River toward Childs Glacier.

But don't go as far north as the Million Dollar Bridge, which twisted and busted on another Good Friday, twenty-five years before the *Exxon Valdez* ran aground and tore apart. Instead, turn right on a road that doesn't show up on the map and hopefully never will: the road that comes to its shoved-up gravel end after just 3 miles. The plan had been to continue constructing the road across Copper River Delta for 50 miles, a linear barrier with two hundred bridges over salmon streams, to access a coal mine controlled by a Korean entrepreneur and hemlock trees controlled by the Chugach Alaska Corporation. Motorized recreation and development would almost certainly follow. The Chugach National Forest gave the go-ahead for the road. Bridges for its construction were shipped to Cordova.

Enter the Eyak Preservation Council, founded by two traditional Eyak (a brother and sister, Dune Lankard and Pamela Smith) and others who value subsistence living and wildness over corporate extraction, industrial recreation, and extinction. Lankard's focus had changed forever in 1989, when, as a commercial fisherman, he heard the news that oil was pouring out of the *Exxon Valdez* into his life. He determined to help save the Copper River Delta. Its millions of sockeye, king, and coho salmon; shorebirds, trumpeter swans, and other waterfowl. Its water flows, islands, willows, seals, otters, beavers, brown bear, and wolves.

The Eyak Preservation Council protested the construction of the 55-mile extraction road (29 miles of which are on National Forest land), contacted media, staged a lockdown to a bridge along the road, and generally raised hell; and the road-builders quit for a while. The bridges stored in Cordova were eventually shipped away, but bridges can always return.

By this time the Eyak Preservation Council and another local group with vision, the Coastal Coalition, had joined forces and sold

National Wildlife Federation on the idea of gathering even more groups into a nationwide campaign to protect the delta as a whole. Thus the Copper River Delta Coalition was formed, and by December 2000, when the public comment period for a new Chugach National Forest Plan had ended, more than 33,000 comments had been submitted. Of these, 30,956 addressed the question of whether the Copper River Delta should be designated as wilderness: 93.4 percent of the Alaskan respondents and 99.6 percent of all respondents favored wilderness designation.

The ultimate fate of that fragile gravel pile at the end of the three-mile road is still under the watchful, strategic eye of the Eyak Preservation Council.

AUGUST 9, 2000

It's evening and we're back in Cordova after floating several days down the Copper River from Chitina to the delta. My husband O'B, David Titcomb of the Eyak Preservation Council, and I are paddling three kayaks across Eyak Lake. We enter an inlet where sockeye are dead or quietly drifting, their dark red, muscular lives coming to a successful end. Young fish are feeding on their elders who have finished. Silence.

Earlier in the day, Lankard had met us, excited, at our float trip takeout. He had heard reports that coho, the season's next spawners, were now entering the Copper River Delta. I wonder how soon they'll arrive at this inlet and this quiet drifting. We beach our kayaks and hike up a wet, faint track past several levels of a waterfall. Salmonberries and blueberries dangle beside us and slide down our throats. We lie on our backs in the moss and wait. Dinner that night at Titcomb's home is coho and a deep green salad. The aurora borealis pulses silently in the sky at 1:30 a.m.

AUGUST 10, 2000

About to fly home to Eugene, Oregon, I pick up the August 2000 issue of *Alaska Business* in the Cordova airport, and read one of its lead articles, titled "The Corporate Retreat: An Alaska Adventure." It's about the booming market for "adventure travel" to places like Alaska for corporate executives: lodges; personal fishing boats fitted with electronic fish-finders; cabins "historically used by cannery workers, but now retrofitted to a quiet luxury"; and groomed nature hike routes.

The article features Chuck Baird, an Alaskan marketer for this industry. He recalls a trip for Ford executives his company helped arrange at Yes Bay Lodge on "pristine" Cleveland Peninsula near Ketchikan in southeastern Alaska. To create a "lasting impression," the trip coordinators barged a new Ford truck to the remote site and parked it on a rocky, scenic point 60 miles away from the nearest road. "For the three or four days they were having a Yes Bay experience," Baird recalls, "that truck was like their Statue of Liberty. Obviously for those guys . . . to stand on the veranda, smoke a cigar, have some fine cognac and to see their truck across the stream there . . . that's special. That's incentive."

I wonder whether coal executives might like to see a crusher dangled tastefully from a cliff at the end of some access road they had completed. Or maybe a necklace of chainsaws draping a bluff for timber corporation managers. Something for incentive. Or as a small reward.

Late in the afternoon, we're flying south above Oregon's Willamette Valley, where I live. Dark green, sinuous lines can be seen in the agricultural fields: ghosts of creek meanders. Not too long ago, the Willamette Valley was thick with wetlands, braided creeks, and rivers. Ninety-nine percent of these wetlands are now gone. The coho I ate on the Copper River and Eyak Lake are now extinct throughout most of Oregon and Willamette Valley. The Copper River Delta is how this valley once was: wild and mostly roadless, with waterfowl, bears, and wolves.

Farther south and almost home, we fly over Findley Wildlife Refuge, bought in 1964 from private landowners and farmers as a refuge for dusky Canada geese, a large, dark subspecies of *Branta canadensis*. Three months from now they'll be arriving here, one of their few winter homes, from their only summer home: the still-wild, still mostly roadless Copper River Delta.

Some connections remain. We are sustained. Holy world.

The Nakina Trail

Brooke Williams

JOHN'S CAMP, JULY 15, 2004

Although this is not the beginning of the Nakina Trail, for me it is the beginning of this story. The trail actually begins at Kuthai, a small lake a three-hour drive from a small town, Atlin, in extreme northwestern British Columbia. It was once the main village for the 30,000 people of the Taku River Tlingit First Nation (TRTFN), and five miles from which many of the 400 remaining Tlingit members reside on a reserve, and where Farley Mowat's book, *Never Cry Wolf*, was made into a movie. For most who make this walk, John's Camp is the first of two overnight stops. There are ten of us—four Round River Conservation Studies students, four leaders, a Canadian conservationist, two American filmmakers, and two Tlingits—Peter Kirby, Vancouver-educated, in charge of TRTFN special projects, and John Ward, Crow Clan leader and spokesperson, and this camp's namesake. This is his twenty-first trip to the river.

We have been on the trail ten hours, most of it difficult to follow if not for the bright red ribbons tied strategically to trees, a few sawed logs, old footprints in the mud where the trail dips into swamp, and grizzly scat at what seem to be frequent and regular intervals. We have spent some of that time on the ground, propped up by backpacks or trees, absorbing what feel like essential elements from this 18,000-square-kilometer wilderness, perhaps the largest intact ecosystem in North America. After less than an hour in camp, we have a perfect fire built from the only dry twigs within a twenty-yard radius. A pot of water is within minutes of boiling. And light rain is tapping on the

110

world's largest blue tarp, which has been draped perfectly across a framework of pine poles to form a shelter from what, based on the deep gray clouds forming on half the horizon, appears to be a major storm. We are ready.

I am sitting on the flat side of a log, chainsawed lengthwise to form a bench, looking out across a meadow of high grasses hoping to see a moose or a grizzly, which is a hundred times more likely than seeing another human. To my left and behind me, the meadow is bordered by deep forests that, from where I sit, my vision does not penetrate. To my right a small, willow-lined stream drops into the meadow after coming off a small elevation dotted with boulders and lodge pole pines. The meadow runs long, from my left to my right. It seems to be a mile across, but in this country measuring distances is impossible. It may run three miles before curving and dropping through an opening in the view exposing what I've been told are the peaks of the Coastal Range, which could be one hundred or one thousand miles away—I can't tell which.

Besides this camp with its fire pit, wooden benches, pole-and-pit outhouse, and sealed twenty-five-gallon drum containing the huge tarp and whatever else might be needed (which, until we arrived, was perched high in a tree), there is no sign that we are not the first. This may be the wildest place I've ever been. A lesser scaup flies right to left across my vision.

John Ward joins me. "The road will run out of those trees," he says, pointing left, "and straight down the middle of that meadow."

NOVEMBER 17, 2004

The "road" John refers to is the one planned to cut through pristine forests and mountain passes between Atlin and the Tulsequah Chief mine located just north of where the Tulsequah River joins the Taku, which will cross the U.S.-Canada border before flowing into the Pacific just south of Juneau, Alaska.

According to Scott Deveau, writing in today's *Tyee*, a local Vancouver newspaper:

> To develop the Tulsequah Chief project, which the B.C. NDP government approved in principle in 1998, Redfern Resources Ltd. plans to carve a 160-km road from Atlin to Tulsequah, through pristine forest in the Taku River watershed. Redfern says the multi-metal

mine will generate $1.5 billion in revenue and create 260 jobs in the region. . . . Some Tlingit worry the road will not only damage salmon stocks but will also disrupt the migration of an at-risk sub-species of caribou that the Tlingit rely on for sustenance, said John Ward, spokesperson for the Tlingit First Nation.

This article does not mention the Nakina Trail, John's Camp, or any of the seven points at which the Tulsequah Road conflicts with traditional Tlingit trails. None of the articles published in the local and national press mention the Nakina Trail and what it means to the Tlingit culture.

1875
". . . the annual report of the Minister of Mines for British Columbia mentions discoveries of gold on 'Tacoo' River."

1935
This spring, as they have done every spring for hundreds of generations, with their new nets and the little they will need while spending the summer fishing, Tlingits leave their homes in what will become Atlin and walk the 80 kilometers to Canoe Landing near where the clear Nakina River meets the milky and glacial Sloko. The Nakina Trail is wide and smooth after centuries of use by the Tlingits, and the walk may take just two days. At Canoe Landing, they find their spectacular canoes where they left them the previous autumn. Their canoes are carved and painted with the forms of salmon and raven and bear. Here the Tlingits launch and swift currents carry them farther downstream, joining the waters of the Inklin River coming in from the southeast. What were once three individual rivers became one: the great and mighty Taku.

This summer-long journey would be a great deal of effort if "fish" were the only goal—as Atlin sits on the shore of the largest lake in what is now British Columbia, which teems with fish. But "fish" is not what the Tlingit need.

The Tlingit need salmon. They need it with more than their physical bodies. They need salmon with their entire beings.

This autumn, Tlingit families will climb into their salmon-laden canoes—sockeye, king, pink—caught and dried during one hundred long days. Using shifted winds, eddies, their strong arms, and the occasional sail, they will move upstream, arriving back at Canoe Landing. They will stow their canoes as they always have, load their fish bundles into packs as they always have, and hoist onto their backs the protein embodied in salmon that will see them through the coming long winter, as they always have. I imagine that as they climb that first short, steep hill, they will stop at the top and look down toward their canoes and then beyond toward the river. I wonder if they know that they are about to become the last group to walk along this Nakina Trail for fifty years.

1951
The Tulsequah Chief mine opens.

1957
The Tulsequah Chief mine closes.

1981
Redfern begins reconnaissance on the Tulsequah Chief mine, which produces positive results. Redfern initiates negotiations with the previous owners.

Hugh Brody publishes *Maps and Dreams: Indians and the British Columbia Frontier*. In it he is very clear about the effect of roads on the traditional hunting practices of First Nations people: "The hunting territories that lie beyond all roads and trails are comparatively untouched by white hunting. Those that are now within easy reach of a four-wheel drive vehicle are hunted very intensively. The new frontier has allowed hundreds, even thousands of Whites to hunt or fish deep inside the heartlands of many Indian hunting territories and traplines. . . . This access causes the most direct threat to the Indian interest in northeast British Columbia."

1983
Tlingits enter into treaty negotiations to settle their land claim with the British Columbia Treaty Commission (to "change the course of history" and to "legally protect our way of life," according to John Ward).

1987
Feasibility assessment work begins at the Tulsequah Chief mine.

1988

Having heard stories about the Nakina Trail from the time he was twelve years old and living in a one-room, wood-heated cabin, John Ward of the Crow Clan sets out to rediscover the trail with his best friend, Brian Jack, a Wolf Clan member. "Until now," John says, "my family stayed away—too many bears." John and Brian believe that modern laws make it difficult for First Nations to reestablish connections to traditional lands without "reinhabiting" them. "Opening the trail reestablishes our customs. We need the right to manage our trail."

Together, John and Brian explore what they can find of the original trail. Fifty years of growth has all but obliterated it, making the exact original route nearly impossible to follow.

When they began, only a few remnants remained: nearly overgrown treeslashes. Occasionally they'd come upon artifacts of those who came before, rusted metal traps, the occasional bottle or can. Once they'd marked a reasonable route for the trail, they began clearing it using axes and chainsaws. When they can raise money, they have a helicopter drop them with their equipment at remote points along the trail where they work for a week before being picked up.

1994

Full feasibility studies are under way and an application is made to obtain a Mine Development Certificate under the prevailing environmental assessment regulation.

July 7, 1997

Today, as part of the treaty negotiations, the Tlingit leaders submitted a revised Statement of Intent map of their traditional territory. This map defines Tlingit territory as the Taku River and the land drained by all its tributaries. The Tulsequah Chief mine and the corridor for the proposed road are part of Tlingit traditional territory.

1997

Endless discussion and reports, including an Impact Report for the Office of Environmental Assessment, question the impacts of the mine itself on the traditional Taku River fishing industry caused mainly by the mine drainage, which continues to leak acids and high concentrations of toxic metals from early operations. The planned road has impacts that will affect the Taku River Tlingit in ways that are more difficult to measure and understand. The Impact Report states: "Currently, the general area of the road corridor is relatively inaccessible. TRTFN members walk the area both as they hunt, fish and gather in the area, and as they traverse the area en route to more distant reaches of the traditional territory. . . . Factors in this assessment include: resource competition; hunting, forestry, mining, tourism, hydro, etc.; land use conflicts; impacts on habitat; impacts on wildlife; impacts on the TRTFN community."

2000

Dennis Sizemore, who founded Round River Conservation Studies because of his personal commitment to "big wilderness," begins talks with Taku River Tlingit regarding the creation of what began as a two-pronged program that would bring college students working on degrees in environmental studies to learn about the Taku, while Round River scientists and cartographers would create a "conservation area design," or CAD, which involves the mapping of as many dimensions of the area as possible. The goal is to establish baseline information that will contribute to the preservation of the Taku River watershed, perhaps the largest intact ecosystem in North America. The idea is to use the CAD as the basis for a land plan that would ideally contribute to reestablishing Tlingit rights over their traditional territory.

2002

The CAD is nearly finished. John Ward is talking to Dennis about the next steps.

John: So Dennis, once you're done with this conservation study, then what? I mean, you'll have your report, and is it on to your next wilderness?

Dennis: What are you thinking?

John: We all work well together, don't you think?

Dennis: We do.

John: That plus, God knows, we need you guys helping us. Why don't you stay a while?

Dennis: How long?

John: What say we start with one generation?

2003

Dennis signs a long-term lease on a house in Atlin and hires Chris Lockhart, a medical anthropologist, to work full-time on Tlingit social and educational issues.

2004

Dennis hires me to work on economic development in an effort to create opportunities for Tlingits to match promises made by the president of Redfern.

NOVEMBER 18, 2004

From CBC News: "Leaders with the Taku River Tlingit are disappointed with a Supreme Court of Canada decision on their case. The first nation challenged the B.C. government approval for the Tulsequah Chief Mine near Atlin. Canada's highest court has decided governments do have an obligation to consult [with First Nations] but industry does not."

The decision paves the way for road construction to begin. It comes as a surprise.

APRIL 3, 2005

Round River is meeting in Seattle with its partners on the Taku River Tlingit project. After hours of background and strategy, the meeting moves toward determining the next steps. "Any plans we make," says Dennis, "ought to be made on the assumption that the Tulsequah road is going to be built."

"Excuse me."

It is Nola Poirier of the Transboundary Watershed Alliance, a striking young woman who has been quietly listening during most of the meeting, the same Nola Poirier who once dressed up as a caribou to ask Canada's premier, who supports the road ("like a dagger to the heart") of the Taku River watershed, "Why are you not upholding your duty to wildlife?"

"We don't need to accept this road—not now." She is firm, without emotion. "There are approaches we have yet to consider. . . . We can't give up on this."

MAY 18, 2005

From CBC News: WHITEHORSE—Fickle finances threaten Tulsequah mine project.

. . . For more than a decade, the Taku River Tlingit and a variety of environmental organizations have been fighting plans to build a road and re-open the Tulsequah Chief mine near Atlin. The battle went all the way to the Supreme Court of Canada but failed to stop the mine owner's plans. . . . Company President Terry Chandler notified investors Tuesday that increased capital and operating costs, and a lower estimate of available ore, seems to make the project unworkable.

JULY 8, 2005

John Ward begins his twenty-second trip to Canoe Landing. As always, this trips begins near Atlin. But unlike those taken by his ancestors, he is driving a pickup full of people and gear. Fifteen minutes from town, he turns off the main highway onto a relatively smooth, two-track dirt road. Recent rains have formed puddles that explode when the truck John is driving hits them at high speed in his haste to return to his trail, his roots.

This is my second trip.

For the first hour the road is smooth enough for most cars. We pass hunting camps, spur roads, and a small group of dilapidated cabins. Then it dips into the McDonnell River, which creates an insurmountable obstacle for standard street vehicles. Years ago during high water, John, atop his quad runner, was washed downstream and almost drowned. Beyond the river the road gets rough and occasionally plunges into swamps. We get temporarily stuck three times. And five times we stop to unload the chainsaw to clear a downed tree blocking our way. Still, there are spur roads and the bones of hunting camps. "We don't see many animals here now," John says, not taking his eyes off the road. "Too many people." John's few words speak volumes about how now his people must travel much farther to hunt.

We finally arrive at Kuthai, a long, bean-shaped lake that, until the road was pushed through the wilderness, was in the middle of nowhere. We fire a bear banger to let Harry Carlick know that we're here. Harry, a Tlingit elder, spends part of the summer and fall camped at the opposite end, counting salmon coming through his weir on their way back to spawn. In ten minutes Alicia Carlick, Harry's sixteen-year-old niece, is pulling a small motorboat onto the shore where we wait. Getting all of us to camp will take three trips.

Once in camp, most of us relax. John and Peter fire up Harry's quad runner and take off with the chainsaw to work on the trail. They won't be back until nearly dark—around ten. Some of us sit around the smoky fire to minimize the suffering caused by mosquitoes. And some of us find our way along the Silver Salmon River, up which sockeyes will soon be coming to breed and die in the shallows where the river meets the lake. One of the students asks, "Do you think that the salmon know that they're coming here to die?"

We talk about intention.

Then we eat, sharing our lightweight backpacking food with Harry and his crew in exchange for their macaroni and cheese laced with Vienna sausages. Harry retires early to his small cabin. We sit up to see how dropping light changes the color of water. Twice, dark circles form as fish rise. A bald eagle chirps in the trees to our right.

Back in camp, by firelight, we look at the map. The proposed road would be within a mile of here.

JULY 9, 2005

After a crack-of-eleven start, Alicia, in her hipwaders, pulls a boat full of us and our gear across the river to the trailhead. We hoist our packs to our shoulders and move out on the trail, John in the lead. We take turns using small handsaws to clear away the errant alder, the bent spruce, opening the trail a bit more than it was.

After miles and miles of walking, stops including tea and soup, and a swim at Arrowhead Lake, we arrive at John's Camp.

Although there have been Tlingits through here this year, it seems the same as it was a year ago when I was here.

Yet, something about it has changed. Perhaps the word of financial woes from Redfern makes the road a bit less likely. Am I feeling the effect of the diminished threat to this particular place?

David Mackinnon, Transboundary Watershed Alliance executive director, is standing, staring into the huge meadow in the distance, the meadow that recently received a stay of execution.

"What a difference, knowing this place is safe," I say to him.

David, who spends most of his life in Whitehorse finding creative ways to protect this place, walks the trail every year to remind himself why he does what he does. His commitment to the Taku has many dimensions. As nearly as I can tell from the math, he and his partner, Tanus, conceived their child on the Nakina Trail last year.

"Anything is possible with the mining industry," he says. "It could all change tomorrow. . . . We didn't give up when the rulings went against us. And we can't give up now."

JULY 17, 2005

It is our third hiking day. When I close my eyes, I see the red tape markers suggesting a trail. We are muddy and wet from the periodic rain, but more from passing against shoulder-high grasses, each with a thousand droplets, and devil's club, whose plate-sized leaves collect enough water to drink. We walk with a rhythm that our bodies have discovered only in the past day. A trance. I realize that the red tape tied around the barrel of John's shotgun is the same as that which marks the trail. For a moment I wonder if I have really seen any actual tape markers hanging from pine branches or tied to alder or birch, or if I have only been following the flash of John's barrel marking the trail.

"Look." John has stopped and lowered himself to the ground on one knee, his shotgun resting across his opposite thigh. The grizzly scat we have seen regularly along the trail no longer consists of gray, hair-filled lobular segments but is now a mash of deep purple dotted with light seeds. "The Saskatoon berries right on the river ripen first," he says. "We are getting close."

Somehow I find myself with the small saw, stopped in front of an obstacle on the trail: a three-inch-diameter alder horizontal, two feet above the trail. I stop to cut it. Halfway through my task, I am overcome with metaphor.

"This is it," I tell myself. These alders and pines and devil's club and downed spruce represent all that has covered what is meaningful to Tlingit during the past fifty years. Cutting them away symbolizes the work that John (Ward), Brian (Jack), and Peter (Kirby), and other Tlingits are doing to expose the true essence of their people. This Nakina Trail and the salmon represent the essence of Tlingit people, which is once again coming alive.

EPILOGUE

July 10, 2005, 7 P.M.

We arrive atop the hill overlooking Canoe Landing. We leave our packs while John allows us to pay homage to his elders, who are buried in grave houses on the ridge overlooking the small cottages built in the past decades on Canoe Landing. The grave house is designed to hold the elder's body and possessions that were symbolic of his or her life. One small house holds a set of golf clubs made with wooden shafts. There are four or five in various states of decomposition—designed to eventually crumble and disappear into the forest floor.

7:30 P.M.

Below us, there are a few cabins, a fish drying hut, and today the tent of some fat B.C. fishermen who've come by helicopter. A group of Tlingits—men, women, children, and dogs—wave and smile at us. We drop down the hill and the two eager and friendly dogs meet us. Fish flesh is obvious in the drying shed. Michael and Yvonne, who walked in here ten days before, explain that the fishing is not good, that the meat hanging represents only four big kings. And that they've had to compete with a mother griz and her two fresh cubs for berries. I find it difficult to reconcile their complaints with their attitude, which seems content, glad to be here, doing what needs to be done.

8:00 P.M.

After sharing Saskatoon pie, cinnamon rolls, and hot tea, for the last time, we shoulder our packs and bunch up—a better strategy for encountering a mother grizzly and her two young cubs. It is a half mile to camp.

There are no bears during the last leg of our journey, only fishers from Atlin. They are sitting, drinking at their camp. They raise a glass to us, having walked here.

At camp we divide up. Some of us will fish for dinner and some of us will cut wood for the fire (for cooking dinner) and for the sauna (a small room built on the bank of the Nakina).

I am worried. According to the fishers from Atlin and the Tlingits staying at Canoe Landing, the kings seem to have passed. The sockeye may still be a week away. If I had to, I could eat rice one more night.

9:30 P.M.

I've been cutting wood. The sauna stove is burning—from last year I know that we're two hours from true heat. I'm sweating, exhausted, and taking a break when I hear what can only be the shrieks of Nicky or Linky who has witnessed the catching of a fish.

10:00 P.M.

Doug Milek, education director for Round River students, is preparing the fish. Doug has been coming to the Taku for nearly a third of his young life. It turns out that we have two fish for dinner. David, a vegan except when it comes to fresh salmon, has caught one, and John and Nicky have caught the other. They are kings: huge and reddish, ready. Nicky, sleeves rolled up, arms blood-covered from cleaning the fish, grins ear to ear.

The mother bear and her babies are wandering up the beach toward us. "Hey!" John's voice is like a gunshot, with more aggression than I thought him capable of. The mother stands up and stares and points her nose toward us. Then she turns and scurries off, her young in hot pursuit. She'd been coming to clean up after the Atlin fishermen who'd left salmon eggs and their uneaten lunch.

11:00 P.M.

Doug has tin foil in which he wraps the fish before placing them on a metal grill above glowing coals. No need for spices or oil. He gauges from their size that even a bowl of rice will be too much for dinner. For the twelve of us. Utter abundance.

11:15 P.M.

Doug turns the fish in their silver coffins.

11:30 P.M.

The fish are ready. Doug, in his way, suggests that we give thanks for the first fish of the year. Based on how I feel about him, I know that he must give thanks for each and every fish, every year. He makes us all think of the lives given up to satisfy, to please, and to enliven us. I think about City Market in Moab, where I live—reading the labels: Is it Atlantic (farm-raised, artificially colored) or wild? Then I think about the distance that this food has traveled to meet my needs. (Forty-six steps—I counted.) I wonder out loud with the young students about distance. About how that minimal distance must—does—contribute to my nutrition. My gut tells me that part of nutritional value is inversely proportional to the distance between life and death, how far the food has traveled, and the time it took to.

And what about power?

11:40 A.M.–1:30 A.M.

After Doug opens the foil, exposing fish flesh, we all take a first piece in turn, a sacrament. Some prefer pink flesh, well done. Some like it deep orange and a bit raw. We eat and eat, picking flesh with our fingers a piece at a time. Talking and laughing, we notice the perfect moment and know how life was always meant to be lived.

In the sauna we seem to vibrate with the power we took on when we ate that fish flesh.

6:30 A.M.

I'm up to pack. In an hour a helicopter will come, bringing David's wife and child and some boxed food. John, Peter, and I will fly back to Atlin.

We'll fly down the Taku to check a vacant Round River camp and see that the boat is gone, perhaps washed away by the same high flow that undermined the bank, causing a huge spruce to fall and crush the equipment cache. We'll fly over mountains, the sides of which are crisscrossed by mountain goat paths. We'll see a huge moose in a lake right before dropping down next to what we think is Arrowhead Lake, where John will get out with his gear to spend the next few days working on his trail.

We'll leave him waving his shotgun in one hand and holding on to his hat with the other. Then we'll drop into the clearing on Kuthai Lake where Harry will be waiting. Peter will jump out and hand him a plastic bag containing the heads from last night's feast and a large king caught this morning.

During the entire flight, I'll be wondering how to explain just how beautiful and big and wild this place is. I'll try but fail to imagine a road cut through its heart.

Pining for an Oak Meadow

Guy Hand

A western bluebird floats inches above October meadow grass, hovering there, its iridescent blue wings a soft blur, its head cocked downward, its eyes locked onto something hidden from my view. Then it dives and disappears. I hear the dry rustle of fallen leaves, see a shivering in the straw-blond grass, and as the bird pops back into view, I spot the fat green grasshopper clasped within its bill. Another bluebird glides down from the immense oak, kites above the grass for a heartbeat, then dives. Then another. As my eyes adjust to the deep shade gathered under the canopy of this old tree, I see half a dozen bluebirds perched within its dusky light, embraced by thick serpentine limbs and dark leaves, like arboreal sprites, each waiting a turn.

This wide, wondrous meadow. *There is so much life here.* Even at the far end of another rainless California summer, another of this country's annual and utterly uncompromising six-month droughts, this place is teeming. That an oak woodland and all its attendant flora and fauna can survive a waterless half year is miraculous to me, as if the rigid rules of survival have been, in deference to the beauty of this place, waived. The more pragmatic of my biologist friends would call it simple adaptation, the machinations of millennia, the inevitable evolutionary drift that pairs all species to place. I wonder. Over my right shoulder I hear the snare-drum call of a Nuttall's woodpecker as it launches into the air. Over my left comes the querulous cry of a northern flicker. In this meadow I've found mountain lion tracks pressed into soft clay; I've caught the metallic light of the full moon glinting in the eyes of mule deer, fox, raccoon, skunk.

When we bought our cabin, I was slow to warm to the chaparral- and oak-studded mountains that surround us, this wild swath of central California backcountry. I measured all landscapes by the deep green pine forests and rushing rivers of my Idaho youth (don't all judge the world, consciously or not, from their childhood's perch?) and found much of this land, by comparison, as harsh and uninviting as a summer sore throat. Even the oaks displayed the blue-gray, tough-leaved look of an alien world.

This meadow changed all that. The day I stumbled into it, after a steep climb up a trail not marked on my Geological Survey map, I gave an involuntary hoot. Nearly flat, embraced by mountains, it was a secret kingdom, a little Xanadu hidden in the folds of the Los Padres National Forest. Wildflowers filled the meadow floor with color while moss-strung blue oaks broke the light into soft, shimmering pools. Here, between hard slabs of sandstone, was a perfect savannah, a landscape that some say resonates back to the beginnings of human memory. It certainly rippled through me. This meadow became my backcountry base, my *locus mundi*; and the passageway through which I traveled toward an understanding of a rare and radiant land.

At the time, I barely noticed the road. It was nothing more than a pair of faint tracks snaking through the grass beneath my feet. On the meadow's far side, those tracks thickened, then coalesced into an actual road, but a very rough, disused one. An old fire road, I thought, assuming that because so much of this nearly vacant land is national forest, this was too. Many months and many visits passed before I learned I was wrong.

One crisp winter morning, as my wife and I made our way into the meadow, we noticed something odd: a half dozen black plastic pots huddled along the roadside, each with a young pine tree quivering in the breeze. As we walked farther we found more, dozens more, and accompanying them an arsenal of shovels and spades. With every turn of the road we spotted more pots, more shovels, more trees. They were a ragtag lot: a menagerie of potted conifers of dubious provenance, some with houseplants sharing their soil, some with faded Christmas ribbons tied around their slim trunks, some already broken and dying. A mission of mercy, perhaps, but we counted 185 saplings and couldn't believe that the Forest Service would take on the mass planting of non-native trees.

A few phone calls later, I learned that the project was indeed not Forest Service–sanctioned. The meadow was, in fact, an island of private property and the planting a new owner's scheme. I learned that the land had changed hands often over the years, but because of its inaccessibility had never been developed. Obviously this owner planned to change that.

Weeks passed as the pines stood at the side of the road, unplanted. Then one day a notice appeared, tacked to the thick trunk of the meadow's largest oak. In an imperious tone it declared that the property would "now be known as the Pathways Forest Wilderness Retreat," and that although the new owners admitted having "fielded complaints . . . about our choice to plant non-native trees," they still intended to replace what they called "nonproductive land" with "a healthy coniferous forest."

The irony stung. I, who once wished I could cloak the world in the pines of my youth, had found someone willing to do so. Yet my perspective had changed. I'd learned that California's oak ecosystem is hardly "nonproductive," but is actually one of the rarest, most diverse habitats in the world. It harbors thousands of species, each fine-tuned to the vagaries of a climate capable of both decade-long drought and biblical deluge. It is also a habitat in danger: like this meadow, 80 percent of California's oak woodland is privately owned and weakly regulated; in the past half century, one to two million acres have been lost to development. With so little oversight, no one knows for sure.

I tried to contact the new owners but they chose not to return my calls or respond to my letters. Never once did I see them in the meadow. And at the end of their first summer, the nearly two hundred potted pines—still unplanted and unwatered—were dead, every one of them reduced to a standing skeleton. I can only hope that the meadow's reticent owners had second thoughts. I hope that as they hauled truckload after truckload of ill-fated young trees down this rutted road, they noticed the bluebirds gliding beneath the old oak. I hope they heard the frogs and the flickers. I hope they saw the flaws in their own belief that native land is unproductive land, that property value is tied always to human tinkering. I hope this meadow taught them, as it has me, that oak woodland is the essence, the pure truth of this place.

Yet, as long as roads cut through wild country, they will hold the land vulnerable to future whims. The road running through this meadow is nothing more than a potholed portal for bad ideas, a puncture wound that won't heal, allowing human fallibility to flow unchecked into the delicate heart of healthy land.

I hear the fluttering of wings. Another bluebird glides down from its oak perch, hovers above the grass, then disappears.

Part Four: Much Ado About Access

> "We now live in an America that is so vastly roaded and so
> thoroughly motorized that there is almost no place beyond easy
> reach of the recreational driver."
> —David Havlick, "Getting There"

Increasing miles of wildland roads means increasing recreational opportunities on them—and in this case these writers mean recreation via motors. You've seen and heard the ads: four-wheel-drive vehicles perched high on hard-rock ledges with soaring sunset views, encouraging us to drive off-road and, really, anywhere we want. Off-road vehicles (dirt bikes, snowmobiles, jet skis, and four-wheelers) do just that: motor mostly *off*-road, which often means through streams, cross-country through woods, or churning through sand dunes and beaches. But to get there they need a road, any road.

So these off-road vehicle recreationists cry foul nearly anytime an agency or private landowner tries to close a road or route, even if it's for safety reasons. They want the public to believe that access is possible only with motors, and therefore if motors aren't allowed, people aren't allowed. But closing and removing roads is not about cutting off human access to wild places. It is about re-creating wild places so humans and nonhumans alike can continue to have access to them—access that does not depend on motors.

Polemic,
Industrial Tourism
and the National Parks (excerpt)

Edward Abbey

The Park Service, established by Congress in 1916, was directed not only to administer the parks but also to "provide for the enjoyment of same in such manner and by such means as will leave them unimpaired for the enjoyment of future generations." This appropriately ambiguous language, employed long before the onslaught of the automobile, has been understood in various and often opposing ways ever since. The Park Service, like any other big organization, includes factions and factions. The Developers, the dominant faction, place their emphasis on the words *"provide for the enjoyment."* The Preservers, a minority but also strong, emphasize the words *"leave them unimpaired."* It is apparent, then, that we cannot decide the question of development versus preservation by a simple referral to holy writ or an attempt to guess the intention of the founding fathers; we must make up our own minds and decide for ourselves what the national parks should be and what purpose they should serve.

The first issue that appears when we get into this matter, the most important issue and perhaps the only issue, is the one called accessibility. The Developers insist that the parks must be made fully accessible not only to people but also to their machines, that is, to automobiles, motorboats, etc. The Preservers argue, in principle at least, that wilderness and motors are incompatible and that the former can best be experienced, understood, and enjoyed when the machines are left behind where they belong—on the superhighways and in the parking lots, on the reservoirs and in the marinas.

What does accessibility mean? Is there any spot on earth that men have not proved accessible by the simplest means—feet and legs and heart? Even Mt. McKinley, even Everest, have been surmounted by men on foot. (Some of them, incidentally, rank amateurs, to the horror and indignation of the professional mountaineers.) The interior of the Grand Canyon, a fiercely hot and hostile abyss, is visited each summer by thousands and thousands of tourists of the most banal and unadventurous type, many of them on foot—self-propelled, so to speak—and the others on the backs of mules. Thousands climb each summer to the summit of Mt. Whitney, highest point in the forty-eight United States, while multitudes of others wander on foot or on horseback through the ranges of the Sierras, the Rockies, the Big Smokies, the Cascades, and the mountains of New England. Still more hundreds and thousands float or paddle each year down the currents of the Salmon, the Snake, the Allagash, the Yampa, the Green, the Rio Grande, the Ozark, the St. Croix, and those portions of the Colorado that have not yet been destroyed by the dam builders. And most significant, these hordes of nonmotorized tourists, hungry for a taste of the difficult, the original, the real, do not consist solely of people young and athletic but also of old folks, fat folks, pale-faced office clerks who don't know a rucksack from a haversack, and even children. The one thing they all have in common is the refusal to live always like sardines in a can—they are determined to get outside of their motorcars for at least a few weeks each year.

This being the case, why is the Park Service generally so anxious to accommodate that other crowd, the indolent millions born on wheels and suckled on gasoline, who expect and demand paved highways to lead them in comfort, ease, and safety into every nook and corner of the national parks? For the answer to that we must consider the character of what I call Industrial Tourism and the quality of the mechanized tourists—the Wheelchair Explorers—who are at once the consumers, the raw material, and the victims of Industrial Tourism.

Industrial Tourism is a big business. It means money. It includes the motel and restaurant owners, the gasoline retailers, the oil corporations, the road-building contractors, the heavy equipment manufacturers, the state and federal engineering agencies, and the sovereign, all-powerful automotive industry. These various interests are well organized, command more wealth than most modern nations, and are represented in Congress with a strength far greater than is justified in any constitutional or democratic sense. (Modern politics is expensive—power follows money.) Through Congress the tourism industry can bring enormous pressure to bear upon such a slender reed in the executive branch as the poor old Park Service, a pressure that is also exerted on every other possible level—local, state, regional—and through advertising and the well-established habits of a wasteful nation.

When a new national park, national monument, national seashore, or whatever it may be called is set up, the various forces of Industrial Tourism, on all levels, immediately expect action—meaning specifically a road-building program. Where trails or primitive dirt roads already exist, the Industry expects—it hardly needs to ask—that these be developed into modern paved highways. On the local level, for example, the first thing that the superintendent of a new park can anticipate being asked, when he attends his first meeting of the area's Chamber of Commerce, is not "Will roads be built?" but rather "When does construction begin?" and "Why the delay?"

(The Natural Money-Mint. With supersensitive antennae these operatives from the C. of C. look into red canyons and see only green, stand among flowers snorting out the smell of money, and hear, while thunderstorms rumble over mountains, the fall of a dollar bill on motel carpeting.)

Accustomed to this sort of relentless pressure since its founding, it is little wonder that the Park Service, through a process of natural selection, has tended to evolve a type of administration that, far from resisting such pressure, has usually been more than willing to accommodate it, even to encourage it. Not from any peculiar moral weakness but simply because such well-adapted administrators are themselves believers in a policy of economic development. "Resource management" is the current term. Old foot trails may be neglected, backcountry ranger stations left unmanned, and interpretive and protective services inadequately staffed, but the administrators know from long experience that millions for asphalt can always be found; Congress is always willing to appropriate money for more and bigger paved roads, anywhere—particularly if they form loops. Loop drives are extremely popular with the petroleum industry—they bring the motorist right back to the same gas station from which he started.

Great though it is, however, the power of the tourist business would not in itself be sufficient to shape Park Service policy. To all accusations of excessive development the administrators can reply, as they will if pressed hard enough, that they are giving the public what it wants, that their primary duty is to serve the public not preserve the wilds. "Parks are for people" is the public-relations slogan, which decoded means that the parks are for people-in-automobiles. Behind the slogan is the assumption that the majority of Americans, exactly like the managers of the tourist industry, expect and demand to see their national parks from the comfort, security, and convenience of their automobiles.

Is this assumption correct? Perhaps. Does that justify the continued and increasing erosion of the parks? It does not. Which brings me to the final aspect of the problem of Industrial Tourism: the Industrial Tourists themselves.

They work hard, these people. They roll up incredible mileages on their odometers, rack up state after state in two-week transcontinental motor marathons, knock off one national park after another, take millions of square yards of photographs, and endure patiently the most prolonged discomforts: the tedious traffic jams, the awful food of park cafeterias and roadside eateries, the nocturnal search for a place to sleep or camp, the dreary routine of One-Stop Service, the endless lines of creeping traffic, the smell of exhaust fumes, the ever-proliferating Rules & Regulations, the fees and the bills and the service charges, the boiling radiator and the flat tire and the vapor lock, the surly retorts of room clerks and traffic cops, the incessant jostling of the anxious crowds, the irritation and restlessness of their children, the worry of their wives, and the long drive home at night in a stream of racing cars against the lights of another stream of racing cars in the opposite direction, passing now and then the obscure tangle, the shattered glass, the patrolman's lurid blinker light, of one more wreck.

Hard work. And risky. Too much for some, who have given up the struggle on the highways in exchange for an entirely different kind of vacation—out in the open, on their own feet, following the quiet trail through forest and mountains, bedding down at evening under the stars, when and where they feel like it, at a time when the Industrial Tourists are still hunting for a place to park their automobiles.

Industrial Tourism is a threat to the national parks. But the chief victims of the system are the motorized tourists. They are being robbed and robbing themselves. So long as they are unwilling to crawl out of their cars they will not discover the treasures of the national parks and will never escape the stress and turmoil of the urban-suburban complexes that they had hoped, presumably, to leave behind for a while.

How to pry the tourists out of their automobiles, out of their back-breaking, upholstered mechanized wheelchairs and onto their feet, on the strange warmth and solidity of Mother Earth again? This is the problem that the Park Service should confront directly, not evasively, and which it cannot resolve by simply submitting and conforming to the automobile habit. The automobile, which began as a transportation convenience, has become a bloody tyrant (50,000 lives a year), and it is the responsibility of the Park Service, as well as that of everyone else concerned with preserving both wilderness and civilization, to begin a campaign of resistance. The automotive combine has almost succeeded in strangling our cities; we need not let it also destroy our national parks.

It will be objected that a constantly increasing population makes resistance and conservation a hopeless battle. This is true. Unless a way is found to stabilize the nation's population, the parks cannot be saved. Or anything else worth a damn. Wilderness preservation, like a hundred other good causes, will be forgotten under the overwhelming pressure of a struggle for mere survival and sanity in a completely urbanized, completely industrialized, ever more crowded environment. For my own part I would rather take my chances in a thermonuclear war than live in such a world.

Assuming, however, that population growth will be halted at a tolerable level before catastrophe does it for us, it remains permissible to talk about such things as the national parks. Having indulged myself in a number of harsh judgments upon the Park Service, the tourist industry, and the motoring public, I now feel entitled to make some constructive, practical, sensible proposals for the salvation of both parks and people.

(1) No more cars in national parks. Let the people walk. Or ride horses, bicycles, mules, wild pigs—anything—but keep the automobiles and the motorcycles and all their motorized relative out. We have agreed not to drive our automobiles into cathedrals, concert halls, art museums, legislative assemblies, private bedrooms, and the other sanctums of our culture; we should treat our national parks with the same deference, for they, too, are holy places. An increasingly pagan and hedonistic people (thank God!), we are learning finally that the forests and mountains and desert canyons are holier than our churches. Therefore let us behave accordingly.

Consider a concrete example and what could be done with it: Yosemite Valley in Yosemite National Park. At present a dusty milling confusion of motor vehicles and ponderous camping machinery, it could be returned to relative beauty and order by the simple expedient of requiring all visitors, at the park entrance, to lock up their automobiles and continue their tour on the seats of good workable bicycles supplied free of charge by the United States Government.

Let our people travel light and free on their bicycles—nothing on the back but a shirt, nothing tied to the bike but a slicker, in case of rain. Their bedrolls, their backpacks, their tents, their food and cooking kits will be trucked in for them, free of charge, to the campground of their choice in the Valley, by the Park Service. (Why not? The roads will still be there.) Once in the Valley they will find the concessioners waiting, ready to supply whatever needs might have been overlooked, or to furnish rooms and meals for those who don't want to camp out.

The same thing could be done at Grand Canyon or at Yellowstone or at any of our other shrines to the out-of-doors. There is no compelling reason, for example, why tourists need to drive their automobiles to the very brink of the Grand Canyon's south rim. They could *walk* that last mile. Better yet, the Park Service should build an enormous parking lot about ten miles south of Grand Canyon village and another east of Desert View. At those points, as at Yosemite, our people could emerge from their steaming shells of steel and glass and climb upon horses or bicycles for the final leg of the journey. On the rim, as at present, the hotels and restaurants will remain to serve the physical needs of the park visitors. Trips along the rim would also be made on foot, on horseback, or—utilizing the paved road that already exists—on bicycles. For those willing to go all the way from one parking lot to the other, a distance of some sixty or seventy miles, we might provide bus service back to their cars, a service that would at the same time effect a convenient exchange of bicycles and/or horses between the two terminals.

What about children? What about the aged and inform? Frankly, we need waste little sympathy on these two pressure groups. Children too small to ride bicycles and too heavy to be borne on their parents' backs need only wait a few years—if they are not run over by automobiles they will grow into a lifetime of joyous adventure, if we save the parks and *leave them unimpaired for the enjoyment of future generations.* The aged merit even less sympathy; after all, they had the opportunity to see the country when it was still relatively unspoiled. However, we'll stretch a point for those too old or too sickly to mount a bicycle and let them ride the shuttle buses.

I can foresee complaints. The motorized tourists, reluctant to give up the old ways, will complain that they can't see enough without their automobiles to bear them swiftly (traffic permitting) through the parks. But this is nonsense. A man on foot, on horseback, or on a bicycle will see more, feel more, enjoy more in one mile than the motorized tourists can in a hundred miles. Better to idle through one park in two weeks than try to race through a dozen in the same amount of time. Those who are familiar with both modes of travel know from experience that this is true; the rest have only to make the experiment to discover the same truth for themselves.

They will complain of physical hardship, these sons of the pioneers. Not for long; once they rediscover the pleasures of actually operating their own limbs and senses in a varied, spontaneous, voluntary style, they will complain instead of crawling back into a car; they may even object to returning to desk and office and that dry-wall box on Mossy Brook Circle. The fires of revolt may be kindled—which means hope for us all.

(2) No more new roads in national parks. After banning private automobiles the second step should be easy. Where paved roads are already in existence they will be reserved for the bicycles and essential in-park services, such as shuttle buses, the trucking of camping gear, and concessioners' supplies. Where dirt roads already exist they too will be reserved for nonmotorized traffic. Plans for new roads can be discarded and in their place a program of trail-building begun, badly needed in some of the parks and in many of the national monuments. In mountainous areas it may be desirable to build emergency shelters along the trails and bike roads; in desert regions a water supply might have to be provided at certain points—wells drilled and handpumps installed if feasible.

Once people are liberated from the confines of automobiles there will be a greatly increased interest in hiking, exploring, and backcountry pack trips. Fortunately the parks, by the mere elimination of motor traffic, will come to seem far bigger than they are now—there will be more room for more persons, an astonishing expansion of space. This follows from the interesting fact that a motorized vehicle, when not at rest, requires a volume of space far out of proportion to its size. To illustrate: imagine a lake approximately ten miles long and on the average one mile wide. A single motorboat could easily circumnavigate the lake in an hour; ten motorboats would begin to crowd it; twenty or thirty, all in operation, would dominate the lake to the exclusion of any other form of activity; and fifty would create the hazards, confusion, and turmoil that make pleasure impossible. Suppose we banned motorboats and allowed only canoes and rowboats; we would see at once that the lake seemed ten or perhaps a hundred times bigger. The same thing holds true, to an even greater degree, for the automobile. Distance and space are functions of speed and time. Without expending a single dollar from the United States Treasury we could, if we wanted to, multiply the area of our national parks tenfold or a hundredfold—simply by banning the private automobile. The next generation, all 250 million of them, would be grateful to us.

The Entitled

Katie Alvord

The guy drove toward me, his four-wheeler gouging rough tracks across the beach. I'd never seen him before, but I recognized his expression, the attitude apparent in his unwavering eyes.

It was one of entitlement.

So tangible was his belief that his all-terrain recreational wheels could take him wherever he damn well pleased that it almost seemed to precede him. It emanated from his countenance, projecting forward like the high beams of headlights.

I stood in his way, five-feet-two and 120 pounds, blocking a small opening between the end of a fence and the edge of Lake Superior. I hoped I wouldn't cross the line from brave to foolish, but was mostly convinced that I already had. No one else stood or sat or walked within eye- or earshot. This guy was probably twice my weight, unknown and therefore unpredictable, and on a vehicle that could easily run me over.

He slowed as he approached me.

"Hi," I yelled over his engine's growl. "What's your name?"

"My name is Dave," he shouted back. "And you can't stop me."

Nevertheless, he stopped.

Dave sat on a beat-up blue Polaris ATV, having just traveled through a public park to reach the mostly fenced property boundary where I stood. Upper Michigan's Keweenaw Peninsula extended to our east. To our north, just a few feet away, the icy blue waters of Lake Superior lapped up onto coarse gray sand. To the south, across a couple hundred yards of beach, a steep fifty-foot bluff rose to a mixed hardwood and conifer forest. Deep green foliage lined the bluff to the west, part of a three-mile stretch unbroken by development.

I happened to be in Dave's path that afternoon because we'd had recent problems on this beach, which was part of some land my spouse had bought more than a decade before. ATVs had been driving down it, trespassing on territory we'd designated as a nature sanctuary, crushing delicate plants that grew in places on the sand, running rampant where birds nested, compacting soil and leaving tracks that wouldn't disappear for years. We had placed the land in a conservation easement with The Nature Conservancy, and the easement prohibited driving. We'd also built a fence to keep errant vehicles off, but Lake Superior's stormy waters made completing it to the water's edge infeasible. Especially on nice days, ATVs frequently ventured around the fence to use the sanctuary as a playground, wreaking destruction on wild plants and animals meant to be protected.

We'd sought help for this problem in the past, and government officials had told us of Michigan codes that allowed us to prevent trespass on the full beach, to the water's edge; we had happily used these as tools against motorized abuse. Now, in my role as enforcer, I figured I'd need all the tools I had. I was not at all confident Dave would be sympathetic to any of them, and even less sure I could single-handedly keep him from driving past me.

"Maybe you missed the sign," I began my attempt. "This is a private nature sanctuary. The Nature Conservancy holds a conservation easement on this land, and the easement specifies no driving."

"You can't stop me," Dave said again.

"Could you turn off your engine for a minute?" I cupped my ear. "I can't hear you too well."

Dave looked annoyed, but he complied. "I said, you can't stop me. This is public property."

"Here." I pulled a folded paper out of my pocket and handed it to him. "This flyer explains how property boundaries work along Lake Superior, and why we have the right to prevent trespass." I always carried a flyer or two when I went out on the beach, just in case.

Dave took the paper but didn't read it.

"You can't stop me," he said, and glared at me.

"Sorry," I said, shaking my head at him. "That paper says I can. It's a private nature sanctuary on this side of the fence, driving's not allowed, and I have the right to enforce that."

"No friggin' way," Dave blustered. "You can't stop me."

I clenched my teeth. The sun beat down; a herring gull called overhead; waves slapped the sand, again and again and again. We faced each other, at an impasse, each rooted by unyielding determination.

· · · · ·

Some might advise: never argue with a person convinced they're entitled to access. At least Dave didn't carry a chainsaw. That's better than the off-roaders who did a little unauthorized road-building in a Nature Conservancy preserve about fifty miles east of our protected beach, reportedly felling a number of rare trees in the process.

Here's the story.

Just outside Eagle Harbor on the Keweenaw Peninsula sits a 1,350-foot peak with two or three names. Some locals call it Mt. Baldy, others Mt. Lookout; I've always known it as Lookout Mountain. In 2002 The Nature Conservancy purchased a tract of land that included most of the peak. The "Baldy" nomenclature hints at TNC's reason for the purchase: at the mountain's top, fierce climate conditions have created an almost arctic stratum, a pygmy oak forest and above that a cap largely bare of trees, covered instead with low-lying bearberry, scrub juniper, blueberry bushes, and several rare plants.

Climb Lookout Mountain and you can feel why its plants prefer to huddle close to the ground. Prevailing winds gust straight into the peak from Lake Superior, strong and chill. The few trees that grow near the top crowd their stunted shapes into protected areas, leeward of the wind.

The blueberries, a tolerant private landowner, and a sweeping view—south to Keweenaw Bay, north to Isle Royale National Park—have long made Lookout Mountain a popular hiking destination. On my initial visit to the Keweenaw Peninsula in 1994, it was the first long hike I took. The "trail" began as a two-track road, but a couple of miles shy of the top became too narrow for cars; any who drove to that point stopped their vehicles and continued up on foot. As the trail reached the summit, it diminished to a thin track, no wider and in most places narrower than twelve inches.

By nearly ten years later, when TNC made its purchase, ORVs had made major inroads to the top. The trail had been widened, more than doubled in many places. Trees had been cut all along it, and not by the landowner.

On a day shortly after TNC purchased it, one of their staff took a small group for a hike on Lookout Mountain. When the hikers started hearing chainsaws, they became alarmed and followed the noise. This led them to a group of young men who had tooled their four-wheel-drives into the protected pygmy oak forest. By the time the hikers reached them, the saw noise had stopped, but freshly felled pygmy oaks lined the now truck-width trail; the TNC hike leader noticed at least one chainsaw on the ground nearby. The men identified themselves as members of a four-wheel-drive club from a local university. The hike leader informed them that The Nature Conservancy now owned the land, no driving was allowed, and certainly no tree cutting, then asked them to leave. At first they protested vociferously—feeling entitled, apparently (years earlier a member of this club had allegedly argued at a public hearing, "We need the right to cross private property to pursue our sport"). When the TNC group didn't back down, though, the club members left.

The hikers counted thirty-two pygmy oaks that had been cut out of the forest, and other vegetation as well. But despite the overwhelming circumstantial evidence, the four-wheel-drive club did not admit to cutting any trees. After ushering them out, the hike leader had a hunch the incident hadn't ended. The hike broke up, but the leader stayed discreetly behind near the base of the trail. About an hour after she'd told them to go, she watched as some of the same members of the four-wheel-drive club motored back up a trail they now knew was off-limits.

The hike leader reported the incident; law enforcement arrived, but by that time the four-wheel-drivers were out of reach. TNC later met with representatives and a sponsor of the offending club, who still denied any tree cutting or other wrongdoing. The only verifiable misdeed was the trespass onto TNC property, and the club representatives dismissed that as a meaningless infraction. No disciplinary action was taken, nor was any compensation offered to TNC.

While frustrated, TNC decided not to press the issue. But the incident did contribute to their decision, in 2004, to permanently block motor vehicle access up Lookout Mountain.

. . . . .

Out in the woods when no one's around, stretching a point on chainsaw use can be easy. It's hard to tell if the saw in back of a four-wheel-drive pickup or strapped to an ATV is there to clear a windfall from an existing byway or to hack down live trees to widen or create another route. If a tree is felled in the forest but no one sees, is it still illegal? Apparently not for some who feel entitled to even more access for motorized play.

The pressure for motorized access, and this kind of unlawful pursuit of it, is a huge problem in the Keweenaw Peninsula and elsewhere in upper Michigan (also known as Michigan's Upper Peninsula, or "the U.P."). This has been reported on lands both public and private. About a third of the U.P.'s 10 million acres is in federal ownership as two national forests, the Ottawa and the Hiawatha. Another large portion is state forest, where a policy treating routes as "open unless posted closed" to motorized recreation further bolsters the sense of entitlement to access. Still more land is corporate forest, classed as commercial forest reserve, or CFR, which allows a tax break in exchange for granting access to the public. The CFR classification does not promise entry for vehicles of any kind, but that technicality is often disregarded, as motorized recreationists carry an "open unless posted closed" mind-set everywhere (except perhaps when they carry the mind-set "open even if posted closed").

The hodgepodge of various land types, intermingled in an undemarcated checkerboard across the U.P., makes enforcement of any motorized access restrictions tricky. ORVers in the U.P. thus get away with a great deal of illegal access, and this seems only to further feed their sense of entitlement to it. It's reached the point that a vocal segment of motorized recreationists seem to see that entitlement as absolute.

Take, for instance, some who spoke at planning meetings held when the State of Michigan gained ownership of about 6,000 acres of Keweenaw Point, or "the Tip" as they call it locally. It's an undeveloped area beyond the end of the highway and power line, wooded and teeming with black bears, shy loons, soaring eagles. A water trail for kayaks and canoes winds around the Tip from the open waters of Lake Superior into Keweenaw Bay. Hikers go there, as do hunters and anglers, mountain bikers, snowshoers, and cross-country skiers. In recent decades it's also been increasingly trammeled by ORVs. Snowmobiles traverse it in winter, and ATVs take over in summer.

Folks who attended meetings of the Keweenaw Point Advisory Committee (KPAC) heard certain ORV users express strong opposition to any restrictions at all on their ability to go anywhere around the Tip. Some of these motorized recreationists openly declared, in front of state officials and on the record, that they would break any law interfering with their access. They expressed little willingness to respect critical habitat, rare species, or easily erodible shoreline areas with eons-old geological formations.

"If you block someplace off, we'll go there anyway," said one ATV rider at a KPAC meeting.

"You can put gates up, but we can go around any gate," said another.

Representatives of other groups argued for reasonable restrictions, and the ultimate plan for the Tip did include them. But what happens on the ground is often a different story, a tale of entitlement leading essentially to land grabs as ORVs flout restrictions, creating disturbances that push others out.

. . . . .

One day I mentioned the sense of entitlement issue to a state conservation officer. He laughed.

"I know exactly what you're talking about," he said. "That's very common among the locals up here. A significant number of them feel they have an inherited right to go anywhere they want to on a four-wheeler."

This officer has never seen a gate or a barrier that off-road vehicles can't eventually get around. In his experience, he said, if they want to go somewhere, they'll find a way.

"What would make your job of enforcement easier?" I asked him.

"Aircraft patrols," he replied with some enthusiasm. And in other parts of Michigan, he said, they do use aircraft. The planes patrol trouble spots to support ground vehicles in pursuit of errant off-roaders. If the land patrol loses the ORVs, the plane can keep up and guide officers on the ground to the right spot.

This is Hollywood movie stuff: picture a swarm of ATVs going places they shouldn't go; picture law enforcement in hot pursuit, by wing and by wheel, from above and below. These paired patrols have apparently been very effective in the places they're used. These are spots where government officials have decided that aircraft are worth the money, that ORVs do that much damage. And it's another telling indicator of just how costly inflated feelings of entitlement on the part of a motorized few can be to the rest of us, and to the land.

. . . . .

Despite our country's emphasis of individual rights, in practice we must always strike some balance between private rights and the public good. That balance point, I would argue, has been far exceeded in the case of motorized recreation, and the extent of entitlement among some of its practitioners shows by just how much.

Not only in the U.P. but across the country, the sense of entitlement to access sends motorized recreation out of control. It clearly fosters the flouting of laws. It often goes hand in hand with drunk and disorderly behavior, as well as vandalism. It can destroy whole landscapes, as ORVs compact and erode soils, crush plants and animals, pollute air and water. And law enforcement can't keep up with the ability of motorized libertines to do what they will on remote wild land.

From motorcycle races ravaging parts of the California desert, to Yellowstone rangers sickened by snowmobile exhaust, to conflicts involving motorized users throughout the national forests, stories abound of ORV damage and abuse. When it gets this out of control, we need to stop and consider: Just who, really, is entitled to what? Are snowmobilers entitled to sicken Yellowstone rangers for access to the park? Are ORVers entitled to cut trees to drive up a Keweenaw mountain? If so many motorized recreationists can't respect regulations meant to protect the public good, are any entitled to continue the activity?

It's fair to ask these questions. It's fair—perhaps necessary—to consider a ban on some types of access. Our collective decision-making often restricts private pursuits in favor of the public good; society does choose to ban some problem activities. Even a score of "victimless" vices have been made illegal—swearing in public, for instance. In Michigan a person was cited just a few years ago for violating a law that bans swearing in front of women and children. Yet we allow motorized access to routinely desecrate the natural world and for the sake of recreation.

How have priorities gotten so flipped, the sense of entitlement so skewed?

Certainly commercial interests play a role. First are the vehicle manufacturers, fueling entitlement to access with ads showing full-color portraits of four-wheel-drive trucks perched on mountain peaks or fording streams, underscored with aggressive and proprietary slogans such as "Own the country." Then there are local communities who have become dependent on the income from ORV tourism.

Some of the small business people in this position support or take part in motorized recreation, but many others hate the activity and put up with its associated problems for the sake of jobs and economic development. Public lands fee programs can put agency land managers in similar positions, as they too may become dependent on revenue from ORV use.

Our separation from the natural world might skew our priorities as well. Often, now, we approach the wild only via some technologically mediated separation from it, viewing it from inside a car, from a plane or helicopter, in a chairlift, on an ORV, on a movie screen, or on TV. Perhaps it is harder for us to understand the consequences of, say, too many felled trees if we always see those trees from behind a car window, or on a video or TV screen, or through a haze of blue smoke and motor noise from the back of a snowmobile or ATV.

The problem with this is not just the problem for the trees, though that should be enough, in an ideal world, for us to change the activity; trees, too, are entitled to their piece of the landscape. The problem is also that our separation from nature ultimately undermines our own survival. This separation keeps us from remembering connections between, for instance, clear-cuts and landslides, industrial pollution and increasing asthma, plastics use and lower sperm counts, motorized recreation and climate change, snowmobile use and oil-contaminated spring runoff that poisons fish and enters our drinking water, feeding cancer. If motorized access widens the gap between us and nature, then it widens the gap between ourselves and our own survival. When a segment of the populace feels entitled to such access, it can only make the problem worse, skewing priorities that much more.

· · · · ·

Somehow I got lucky when it came to Dave: he barked but didn't bite. I supposed, happily enough, that once he'd turned his engine off, he'd lost the momentum to charge by or run me over. But he did like to talk, and as we faced off on the beach, Dave began to ramble. He told stories about some of his friends. He talked about his domestic problems, his divorce, trouble with his ex-wife. I wasn't sure what else to do but listen. I didn't want to move; I didn't want to let him by.

After a while, though, I began to lose my patience.

"Look," I said, getting back to our argument, frustration edging my voice. "This is a nature sanctuary. Birds nest here, right in the sand.

Rare plants grow here. It's a harsh environment already, and they'll get creamed if they're driven over. We love this place, and we're just trying to protect these plants and animals."

Dave sat in silence.

"Listen," I went on. "If you want to get off your machine and walk down here, carefully and respectfully, that's okay. But. Driving's—not—allowed."

How long had we been out there, talking and arguing? It seemed like hours. I was no longer sure how long I could last.

Suddenly Dave became retrospective.

"Ya know," he said, "we came down one time to pick up broken glass on the beach in the park here." He gestured back over his shoulder. "There was lots of glass out there, beer bottles and trash left by people who didn't care about the place. A whole group of us came out. We spent the afternoon. We wanted to make it safe for our kids."

He hesitated. I held my breath.

"I guess that's like you protecting the beach for the animals and plants," he said. "I can sort of understand that."

I took a deep breath, then, and let it go.

"Thank you," I said.

He looked at me speculatively. "So it's okay if I walk down here?"

"Yes," I repeated. "Just no driving."

He nodded, and then—I still find this hard to believe—we shook hands. I wondered how much persistence had helped us reach this point, whether my listening to Dave had led him to be less hard-nosed, or if the suggestion that he could walk down the beach had played a role. Our conversation over, he fired up his machine, then backed and turned and rumbled off the way he'd come, out through the park.

I never saw him on that beach again.

For every Dave that leaves, I've seen far more trespass, vandalize, or flout public land laws. But there is a point at which, even in the face of feelings of entitlement, sanctuary can trump access. Dave and I managed to reach that point on the beach, at least temporarily. The Nature Conservancy reached that point on Lookout Mountain, too, when they finally decided to bar motor vehicles from going there. As I write this, the top of the mountain has remained free of motorized trespass since volunteers helped to install a hiker-friendly but permanent barrier across the trail.

If we can reach this point in small ways, then ultimately we can reach it in big ones—as a culture, and on our public lands. It may not be easy, it may take unprecedented persistence and big priority shifts, but we can remember that it's possible. We don't have to tolerate out-of-control destruction for the sake of economic development or some distorted notion of individual liberty; we can, if we wish, decide that motorized access is incompatible with the greater good, and legitimately ban it.

And we can do even more by restoring more access to territory for other species: giving them more sanctuary and providing a balance that supports a diversity of life. Because perhaps those most entitled to access, really, are the species we've displaced as we've seized so much access for ourselves.

. . . . .

Not far from the site of my standoff with Dave is a section of woods where people rarely tread, in part because our conservation easement limits human access to it. It's about 200 acres of wooded swamp, small by western standards but big enough in the more densely verdant North Woods to be a wildlife stronghold. Winging into its depths are great gray and sawhet owls, pileated woodpeckers, blackburnian warblers. Merlins nest there and eagles perch on high snags. Fishers prowl, hunting red squirrels, snowshoe hares, prickly porcupines. Black bears roam through. Wolves have begun to return. From deep in those woods, many nights, comes the howling chorus of coyotes, reminding us of what it means to be alive in the wild. Perhaps it is our allowing them that untrammeled space that allows them to remember, as well, and revel in it.

Road Huntin'
Ain't No Huntin' a'Tall:
A Reasoned Rant

David Petersen

As a conservationist, naturalist—and as one unsympathetic neighbor dubs me, "our local wildlife idiot"—I see no contradiction in pointing out that I am also a passionate hunter. Nor am I alone in this realm. Yale sociobiologist Stephen Kellert, an expert on human attitudes toward nature, categorizes a growing minority of hunters as having a strong "nature/naturalistic" orientation. As such, they/I/we comprehend and embrace nature on an ecological scale and tirelessly ruminate the conundrum of killing and eating the very creatures we so love. From my neo-animistic point of view, there is no moral conflict here: death feeds life; life feeds on death; that's how nature works. Respect, empathy, and reciprocity are the keys to moral compatibility in this ancient bloody arena. Done right, there is no more natural, thus no more moral, human-nature relationship than hunting.

But done wrong, hunting can be a horror show. And far too often today, it is done wrong. Sadly, for every "nature" hunter, there are at least two of the type Kellert classifies as "dominionistic/sports." These dilettante weekend warriors know or care woefully little about nature, ecosystem dynamics, or the animals they hunt. (The only other faction of American culture to score as dismally low on Kellert's "nature knowledge" tests as the sports, ironically, are their "animal rights" nemeses!) Worse, a growing number of these clueless nature-dominators, bowing to our consumer-culture paradigm and the amoral outdoor industry's dictum to abandon their lungs, legs, and hearts in favor of engines, wheels, and other cheater technology, undertake most of their "hunting" with their butts planted firmly on the seats of off-highway vehicles (four-by-four pickups, SUVs, and

ATVs), viewing wildlife as little more than moving targets and potential trophies. True hunters are embarrassed and angered by the words, actions, and myopic, self-serving politics of these armed motorheads, who cruise back roads and too often illegally off-road in search of easy targets and unearned bragging rights, and who leave ugly ecological, spiritual, and public-opinion footprints everywhere they go, though their boots rarely touch the ground.

As one crusty old Colorado outfitter friend puts it, "Road huntin' ain't no huntin' a'tall."

For an example of the harassment and harm that roads and their human cargo bring to wildlife—including not only butt-bound pseudo-hunters but so-called nonconsumptive (no such human critter exists) motorized recreationists as well—let's consider the impacts on a popular, tough, and adaptable big-game species that's been the subject of intense long-term studies in relation to road impacts: the elk, or North American wapiti.

On heavily roaded landscapes, elk find themselves lethally sandwiched between almost ceaseless harassment by motorized invaders, especially during hunting season, and decreased hiding cover. The "big four" survival essentials for elk and other wildlife are food, water, cover, and room to roam. Unrestricted legroom is essential to elk (a highly mobile and migratory species) not only to meet the first three needs through all the seasons, but to allow females to "shop around" for the fittest males to father their young. In heavily roaded and logged habitat—and roading and logging are sinister twins—the ability to roam must be bought by elk at the usurious price of greatly increased stress and greatly reduced survival. Either way, move or sit tight, the wapiti too often lose. Moreover, researchers point out that elk and other wildlife often suffer stress and behavioral disruption because of continual motorized traffic noise—the growl and engine-rattle of diesel off-highway-vehicles, the mosquito-whine of ATVs, dirt bikes, and snowmobiles—even should they escape such direct motorized harassment as being shot, run down, or chased around.

Ostensibly to reduce the risks to elk of proposed new roads and timber sales, the Forest Service employs a "vulnerability paradigm" called the Blue Mountain Habitat Effectiveness Model. This rule of thumb, developed via studies conducted in the fecund forests of the Pacific Northwest, proclaims that "good" elk habitat consists of 60 percent forage (with "forage" generally and erroneously considered to be satisfied by clear-cuts) and 40 percent cover. But the radically varying quality of forage and cover across all the many western states occupied by elk is insufficiently addressed. Cow-burned clear-cuts and arid rangelands offer inferior forage (not only in calories per acre, but in digestibility and nutrition-essential variety) compared with moist, ungrazed riparian corridors or rich aspen understory. Likewise, the harsh artificial edges between clear-cuts or road edges and standing timber do not equate to rich natural ecotones; rather, quite the opposite in both fact and ecological effect, as preeminent conservation biologist Dr. Michael Soulé and others have unimpeachably demonstrated.

The Blue Mountain model goes on to specify that elk cover should consist of 20 percent hiding, 10 percent thermal, and 10 percent "either thermal or hiding cover." In yet another omniscient agency dictum, effective hiding cover is decreed to be "vegetation capable of hiding 90 percent of a standing adult deer or elk from the view of a human at a distance equal to or less than 200 yards." Which leaves one to wonder: Is that with the naked eye . . . or through a rifle scope?

Such substantially hypothetical models and definitions would be laughable if they weren't so tragic for the animals they purport to protect. And even these obviously inadequate minimums have traditionally been subverted when they threaten to interfere with bureaucratic business as usual. According to retired Montana USFS biologist Jack Lyon: "We had a lot of trouble recognizing the distinct difference between habitat effectiveness and habitat security for a while. Many wildlife biologists would say, 'No [the 60/40 model] doesn't necessarily provide security,' but district rangers would say, 'Yes it does; we need to get the cut out.' I can't describe how rash the interpretations were. And it was very clear why the interpretations came about, and it didn't have a damn thing to do with elk."[1]

Another former USFS biologist, Alan Christensen, specialized in elk vulnerability. Summarizing his career findings and feelings (also in *Bugle*), Christensen says flatly: "Roads are the single biggest problem on the landscape for elk. It's well documented and everything else pales in comparison."

Citing long-term studies in Idaho, Christensen points out that bull elk survival and average age (that is, "trophy" status) decrease radically with increased road access. "It's simple biology and common

---

[1] Quoted in *Bugle*, March–April 2002, the journal of the Rocky Mountain Elk Foundation.

sense. Roads are the delivery system for people to invade habitat. If a wildlife population is weakened by land management decisions—in this case motorized access—you'll have higher losses from everything: winterkill, predation, hunting, accidents, and disease."

This is no "liberal tree-hugger voodoo." It is scientifically documented, personally observable fact. Even the most thoughtless road "hunter" should be able to understand that if you want some elk to hunt, first you need some elk. And to have and keep elk—and particularly to "produce" trophy bulls—you need viable habitat to support and shelter them, in all seasons and over the long term. And bottom line: roads and clear-cuts have been proven to weaken and, too frequently, utterly destroy elk habitat viability.

And so it is that by attacking the integrity of wildlife habitat in pursuit of a personal passion for effortless motorized access everywhere—mouthing the greedhead "wise use" lie "We can have it all"—all too many sportsmen, sitting all too comfortably on their motorized butts, rumbling blithely along (and often illegally off) tens of thousands of miles of public-lands byways, are pissing on their own butts.

Dip Nets and the
Devil's Own Invention

Susan Cerulean

As Jeff and I strike out on our favorite bike trail just south of Talla-hassee, we're grateful for the subtle gifts of early September. The temperature has dipped five degrees—into the low nineties—for the first time in months. Early flowers of purple liatris promise an eventual autumn for this seriously hot southern landscape, the Munson Sand-hills in the Apalachicola National Forest. Longleaf pines have cast rus-set needles over the narrow sandy track we ride, and catbrier tendrils reach for our shoelaces and the spokes of our wheels.

Jeff pedals out ahead of me on the longer loop of this designated trail, about eight hilly miles. He has exercise on his mind, but today I have a dip net and field guides stuffed in my pack, and a desire to take a better look at the threats to Bruce Means's ponds.

For nearly forty years, renowned Tallahassee herpetologist Dr. Bruce Means has seined and dip-netted and cataloged the vertebrate life of more than 266 unique, ephemeral ponds that dot this landscape just south of Tallahassee. Rare and threatened amphibians, including the striped newt and the gopher frog (both designated candidates as feder-ally threatened species), have struck an evolutionary deal with the ponds' ever-changing water levels, which can include going bone-dry for sev-eral years at a stretch. These animals and quite a few others actually depend on periodic dry-downs to eliminate fish and other aquatic pred-ators from the ponds. In addition, at least ten of Florida's twenty-seven species of native frogs use temporary ponds almost exclusively—four in the very coldest time of the winter and six in the summer months.

But Bruce Means has told me that illegal off-road motoring contin-ues to threaten the very existence of the newts and salamanders and

151

frogs that live here. The U.S. Forest Service rules allow motor vehicles only on established trails within the national forest. Resource damage, which includes driving in or near ponds, is prohibited. When I met with Means in his tiny Tallahassee office, he ran through a set of slides he took of a single pond over the last nine years. The first slide showed an undisturbed wetland, so thickly vegetated that I couldn't really tell where the forest stopped and the pond began. "There was very little off-highway vehicle use of the sandhills in the national forest when I began my study," said Means. "But all of a sudden, about six years ago, boom. Here come all these OHVs. Precipitously."

He told me that what protected the Apalachicola National Forest up until that point was unlimited public access to the commercial paper company lands to the east. In 1998, those private roads were gated and posted by hunting clubs, which had leased the hunting rights and now excluded trespassers.

It was the forest that took the overflow of displaced OHV riders.

"And it's the very ponds the rarest animals live in that these idiots have been destroying with their mud-bogging and joyriding activity!" he said. The last slide in his series showed a forty- or fifty-foot swath of muddy destruction around the perimeter of the sampling pond. I don't need further convincing; it's clear that very little could survive in that war zone.

"What's really scary is the way these guys love to motor around and around these ponds, totally destroying the littoral vegetation, the underpinning of the whole system," said Means.

. . . . .

The first pond I visit this morning looks more like a grassy bowl than a wetland. The standing water at the center is less than eight feet across and a mere four inches deep. It's so small I can almost encircle it with my arms. But the surface of the water thrums with life. Each pass of my net yields a scattering of dragonfly nymphs and a dozen tadpoles with bronze robust bellies and delicately marbled tails. I wish I knew their names. My field guide illustrates only the adult frogs, doesn't distinguish between the tadpoles. As I kneel by the tiny wetland, I can clearly see its seasonal range of movement between the tall pines and arching oaks at its perimeter to this remnant pool at the center. I think about the dissolution of subsurface limestone that caused the ground to slump and create this mild saucer. In other

places, where the ground sinks too much and dips into the under-
ground aquifer, I remember Means saying, a permanent water body
will be formed, creating an entirely different environment.

Farther down the trail I come across a larger, deeper pond. I test
the water temperature with my fingers, then wade straight out until
I'm standing thigh-deep. I've just passed through the littoral zone, the
shallow, highly productive zone where the water is warmest. This is
the engine of temporary ponds where metabolism and primary productivity run hot. Here among the nooks and crannies and hiding
places of bog button, sedge, and grass, life is exploding. And this zone
stays with the pond as it shrinks. Fifty feet in front of me is a circle of
clear water ringed with emerald pads of water lotus and lilies. Out this
deep, I catch nothing with my dip net among the submerged grasses;
this is probably one of those ponds containing fish that Means
described, and it might also be home to an alligator or two. I know
from previous experience that water lilies generally root at depths
well over my head, so I decide against exploring the center. As I
retreat back to shore, I scare up a small dark salamander (what species,
I wonder?) and watch it skitter not toward the water, but upland into
the pines. Means's research, and that of other scientists as well, shows
that the ecological quality of the upland habitats surrounding temporary ponds is as important for vertebrates that use them as is the water
to the animals' larval and aquatic stages.

I get back on my bike and continue deeper into the forest. There's
a big pond on my left, and I push my bike through the palmetto
understory to the water's edge. I see deer tracks in the sand, one white
egret, and a turtle stroking off through the grasses. This pond is much
bigger than the previous two—must be five or more acres—and it's
ringed with a sandy beach that sparkles with shattered bits of green
and brown beer bottles.

I think about approaching Tallahassee by plane, how I'm always
struck by the landscape's piney vastness and the dozens of small lakes
embedded within the forest's interior. Every time I spot those remote
ponds from the air, glittering back the sun, perfectly ringed by white
sandy beach, I remind myself to get out there swimming sometime
with the kids.

But what appears to be perfectly natural sand beach encircling this
pond and so many others in the forest is an artifact, I realize, of past
OHV traffic and a goodly number of parties. As beautiful as they might

seem, they are actually scars in the once-continuous sandhill fabric. Vehicle tires have destroyed the vegetation that grew here and ground down ruts that trap and kill newts, salamanders, and their larvae as the ponds seasonally recede. The wide, sandy trails remain desertlike barriers for the tiny newts and other rare creatures attempting to move between pond and forest, as they must, to complete their intricate life cycles. "These sand rings should not exist," says Bruce Means.

In March 2004, in response to documentation of the damage to sandhill ponds on the forest provided by Means and the Friends of the Apalachicola, the U.S. Forest Service closed about 6,500 acres to off-road vehicles. A story with a happy ending, right? Scientist shares lifework, persuades federal administrators to permanently protect sensitive areas, isn't that how it works? Unfortunately, and unbelievably—given what's at risk—the closure is most likely only temporary. Although the Forest Service's plan for the national forests in Florida changed access for motorized vehicles and bicycles by prohibiting cross-country travel, and established a few restricted areas where travel will be limited to designated roads and trails only, we are still awaiting a final access decision that designates a system of roads and trails within the restricted areas. The document is four years late and appears to be in the hands of Forest Service recreation planners with close ties to the OHV community, rather than the biologists and natural resource specialists who ought to be laying out the needs of the forest's sensitive species as an immutable baseline from which all other decisions should be made.

"In the meantime," says Walter Tschinkel, another longtime forest researcher and president of the Friends of the Apalachicola National Forest, "the temporary restricted area closures and the ban against cross-country travel are violated right and left, and with only two law enforcement officials on the whole 500,000-acre forest, the riders grow more confident and brazen every day. I think these machines are the devil's own invention."

. . . . .

I decide to visit the closest store that sells the offending vehicles, called CycleNation, just a few miles from my home, and just as close to the forest. The shiny new machines in the showroom are impressive beasts, apparently ready for anything, and don't seem to be particularly marketed to the OHV user segments classified in a 2005

Forest Service report as "Upper Middle Class Nature Lovers" (18.2 percent of users), "Middle Age Actives" (23 percent), or "Seniors" (7 percent). I'd guess these machines match the profile of yet another user segment, the "Young Adventure Seekers" (a quarter of OHV users nationwide). These are mostly male, with a mean age of just over nineteen.

That would also include the two teenaged boys sitting across the kitchen table from me at lunch, my nephew Garrett and my son David. They've never ridden an all-terrain vehicle or a motorcycle themselves, but they're quick to recognize advertising when it's aimed their way.

With a peanut butter sandwich in one hand, Garrett pages through the hot catalog of 2005 ATVs I've brought home from CycleNation. At age seventeen, this muscle-cut competitive gymnast is a Young Adventure Seeker himself. He hopes to enroll in the Air Force Academy upon his high school graduation, and has never been one to turn down a physical challenge. He flips through the slick color pages dominated by khaki, camouflage, and flying wet mud and describes for me the backstory.

"See what they're promising you?" he says, indicating the layout of cameo profiles on the cover. I study the airborne motorcycle, the wet mud everywhere, the guy muscling a Jet Ski through strong surf with a smiling girl clutching his waist.

"It's all about sweet tricks and sex," he says. "They're saying, 'Look at me, I'm conquering the country!'"

The boys continue chewing their sandwiches, still absorbed in the shiny ad piece. "It's like video games," the two agree. "The ones where you get to do stuff you don't usually get to do in real life—fly a jet, kill the bad guys, really test yourself. It's all about 'can I handle it?'"

"And maybe most of all the advertisers are telling you: buy one of these and you'll be able to create your own trail in the wilderness."

Exactly.

Manufacturers and retail outlets imply through advertising that you can take your expensive new ATV anywhere, just as car manufacturers would have us believe. Technologically it's true, but riders are finding it's not so easy once you trailer up your pricey new machine and head for the woods.

As the boys head out the door, returning to school for the afternoon, I read the literature more closely and think about the raising of Young Adventure Seekers in the modern-day world.

I've watched these kneeboarding boys' faces light up with pure thrill as they survive the bumpy wake of our old motorboat on the Ochlockonee River. I remember riding with David on the St. Marks' Trail, pedaling fast together down the six-foot-wide pavement, noticing how quickly it bored him. I could count on him striking out for the head-high sand berms just to the left of the trail, seeing how far he could push himself up and over that edge. I've long recognized their pleasure in going fast, testing themselves. And in their instincts to challenge themselves and move cross-country, I think I see the very starter pine the ATV industry hopes to fan into flames.

. . . . .

Off-highway vehicle use has risen dramatically in recent decades. In 1960, so few people rode them that they were not even addressed in a nationwide survey on recreation. According to the Motorcycle Industry Council, the primary trade organization that represents the ATV and motorcycle industries in the United States, OHV annual sales more than tripled between 1995 and 2003; more than 1.1 million vehicles were sold in 2003. ATVs continue to account for more than 70 percent of the OHV market. In just ten years the number of OHVs has grown from fewer than 3 million vehicles to more than 8 million in 2003.

Most of these off-highway vehicles have swarmed onto public land like a displaced hive of bees, nimble and powerful and numerous. The land-managing agencies have had no time to develop intentional and thoughtfully designed trail systems or any other way to manage the new users.

"It just 'happened,'" says Jerrie Lindsey, director of the Office of Recreation Services for the Florida Fish and Wildlife Conservation Commission. "The quick proliferation of off-road users took us all by surprise," she says, citing the unbelievable damage to the Croom Wildlife Management Area and the Ocala National Forest in central Florida. "If these guys were all running around in electric golf carts at 20 miles per hour, we'd have no problem. But our law enforcement people arrest them all the time going 50 and 60 miles per hour on levees in south Florida, and parts of our public lands are being turned into virtual wastelands.

"You cannot add a recreational activity of any sort that requires a lot of management and just expect the agencies to keep up."

Some representatives of the OHV community understand this, and as OHVs have gained in popularity, the growth and profitability of the industry have given rise to an immensely powerful lobby shaping not only its own profits but also public policy. A bill passed by the Florida legislature in 2002 calls for establishing a number of OHV areas on Florida's public lands. When this act was passed in 2002 with full industry backing, the OHV community was giving notice: "We want to have a voice." The act requires each ATV and OHV owner to purchase a title, similar to those required by car buyers, prior to riding on any public lands that have designated areas for OHV trails. In this way, users can make their case for the need to support this activity. The proceeds will contribute some dollars to develop and manage trail systems, although not enough to buy and set aside land for OHV use. The first of these trail systems—fifty miles of designated trails—was just opened by the Florida Division of Forestry on existing roads in Tate's Hell State Forest west of Tallahassee.

"Public lands belong to the people of Florida," says Chris Reed, the division's new OHV coordinator. "They have a right to recreate where it's suitable. We are hoping that with proper planning and management that maybe we can sustain this kind of use."

Some view this as another step in legitimizing a user group on public lands that just may not be compatible with the purposes for which these lands were set aside. ("How can we integrate OHVs into the ecosystem?" says Bruce Means. "We can't. They don't belong in the ecosystem at all!")

· · · · ·

There's another solution that some land managers believe could mitigate this problem, at least somewhat. "What we're looking at now are lands that can be basically dedicated or sacrificed for this use, like former phosphate mines," says the state wildlife agency's Jerrie Lindsey. "Teneroc Fish Management Area near Lakeland is a good example—a reclaimed phosphate mine that is never going to be a pristine pine forest again. What you see down there are pines with waving stands of invasive cogan grass underneath. It would cost billions to restore it for other uses. It just might be the place for off-road riders." Lindsey and her colleagues in government agencies know that pretending this problem is going to go away will never work. "Pandora's box has been opened," she says. "If we don't try to help, then we're part of the problem."

I just can hardly stand the thought of sacrificing *any* of our Apalachicola as an off-road playground, and I say so to Chuck Hess, a former wildlife biologist with the forest. He tells me, "If you don't let them into the forest at all, you lose supporters for natural areas. You've got to pick an area that's already trashed. You've got to give it to these guys. You've got to set up areas to do it in and eliminate it everywhere else. I just don't think the concept of trail systems is going to work. You'd have to count on the people who use the trails to behave responsibly. It's not enforceable; unless we issue draconian threats and hire twenty times the present law enforcement personnel, we don't have a chance."

Pretty grim prospects. Given that OHVs are designed to trample the landscape; given that the number of riders has far outgrown law enforcement capabilities of public land agencies; given that the Bush administration is not only loosening protective regulations, cowing its employees, and gutting their budgets, but attempting to rewrite their very mission statements. I wonder if we as a culture will have to let this one play itself out to its sorrowful, sorry conclusion, just as we are with the automobile.

I think back to my last visit to Bruce Means's tiny second-floor Coastal Plains Institute in a funky, unassuming downtown neighborhood. Hurricane Katrina was just bearing down on New Orleans, her fringes bending the trees outside the windows while we talked. As we paged through reports and images of the habitats and creatures he's come to know so intimately, Bruce's lifework seemed as vulnerable and essential as one of his beloved ephemeral ponds. I looked at the tiny rooms honeycombed with white shelving, the carefully arranged libraries and data collections, the hundreds and hundreds of boxed slide carousels. All on behalf of rattlesnakes, newts, gopher frogs, and salamanders, and why? "They've had the same evolutionary run on the planet that we've had," says Means. "We owe them everything we can do."

Getting There

David Havlick

In New England, where I now live, the old-timers are known for being kind of cagey. When "leaf-peepers" arrive each autumn—tourists come north to check out the fall foliage—they invariably get lost on winding country roads. When these city slickers ask a local for directions, they can expect a response along the lines of "Ya cain't get theah from heah." It's not a particularly helpful set of directions, but it's all part of New England's charm. You've got to work a little to find the beauty up here.

As it turns out, charming or not, the New Englanders' response isn't very accurate. Whether you happen to be in the eastern United States, the Rocky Mountains, the Pacific Northwest, southwestern deserts, Great Plains, Deep South, or Midwest, the actual answer almost surely is that you can get there from here. We now live in an America that is so vastly roaded and so thoroughly motorized that there is almost no place beyond easy reach of the recreational driver. At last count, using the digital GIS mapping systems that have charted our planet, the farthest point from a road in the lower forty-eight states is twenty miles—near the southeast corner of Yellowstone National Park. Second most distant is about eighteen miles (in the Bob Marshall Wilderness of northern Montana), and it tails off steadily from there. Beyond a few bug-infested corners of Florida and Maine, you won't find yourself more than five miles from a road anywhere east or south of Minnesota. That's not even a long walk.

Roads, for that matter, are only the opening wedge of the broader point of motorized access. In the past thirty years we have also developed a powerful fleet of all-terrain vehicles and snowmobiles that carry us far beyond the road's end into places that once seemed—and actually were—remote. You can get there from here, and chances are good you won't even need to get off your cushioned, thermostatically controlled seat to arrive, whether there's a road that takes you there or not. Outside of the 4 percent of U.S. lands formally designated as Wilderness where motor vehicles are forbidden, you'll be hard-pressed to head into the woods without running into some sign of motorized activity—whether by sound, sight, or smell.

There are more than 700,000 miles of road already built into America's national forests, parks, wildlife refuges, and other federal lands, and each year Americans buy more than 700,000 new ATVs to roam far beyond those roads. You can do the math, but the land just is not large enough to absorb all that without a trace.

So what are we to do about all this motorized access? Go back to the age of steamships! Model Ts! Get yourself a good horse! What greater access could a human want?

No. What I want to do, actually, is try to think like an off-roader. It's not so crazy. The demographics of recreational off-roaders make them sound an awful lot like me: about forty years old, male, college-educated, and professing an appreciation for the outdoors. In many respects we're not that different, but here's the rub: I say motorized recreation should be strictly regulated, limited to occur only on roads, and that hundreds of thousands of miles of the roads currently criss-crossing public lands (and many private lands) should be removed. Suddenly I seem a lot less like my ATV-wielding doppelgänger. That's fine. I'm not trying to become him; I just want to think like him, work to understand his views, and figure out why I disagree with them.

In many respects the easiest case against off-road vehicles and extensive motorized access is ecological. From soil and snow com-paction, to rapidly spreading invasive plants to motorists' direct and inadvertent harassment of sensitive species, to air and water pollution, the litany of adverse ecological effects of both roads and motorized activity is well documented and ably covered elsewhere. But, for the ecological effects of roads and motorized recreation to carry the argu-ment, you have to hold a certain set of values. You have to care about ecology, for instance, or at least believe that causing harm to other animals, plants, their habitats, and the processes upon which they depend ought to be minimized or avoided wherever possible. That set of values doesn't come automatically with U.S. citizenship.

Beyond ecology there's also a deep rap sheet of social claims against off-road vehicles. Even when off-roaders are polite and law-abiding, their activity disrupts and displaces hikers, skiers, equestrians, bird-watchers, anglers, and a number of hunters and other folks who turn to the backcountry for recreation, education, inspiration, or suste-nance. In some instances, the noise, smoke, and speed of off-road vehicles can pose a true hazard to other people. In many other cases there is simply an abrupt sense of violation when nonmotorized visi-tors encounter vehicles beyond the reach of roads. It's like finding a cigarette butt in your soup—it's not necessarily illegal or maybe even dangerous for it to be there, but it ruins your appetite for a while.

Social issues may be more difficult than ecological ones for most people to cast aside; I mean we all just want to get along, right? But even here, for off-roaders it's possible to cast a skeptical eye upon the claims of nonmotorized users who say they're displaced. Shouldn't there be some reciprocity, after all? If an ATV driver doesn't feel dis-turbed when passing a group of backpackers, why should the hikers feel so put out by that same encounter? If motorists are willing to share these places, why aren't the hikers or skiers?

This asymmetry of experience surely accounts for some of the con-flict and complexity of the motorized access question. People of decent character can have vastly different experiences on the exact same trail at the exact same time simply by virtue of their relationship to a certain piece of machinery—namely, whether they are straddling it or standing apart from it.

It's actually pretty difficult for hikers to disrupt an off-roader's day in any fundamental way. Hikers can make rude comments or gestures, but a hiker's or skier's tracks will be little noticed by the passing ATVer or snowmobiler. Meanwhile, vehicle tracks can radically change the quality and character of the hiker's or skier's route, and if the vehicle is still within earshot, the noise and/or fumes can further degrade the quiet recreationist's experience. It's not fair, to be sure, and that's part of the problem.

What we might call the "recreational injustice" of motorized recre-ation is, in fact, a piece of the explanation, but it doesn't fully account for how roads and motorized access affect us and why many of these impacts ought to be regulated.

What is it, after all, that makes a motorized outing in the woods different from a nonmotorized one? How does relying upon a machine to take us somewhere alter our relationships to the places we reach or people we meet along the way? What does it mean to gain *access* to a place?

We're getting there. We've nearly arrived. We've almost made it.

Sometimes I imagine Sir Edmund Hillary gasping such things to Tenzing Norgay as they staggered those final feet toward the summit of Everest. I hear an earnestness to his words, exhilaration wrapped in fatigue and days on end of trial, perhaps a sense of gratitude and relief that they were about to arrive. It makes me think that access is not just about getting to a place or knowing that a place is available. Access in its deeper sense must include the drawn-out acts of arriving. It's a lesson that might not take more than a meandering September drive through red oaks and sugar maples to learn.

We want to reach places because we think it will be meaningful not just to be there, but because there is something worthwhile in the journey. How long, after all their efforts, did Hillary and Tenzing linger at the summit of Everest, their "destination"? Hillary later claimed that he sought to climb Everest *because it was there*, but how different would his accomplishment have been had he motored to the top in a snowmobile or been set gently on the summit ridge by a helicopter? (Neither, thankfully, is yet possible.) *Getting there* often isn't the whole of the experience, or even the most valuable portion of it.

A number of years ago, two friends and I walked from Mexico to Canada along the Continental Divide. Nearly two thousand miles into our trek, we needed to cross Interstate 15 at Monida Pass on the Montana-Idaho border. As we approached the highway on a rain-swept gravel road, a man pulled alongside in a pickup to ask where we were headed. "Canada!" we told him. "We're hiking the Continental Divide." The driver seemed a bit puzzled and asked, "How long's that gonna take?" We figured we had another six or seven hundred miles to go on our meandering ridgeline route and told him it would take us five or six weeks. He seemed perplexed, then brightened with a suggestion. "Hey! If you just hike up I-15 here, it'd be way shorter. You might get to Canada in only three or four days. You know, I'm heading that way myself. If you want to cover some of the gas, I could get you there in a couple of hours."

We appreciated his offer, truly we did, but we declined. It seemed clear that he didn't understand what we were trying to do. We weren't just trying to get to Canada. Getting to Canada was our goal, but only in the context of a broader activity and a whole suite of experiences along the way.

What, then, are some of the experiences commonly sought by motorized recreationists? Surveys consistently show a handful of responses: spending time outdoors with family or friends; assisting other activities such as hunting or fishing or ranch and farmwork; and what one study categorized as "achievement and stimulation," or more simply, skills, thrills, and speed. Few accounts report that motorized users consider their machines essential to actually arriving at a particular place. What ORVers frame as a matter of access, then, often means not so much the ability to get somewhere as it means getting somewhere in a certain way—with a particular degree of ease or speed. As Hillary and many others have demonstrated over the years, you can get nearly everywhere on earth using your own two feet; you just might not get there easily or quickly.

As a rule, driving along a road or riding a powerful machine to reach your destination makes access easy and fast. At times this can be a fine combination. My wife and I drove to Canada just last week, in fact, and I don't recall a single moment of the trip when I would rather have been lugging a pile of conference papers and a three-month-old baby on foot along the New York Thruway. In this case, all we really were trying to do was reach our destination. But isn't that a different kind of access? Shouldn't we be able to distinguish between those journeys for which speed and ease of travel are our highest priorities and those for which we're seeking something else? This lack of distinction is what brings ATVs and backcountry roads into serious question.

If we could make such distinctions more clearly, it might almost seem odd to note that the pitched battle over motorized access in recent years has focused on how extensively ATVs and snowmobiles should be permitted to reach into the remaining backcountry areas of the United States. After all, if one of the fundamental points of driving a vehicle is to make it easier or faster to arrive at your destination, then why would you even bother trying to go to a backcountry region that is, by definition, out of the way or hard to reach? Once you make it easy and quick to get there, doesn't it become just another version of a drive-thru?

Off-road vehicle enthusiasts tend to respond to comments like this by noting their appreciation of the outdoors or highlighting the merits of scenic loop rides through the mountains. In this, off-roaders are not so different in their desires from millions of other motor tourists who visit national parks each year or cruise scenic routes such as Shenandoah's Skyline Drive or the Blue Ridge Parkway. The key difference is that these latter routes have been carefully designed and intentionally maintained to attract and accommodate just this kind of use. These roads come with their own supply of impacts and costs, to be sure, but they have long been built explicitly into our society's infrastructure of laws, appropriations, and public works. As a broader public, we have effectively agreed that we value scenic roads in these places and are willing to support them.

The case of off-road vehicles accessing public lands is rather different. ATVs and snowmobiles emerged abruptly in the past three decades as a form of technology that enabled individuals to reach new places in new ways. These machines carried with them a host of impacts and costs that laws and land managers have never adequately accounted for or successfully brought under control. Even where trails have eventually been opened up to legal motorized use, this access was commonly forced upon managers first by illegal or unplanned motorized activity. Outside the handful of off-road vehicle "play areas" or trail systems that have been designed, funded, and built from the outset with this type of activity in mind, what we find in the growing armada of ATV and snowmobile users is a widespread application of renegade ethics that disregards many social, legal, and economic boundaries.

The renegade creed of off-road motorists often rides beneath a familiar American banner of individual freedoms and the liberal pursuit of happiness. But we are, when last I checked, a nation dedicated to laws more than to hedonism. The fact that driving a snowmobile at fifty miles per hour across an alpine meadow could bring me great thrills doesn't justify its acceptability any more than if my preferred source of adrenaline were throwing bricks through storefront windows. We live in a nation that cherishes its freedoms, but always within limits.

It is just that trait—the disavowal of living within limits—that I find most profoundly troubling about motorized access and its proliferation. We not only make ourselves vulnerable in the world when we engage it without humility, we also place an undue burden upon our environmental and social supports. And for most men, at least, nothing seems to breed hubris more swiftly than wedging a powerful engine between our legs. In what sounds like only a curious aside but surely ought to give us some pause, surveys consistently show that the vast majority of off-roaders—by more than a nine to one margin—are men.

I'd like to think there's a better way to get from where we are to wherever it is we're going.

I would like to know what it means to try to get somewhere, not just easily or fast, but as a more drawn-out process of arriving. *Access* for too long has meant that we expect to go anywhere to do anything no matter the cost. Fast and easy, in access as in food, often finds us quickly fulfilled but with a lingering case of dis-ease. Surely access can mean something else. Perhaps access can teach us not just about our own limitless desires, but also about the places we're trying to reach. So just how do we build a foundation of understanding into our mad dashes to reach new places?

Slowing down may help—not always, but in those cases when a bit of lingering can lead to a deeper connection to or respect for the surroundings. I'm not sure that if I had walked to Ontario via the New York Thruway last week I would appreciate many of those places more—it's pretty tough to bond with concrete Jersey barriers and roaring eighteen-wheelers. But in other places, taking your time can make a great difference. I suspect that few events in my life will affect me as deeply as that six-month Continental Divide hike up the length of the Rockies, not because we were surrounded at all times by wilderness—for many long stretches we weren't—but because of the pace of our progress. We passed through the land at a rate that seemed to make sense to my body, step by step, so that my legs and my shoulders and my mind could fully absorb the shifts of light and scents and rise and fall of mountains, as well as the activities of people and how we fit into these places. For years afterward I could still recall every night's camp for the length of the trip. It created a string of memories that linked Apache pine forests to stands of subalpine larch and pulled together the scratchings of javelina and those of grizzly bear along a single winding path. It made a map of my world for me in a way that no trip in a car or a snowmobile has ever managed.

I'm not saying that we all need to get out and hike for six months to appreciate the world. Far from it. But having had the luxury to do just that, I realize more vividly how speeding up can change and reduce the scale of our lives. As Einstein aptly proved, time and space are intricately connected. When we speed up, our world shrinks.

In some ways, where I think we ought to go needn't even be a difficult journey. As poet Mary Oliver has reminded us, "You do not have to be good/You do not have to walk on your knees/for a hundred miles through the desert, repenting." All we really need is to maintain those places in our lives and in our lands where we recognize the power of restraint.

We don't need to get everywhere from here. Maybe that's what the old New Englanders are trying to tell us. Maybe we've been taking them too literally all this time. Maybe we just need to figure out how to find satisfaction and inspiration and beauty in ways that don't ride roughshod over our neighbors or have us motoring frantically past the flame-orange leaves of autumn maples.

I'd like to think we have access to much of this already if we could just take the necessary time and care. It almost certainly doesn't require a powerful machine or hundreds of thousands of miles of backcountry roads to reach fine scenery or create satisfying routes or find good times with friends and family.

I would like us to think again about where we need to go, and by what means, in order to live well in this world. I think we can get there. I would like to try to get to that place.

Part Five: Ripped, Restored, Revived

"In 1988, the local watershed group had inventoried catastrophic earth slides in the basin and found that 87 percent of them were related to roads. Some ten years later, state and federal funding agencies had begun to think in terms of watershed economics. Wouldn't it be more cost-effective in the long run to stem the chronic flow of sediment into waterways than it would be to apply bandages after the bleeding had begun?"
— Freeman House, "More Than Numbers"

The first four parts of this book focus on the impacts of roads and motorized recreation, but thankfully, damaging roads can be removed, and places restored. Restoration is a hot topic among scientists, activists, land managers, decision-makers, and even nature writers. But sometimes there are vastly different perspectives on what is, or is not, restoration. Often wildland restoration is focused just on trees, which ones to cut and which ones to leave. The writers in Part Five put bright lines around road removal, highlighting it as a different, but key component to watershed restoration. And, as we've read in previous sections, there are plenty of roads to go around and hence plenty of roads to remove.

For instance, in 2000 the Forest Service called for removing more than 140,000 miles of roads over the next twenty to forty years. If Congress fully invested in such restoration efforts, which require bulldozers, excavators, and other heavy equipment, road removal could provide decades-long family-wage jobs that restore not only the land but the communities that surround it. And while the physical landscape is being restored, some writers wonder about the "spirit" of that landscape. Can it be restored too?

The End of the Road

T. H. Watkins

I found it difficult not to compare the thing in front of me to some kind of unclassifiable dinosaur clawing its way through the landscape. But it was just a track hoe, a 50,000-pound excavator with huge treads and a fifty-foot arm from which a big bucket depended like an enormous fist. The operator sat in the cab and yanked levers as the critter growled down the ancient logging road, its bucket swinging from side to side to knock over trees like Godzilla slapping down office buildings.

Anne Connor grinned at my openmouthed awe. "On a stretch like this," she said, "he can clear a quarter-mile an hour." That seemed to please her. We were on the side of a mountain in Idaho's Clearwater National Forest. With me were Connor, a civil engineer with the U.S. Forest Service; Ira Jones, director of watershed programs for the Nez Perce tribe; and Emmit Taylor, Jr., a watershed project leader for the tribe. With impetus and funding from the Forest Service and the Bonneville Power Authority, these three were joining forces to turn history on its head.

They were killing roads—though "obliteration" and "decommissioning" are the preferred terms. This is not an activity for which Uncle Sam has been noted. Quite the opposite, in fact—a truth that had come through with particular force earlier that day when I drove through portions of the Clearwater. The brow of just about every mountain I saw was scarred by tier upon tier of roads.

It had all been part of the most ambitious logging program in Forest Service history. After World War II the agency, citing the national demand for housing, began to convert much of its 180-million-acre

169

domain into clear-cuts made accessible by roads. By the mid-1990s, there were some 383,000 miles of official forest roads, plus at least another 52,000 miles of "unclassified" roads, many of them created unofficially by fast-moving logging and mining companies, or by recreational ATV drivers.

"Roads have been identified as *the* major impact on the forest environment," a hydrologist at Montana's Kootenai National Forest wrote in 1995. Many of those built during the first frenzied decades of the logging boom were simply abandoned. Maintenance budgets were inadequate even to keep stable roads in good condition, and thousands of miles were unstable. Culverts plugged up with debris. Roads sagged. Rainfall washed increasing levels of sediment down mountain slopes, clogging rivers and smothering fisheries. Occasionally, huge chunks of deteriorating roadbeds collapsed, sending an avalanche of mud, rocks, and trees crashing into some hapless stream.

By the 1980s, it was clear to many that something had to be done, but for years not much was. Then in 1997, the Forest Service's new chief, Mike Dombeck, asked for an increase of $22 million in his budget to remove 3,500 miles of roads, which Dombeck characterized as only a fraction of those eligible for closure. "It was an excellent start," observes Bethanie Walder, director of the Wildlands Center for Preventing Roads, in Missoula, Montana. "But if you don't address the potential hydrological impacts of every road, no matter how stable it seems, you're just creating time bombs."

The Clearwater is one of the most thoroughly roaded of all the national forests and, at the same time, the one with perhaps the most vigorous obliteration program. Nature had helped, Anne Connor told me. For years, road obliteration had been low on the Clearwater's budgetary totem pole, but in the mid-1990s rainfall greatly exceeded normal levels. Nearly a thousand landslides resulted, and more than five hundred of those fiascoes were road-related.

"I can remember thinking in my early years that if one road failed, the debris would be stopped by the road below," Connor said. "After the floods, I knew that just wasn't true. You get a failure on the top road, and it just slams through the whole series and takes every other road right on down the line."

Connor began an inventory that soon identified nearly 2,000 miles of road-obliteration candidates. Most were old "jammer" roads, primitively engineered tracks that had been hurriedly gouged into the mountains from the 1950s to the 1970s for timber harvest. Trees were cut from the slopes below each road, then hauled up by cable for loading onto trucks. Because the cables of that time were short, it took a lot of roads to strip a single slope of its timber. The roads were so closely packed that, in at least one of the worst areas, there were 60 miles of roads in a single square mile, taking up a full third of the total land base.

By the time of my visit, crews had obliterated 225 miles of roads in the Clearwater. A messy business, I learned. First, in order to gain access, you go in with the track hoe and wipe out all the trees on the roadbed, as I had just seen happen—bad moment for an old tree-hugger like me. "You have to remember," Emmit Taylor told me as some good-looking trees were knocked over by the big machine, "we're talking about a hundred-year recovery plan here. So sometimes you have to sacrifice thirty-year-old trees to do the job right."

Once the road has been cleared, the track hoe reverses itself, pulling up dirt and woody debris from the road's downhill, or cliff, side and piling it against the other side. This partially recontoured roadbed is then seeded, and shrubs are transplanted, for revegetation. At every stream crossing, the machine rips up even more of the roadbed and rebuilds the site to mimic a natural watercourse. Rocks, straw bales, downed trees, and other vegetation are manipulated into place to help control erosion. It all happens swiftly and noisily, and if the immediate effect is to create an area as ugly as a war zone, recovery is astonishingly fast.

Later that day, Connor and her fellow road-killers showed me one they had obliterated less than a year earlier. I saw hardly a sign that there had ever been a road. Everywhere, grasses abounded, and tiny sprouts of ponderosa pine and white pine poked their heads above the artful rubble.

Emmit Taylor had done much of the work here, and his obvious pleasure in showing off the results put me in mind of something Dombeck said back in 1998, around the time he first proposed a controversial road-building moratorium that now affects millions of acres of forest land. "In fifty years, we will not be remembered for the resources we developed; we will be thanked for those we maintained and restored for future generations."

Thanks, Emmit.

The Two-Track and the Beer Can: What Ripping a Road Affirms

Kraig Klungness

I clearly remember my first anger at a road. It was a crisp November morning in 1967, not far from my grandfather's cabin near the Michigamme River in Michigan's Upper Peninsula. I was fourteen and ecstatic over the newfound independence of finally being allowed to venture into the woods alone to hunt whitetail deer.

After sitting perfectly still for three early morning hours by an old white pine overlooking a deer run, I got antsy and decided to stalk eastward onto adjacent state lands and unfamiliar ground. I wanted deeper woods and greater distance from the other hunters I knew were around, to experience a more wild hunt.

I meandered through mixed hardwoods, teetered atop the springy sphagnum moss of a spruce bog, and traversed a rise of birch. Emerging from a dense grouping of spruce and fir, I pulled some dry bracken fern from my bootlaces and found myself on the edge of a two-track logging road. Startled, I heard an engine just around the bend, coming my way. I wanted to duck behind a spruce and hide as the vehicle passed, but it was too late for that. So I stood there, awkwardly, as a large four-wheel-drive wagon with three hunters pulled up and stopped.

The driver asked if I'd seen any deer and I gave what from then on became my standard answer for such questions: no. He grunted a response and threw an empty Hamm's beer can—you know, the land of sky-blue waters—into the woods. In perfect mimicry, his red-capped buddy in the backseat did the same. I stood there, angry and dismayed, as I watched the vehicle move on, waddling from side to side through puddles and potholes.

Though only fourteen, I had been coming to my grandfather's cabin and joyfully immersing myself in the surrounding woods for ten years. The older I got, the more I explored on my own. By the time of this incident, I felt a budding knowledge and love of the ways and beings of this place—the old-growth we called "the pines," the tag alder swamp and a chunk of upland in its middle we called "the island," the gray jays we called "whiskey jacks," the river, the red squirrels, the weasels, the woodchuck, the bobcat, the black bear, the Canada lynx that held my grandfather and me spellbound as it passed through fresh snow within one hundred feet of us on one year's trek to get a Christmas tree.

It was always exciting to expand my range of travel, to go farther out and discover more. But that one incident—those beer cans, their ill-mannered tossing, the power wagon, the goddamn road—changed my whole world right there. The place seemed smaller, less enchanted, less wild, more threatened.

It wasn't just the two-track and the littering, but the attitude they symbolized. It was the same attitude that resulted in the clear-cuts I later found down that same road, the stagnated water where the roadbed dammed a marsh's natural drainage, and the nearby gunny-sack of rotting meat hanging from a tree limb over steel-jawed traps set for coyotes.

At fourteen I could not clearly articulate all the nuances and implications of what I felt that day. But I knew in my gut that what had happened was part of a much larger form of disregard that was not good for me, those woods, or any other wild place. Now, after thirty more years marked with similar experiences, much thought about them, and much reading, I have more to say.

Just as that two-track was part of a much larger monster, working for the prevention, removal, and revegetation of roads—"road-ripping" for short—is part of a much larger configuration of ecological acts and values. It symbolizes their enlivenment just as those boorishly tossed beer cans symbolize their defacement. The strength I feel in opposition to this defacement lies not in the opposition itself, but in what it affirms.

First, the work of road-ripping affirms the inviolate identity of a wild place you know and love. Most of us have had experiences similar to mine, and similar feelings. Those feelings tell you something, that something is wrong, and you can use the energy they give to respond. It's personal sweat-and-tears work to remedy an injury to a place that, when it hurts, you hurt.

Second, road-ripping affirms tolerance: tolerance for natural diversity in all its varied forms. It helps create the space for manifold wild beings, including humans, to thrive and evolve and celebrate their own call of the wild. At the same time we learn what cannot be tolerated in order to conserve a collective good that includes the nonhuman.

Third, road-ripping affirms quietude. A place without roads and motors is a much softer, quieter, more welcoming place for people and wild things. Engine noise clutters the air with mechanical uncleanliness, shrinking spaciousness down to the bark of internal combustion. Getting engines off the land takes us a long way toward hearing nature, toward solitude and silence, toward a practice of quietude.

Fourth, road-ripping affirms the intrinsic value of wild nature— wilderness for its own sake and not for what it can become to the human enterprise. By preventing the intrusions that accompany roads, we allow the land community to flourish independent of commercial, recreational, and scenic values.

Nature's intrinsic worth is so important. It's fundamental, not just intellectual. Breathe it, feel it, walk it. It's inherent in the domain of the more-than-human, of goshawk, river otter, butterwort, piñon pine, wood turtle, panther, bull trout, mountain, and river. Road-ripping works to prevent their desecration in a spirit of good ecological manners.

Fifth, road-ripping affirms and accepts limits, something that industrial society abhors. By promoting unlimited access, industrial society strives for unconditional power over wild nature, the ultimate violation of its intrinsic value. By thwarting this power, road-ripping goes a long way toward making wildland access ecologically accountable.

Road-ripping stops access for machinery and the churlish romping of ORVs, the trails of which are roads and the self-made routes of which are a form of road-building. Limiting their access to conserve a greater good is a form of respect that goes far deeper than superficial matters of lifestyle or taste. Accepting limits is part of the work of maturing; when we understand this, we see that road-ripping is a mature act.

Sixth, allowing vast areas of roadless country affirms wild nature's self-order. We allow the land to be, without subjecting it to human manipulations. The larger the area of wildland, the greater its self-will, which is the essence of wilderness. Every road obliterated, every roadless acre added to any wild area, enhances that land's self-order, its sovereignty, its wildness.

This, too, is fundamental, and it ties in with all of the previous principles: with love of place, with tolerance for natural diversity, with quietude, with intrinsic value, with limits. If you love a wild place, have tolerance for its natural diversity, respect its quietude, feel its intrinsic worth, and therefore respect the limits that arise from these, then you do not attempt to exert control, you do not dominate, you do not manipulate. You just rip the damn roads as far out as you can and allow the land its autonomy. Managerialism has no place here. Wilderness should truly be a big blank spot on the map.

Since that crisp November day in 1967, I've had my favorite route up Lookout Mountain severed by a forty-foot-wide road corridor. Ditto for East Bluff. The woods surrounding a favorite trout stream were roaded and clear-cut to within twenty feet of the stream's banks. Now there's a movement to open the Boundary Waters Canoe Area Wilderness to trucks and Jeeps. Last week I read that large portions of Alaska's wildlands, our last great wilderness, are spotted with yellow metal pipes signifying road easements. In *The Practice of the Wild*, Gary Snyder laments the "slow-motion explosion of expanding world economies" and pleads: "If the lad or lass is among us who knows where the secret heart of this Growth-Monster is hidden, let them please tell us where to shoot the arrow that will slow it down. And if the secret heart stays secret and our work is made no easier, I for one will keep working for wilderness day by day."

It's an apt metaphor for the situation with roads, the monster's tentacles.

Remember each day what road-ripping affirms, how this plays into your own character and defends what you love. Then practice, day by day. Even little successes help. They are acts of mindful regard for the wildness of place, the natural world, and your own wild self.

That two-track road near the Michigamme River is still there. It's not legally amenable to closure. I now own the hunting cabin, a gift from my departed grandfather. The road to it has grown in with alders and spruce. I helped this to happen. You can't drive there anymore, and I like it that way. It is a small victory but it looms big in my heart.

More Than Numbers: Twelve or Thirteen Ways of Looking at a Watershed
(with apologies to Wallace Stevens)

Freeman House

1.
It was evening all afternoon.
It was snowing.
And it was going to snow.
The blackbird sat
In the cedar-limbs.

It's December again and curdled aluminum cloud cover extends all the way to where it kisses the iron of the ocean horizon. At its mouth, the river runs narrow and clear. If you've lived through many winters here, the sight is anomalous: normal December flows are more likely bank to bank, and are muddy as corporate virtue. A storm had delivered enough wetness around Halloween to blast open the sand berm that separates the river from the sea all summer and fall. The salmon had been waiting and came into the river then.

All through November and December the jet stream has been toying with us, diverting Pacific storms to either the north or south. The fish have been trapped in pools downstream, waiting for more rain to provide enough flow to move them up fifty or sixty miles to their preferred spawning habitat. By now many of the gravid hens will have been moved by the pressure of time and fecundity to build their egg nests, called redds, in the gravels in the lower ten miles of the river. Come true winter storms, too much water is likely to move too much cobble

---

The epigraphs at the beginning of some sections of this essay are from Wallace Stevens' poem, "Thirteen Ways of Looking at a Blackbird."

and mud through these reaches for the fertile eggs to survive. They'll be either buried under deep drifts of gravel or washed away entirely.

I have committed the restorationist's cardinal sin. I have allowed myself a preferred expectation of the way two or more systems will interact. For the last two winters, steady pulses of rain have created flows that were good for the migrating salmon, carrying them all the way upstream before solstice, but a desultory number of fish had entered the river those years. This year, from all reports, the ocean is full of salmon, more than have been seen in twenty years. So I have allowed myself the fantasy of a terrific return combined with excellent flows.

I know better than to hope for conditions that fit my notion of what's good. Perhaps as a reaction to my wishful thinking and its certain spirit-dampening consequences, I am suffering from a certain diminution of ardor.

2.

I am suffering from diminished ardor. As I look out the window on the hourlong drive to Cougar Gap,[1] I'm seeing the glass half empty. As my eyes wander the rolling landscape, they seek out the raw landslides rather than indulging my usual glass-half-full habit of comparing what I'm seeing with my memory of last year's patterns of new growth on the lands cut over forty years ago.

It's one of the skills you gain in twenty years of watershed restoration work: to see the patterns in the landscape and be able to compare them with a fairly accurate memory of what was there last year. I've come to believe that I have restored in myself a pre-Enlightenment neural network that interprets what the eyes see, what the ears hear, what the skin feels in terms of patterns and relationships rather than as isolated phenomena numeralized so that they can be graphed. It's a skill given little credibility in the world of modern science, but it's deeply satisfying nonetheless.

Among the raw scars on the landscape to which my eye is drawn today, some are the result of human activities and some are the natural processes of a rain-whipped, earthquake-prone, sandstone geology. Their patterns don't change that much from year to year; the soil that would allow them to recover rapidly has been washed off the steep

---

[1] Names of persons and places have been changed.

slopes and into the river. It'll take hundreds if not thousands of years for that soil to rebuild itself. It'll take generations for the mud in the river to be flushed out to sea.

These are patterns with cycles longer than the individual human life. It's satisfying and useful to be cognizant of them, too. Such knowledge tempers our human tendency to want to fix—read tamper with—everything in sight.

I'm beginning to feel better. Thinking about numbers has made me realize that it's numbers that have been getting me down.

3.
A man and a woman
Are one.
A man and a woman and a blackbird
Are one.

Numbers have been getting me down. Twenty years of this work. The numbers of returning salmon decreasing each of the first ten of those years. The numbers creeping upward during the second decade so that they stand now at close to the point where we began. The rational insistence of the agencies and foundations that pay for our projects that we quantify our work—numbers of fish, miles of road and streambank treated, numbers of trees planted, percentages that have survived. Our numbers have looked good enough so that our little community-based watershed restoration organization is anticipating a half-million-dollar budget in the next fiscal year. Abandoned roads will be decommissioned; managed roads "stormproofed" to make them less constant conduits of mud into the waterways; trees grown from locally gathered seed will be planted; with luck, more wild salmon will be captured, their eggs fertilized and incubated, and schoolchildren will release the juvenile fish back into the wild. A number of local jobs will be generated. Similar budgets have provided me with an office job for the last two years. High on my job description is the mandate to keep that cash flow coming. I have been successful enough, and I'm really a little old to be planting trees or hefting rock, but after a while there comes to be something demeaning about pursuing public funds for a living.

While there is an increasing number of 50- to 75-dollar-per-hour professional scientists and consultants involved in watershed and ecosystem restoration, any work that involves moving heavy things around or getting wet and dirty is still done by volunteers or locals working for 10 to 20 percent of those amounts.

Some of the amateurs go on to become professionals, make a career of it, but most of the practitioners are satisfied with the rewards of an ever-deepening relationship to the places where they live, by the sense that they are returning some small part of the enormous gift of Creation, by a growing knowledge that humans are capable of reunion with the life systems that support them. At its best, the work is an act of love, of communion, and as such delivers its own rewards. "Work is work," writes Jim Dodge, "but it's a pleasure to sing for one's supper when the song itself provides sustenance."

4.

For most of the twenty-plus years that Rochelle has lived in her country neighborhood, the most logical expectation has been that the industrial timberland owners who owned the remaining old-growth forests nearby would liquidate their inventory. The most efficient and cost-effective way to turn those trees into timber is by clear-cutting, a practice that leaves the steep lands barren under the driving rains of winter. Often, topsoil needed for the recovery of vegetation will end up in the streams, choking salmon habitat.

Rochelle had experienced the prospect as a piercing sadness. It had become clear to her that if corporations couldn't be held responsible for damage they inflicted on the lands they managed, then it was the responsibility of the resident landowners to resist that damage, and in the event that the resistance failed, to plan and implement a strategy for the recovery of the land and waters. The land means everything to Rochelle, and she quietly assumed that her neighbors, surrounded by the same beauty, would eventually come to the same conclusions. It may or may not be possible to stop the corporate practices, she reasoned. One certainly is compelled to try. But if you take the long view, the land itself can become the context and rationale for cooperative management strategies assumed by people who *live* on the land. Cooperative because natural succession proceeds at the level of the landscape and ecosystem rather than within the boundaries of property. When people live on damaged land, they can learn to act as watershed paramedics. As the land recovers, their management can begin to resemble preventive medicine. Some of the people Rochelle talked to were interested in small-scale sustainable timber production; others could not imagine a chainsaw in their hands biting into a living tree.

Rochelle had been talking to the crankiest bunch of individualists I can imagine, and it has taken a lot of persistence and patience. But now, with the recent purchase by conservation buyers of most of the industrial timberlands in the area, including several thousand acres of old-growth forest, her slow work is consolidating like ripening cheese. There are enough landowners talking cooperative conservation-based land management that, together, they might quilt a mosaic of wild and well-managed lands.

. . . . .

The road on which I'll be been traveling once I turn off the paved county road is one of the log-haul roads pushed in on the cheap forty or more years ago. Like most logging and haul roads cut in that frenzied boom time, it had been designed, if that is not too grand a word, for onetime use only and then abandoned. In aerial photos, you can see a spaghetti-like tangle adding up to more than 2,500 miles of such roads in this 300-square mile watershed.

Later, in the 1970s, when large ranches were being subdivided, developers "improved" the roads, adding as few culverts as county codes would allow them, and called them access roads to the parcels that were being snapped up by back-to-the-landers. The improvements proved to be less than adequate in terms of the large amounts of sediment they bleed into the waterways each winter. The far larger numbers of still-abandoned roads periodically hemorrhaged landslides and stream-crossing washouts during the wettest years. At a rate frighteningly rapid in terms of geological time but harder to see in the brief span of human lifetimes, the watershed is slowly bleeding to death.

In 1988 the local watershed restoration group had inventoried catastrophic earth slides in the basin and found that 87 percent of them were related to roads. Some ten years later, state and federal funding agencies had begun to think in terms of watershed economics. Wouldn't it be more cost-effective in the long run to stem the chronic flow of sediment into waterways than it would be to apply bandages after the bleeding had begun?

Everyone involved—the state, the feds, the community groups, the professional consultants—knew that cost-effective didn't necessarily mean cheap; there probably wasn't enough money in the world to put to bed or upgrade all the roads that had been carelessly built in the American West in the last half century. But the local groups had been waiting for such an opportunity for a long time and jumped into the scramble for limited funds with a grand ten-year plan to inventory all the roads in the basin, prioritize the largest bleeders, and launch projects, tributary by tributary, to stormproof the active access roads and remove the stream crossings that hadn't yet blown out on abandoned ones.

It is one of Rochelle's day jobs to enlist the cooperation of neighboring landowners in such projects in the three basins surrounding her place. With the threat of clear-cut logging reduced, it seems to her like a win-win-win opportunity. Not only will landowners get otherwise unaffordable work done on their properties, but they will in the process become well educated about road maintenance. Soil and water and all the myriad creatures, including humans, will benefit. Both terrestrial and aquatic habitats will become more productive and the very need for restoration projects may gradually dwindle.

5.
Among twenty snowy mountains,
The only moving thing
Was the eye of the blackbird.

As usual, I get lost on the way to Rochelle's place. Where the county pavement ends begins a maze of muddy roads, one of those hastily built thirty or more years ago. It's easy to get confused unless you thread this maze every day.

When a few ranches were subdivided in the early seventies, a little land rush was inadvertently created. There were at that time in American history the extraordinary number of young people who had come all willy-nilly to resist the institutionalization of primary experiences like birth and death and providing one's own food and shelter. I have no idea why so many people seemed spontaneously to develop the same actualization of this resistance. But like lemmings, tens of thousands of urban people moved back to the land to test a faith unsupported by any evidence or personal experience that they could provide for themselves and one another and thus reclaim their confidence as humans.

Rochelle is one of the survivors of the hegira, as am I. She's been singing the song that provides its own sustenance for a good part of her time here. After the clear-cuts and fires of the early eighties, she and her community planted tens of thousands of streambank trees, trees that have grown high enough now to cool the water again.

A gorgeous fireplace and chimney, handbuilt from rocks of many shapes and colors, stands eerily alone in her yard. A few yards away, the newer house sits unfinished. It's the third house Rochelle has built in this country. The first, on another property a mile or two away, was burned to the ground in a fire that was supposed to be controlled. The insurance money moved her onto this place, a little larger at ten acres. The house that surrounded the beautiful fireplace fell down in an earthquake in 1991. Her husband, Thomas, is always busy. Whenever I visit he has little time for small talk. Often I'll just catch an occasional glimpse of him moving from task to task. This year the third house will be expanded to include the pretty fireplace that was the heart of the second.

Up until a year ago, industrial timberlands surrounded Rochelle's ten-acre parcel. A good part of those had been cut over carelessly in the eighties, but large parts were still untouched. The piece directly upstream of her, the parcel that protects the steep headwaters of the creek that runs near her place, had worried her. Back when the timber market was steady and before the feds had reduced the cut in the national forests, Rochelle had approached the local corporation that owned the headwaters of her stream, and for a small fee had obtained a piece of paper that gave her last bid should the parcel come up for sale. At the time, neither Rochelle nor the timber company imagined that it would ever come to anything.

6.
At the sight of blackbirds
Flying in a green light,
Even the bawds of euphony[2]
Would cry out sharply.

We get out of the truck and step into drizzle after another five miles of rough road into a wilder terrain. I want to see a certain view. Rochelle wants to look at a certain road. We are at one of the higher elevations near the eastern ridge of the watershed. Despite the drizzle, we can see nearly a hundred miles to the south, and twenty miles to the west (though it seems much farther), where the horizon is the ridge that rises straight up out of the Pacific on the other side of it. I bathe myself in the prospect before me, thinking of Gary Snyder's "mountains and rivers without end." Close in, the landscape breaks into the mosaic of prairie and forest that characterizes the region. Farther into the distance, the mosaic fades into a wash of forest greens and upland prairie browns, differentiated by the deep green of Douglas fir and the celadon green of tan oak.

Although we can't see the ocean, we can get a sense of the weather system coming from it, which is changing before our eyes. Under the overcast the colors are faded, but where there are breaks in the cloud slurry, sunlight pours down to make blazing splashes amidst the gloom. Where the light cuts through columns of mist, it breaks into discretely defined rays like signals from the gods.

You can look at the land spread out below us and imagine that it is uninhabited, or inhabited only by a community with bear and cougar at the top of the food chain. I know better. Parts of the land *are* uninhabited by humans, and those parts are managed either by state and federal agencies or by industrial timber corporations. The inhabited part, more than four-fifths of the land laid out before me, is privately owned by ranchers, back-to-the-landers, outlaws, or some combination of the above: new Indians, new cowboys, dope-growers, new scientists, old pioneer families, traditional rednecks, environmentalists, new rednecks, vegetarians, tree planters, and check here for "other."

---

[2] A bawd is a procuress or prostitute. Euphony is "the quality, esp. in the spoken word of having a pleasant sound" (OED). Wallace is speaking of sweet-talking hustlers here, or perhaps of poets in general. He then separates himself from the crowd with the noneuphonious (to my ear) phrase that follows, "Would cry out sharply." I hear the cry of the western raven, a very black bird.

Language will always fall short of describing the beauty of nature, no matter how skillful the speaker. We are attempting to describe Creation from *within* Creation, one of the binding paradoxes of the human condition. By extension, to call our rehabilitation efforts "ecological restoration" is hubristically to claim a power equal to that of evolution itself. There is no such thing as ecological restoration, except in controlled experiments carefully kept free of random human cultural effects, which more properly describes the science of *restoration ecology*. The rest of us amateurs ("practitioners of love" according to Stephanie Mills) living deep within the variables of diverse human ambitions can only hope to put ourselves into the picture in a way that we hope to be *co*evolutionary. Dennis Martinez uses the phrase "eco-cultural restoration" to describe his work among first peoples, recognizing that the renewal of indigenous cultural practices must be accompanied by the rehabilitation of the indigenous landscape. We newcomers are practicing something else. In my better moments, I like to think that we may finally be discovering a culture appropriately based on the constraints and opportunities of the diverse places in North America.

Because I have been down many of the roads in this part of the water-shed and have talked to the people at the ends of them, I know that the region closest to us is mostly populated with second- and third-generation ranchers and more recently arrived agricultural outlaws. Both groups call themselves environmentalists while being practition-ers of the most conservative sort of private property rights, each group for different reasons. I tend to be slightly more sympathetic to the ranchers, who are more honest about their espousal of John Locke's eighteenth-century philosophy of property and pride.

7.

Economies develop or devolve according to their own rules. Conser-vation buyers have purchased most of the private industrial timber-lands in Rochelle's neighborhood in the last two years to be pre-served for public management. The previous owner was a local corporation with a mill too large to be adequately supplied by its own too small land base. When, due to protection of the northern spotted owl, cheap timber from the national forests had become less readily available, the local corporation found itself competing for logs on the open market with larger corporations that could afford to underbid them.

At the same time, a local environmental group was successfully challenging in court each one of the local corporation's logging plans. The company saw the long window of time opening up to swallow it. The corporation—mills, lands, and all—was put up for sale. Other organizations, some of which included Rochelle, started raising money in an attempt to outbid the same larger corporation that had helped run the smaller one out of business.

The effort attracted the attention of an international forest preser-vation organization that was looking for a project that would establish its presence in North America. These several thousand acres of old-growth Douglas fir, scattered between a state park on the east and a national conservation area on the west, looked like a winner. The international organization developed its strategies around the philos-ophy of the Wildlands Project, which recognizes that even if every unexploited area in the developed world were put out of bounds to economic development immediately, there still wouldn't be a large enough land base to do more than slightly slow the rate of the extinction of species. The Wildlands Project has demonstrated the need for "corridors" between the pristine "core areas," places where human activity is limited in favor of their uses by other species. The theory is scientifically sound in the abstract, and presents a conservation strategy simplified enough to have gained a significant number of adherents in centralized government land management agencies. The purchases were going to require a great deal of money, a large part of it public funds.

Combine the word *corridor* with public funds and the result may or may not make for viable wildlife habitat, but it will certainly create the expectation of public access to places where human presence had heretofore been minimal. Public funds had been used for the acquisitions, generating a vague expectation on the part of the state that at some time in the future, some kind of trail would exist through the reserves. On the part of the locals who lived on parcels separating the newly acquired forests, a well-defined paranoid expectation bloomed: many hikers in expensive outdoor gear closely followed by uniformed rangers on the lookout for illegal activities of all kinds.

Up until the point at which the purchase was secure, the international forest preservation organization had acted in a fashion in keeping with the techniques and strategies of most centralized and urban-based organizations working from high-minded and abstract principles. The climate of political expediency can intensify in direct proportion to the numbers of acres, or dollars, at stake. Soon the end of preserving big parcels of undisturbed habitat was justifying the means of describing the landscape as if it had no human residents. The needs and concerns of the locals had been treated as an irritation. The situation had been described to funders in such a way as to make it legible and attractive to them, ignoring the potential social problems locally.

To its enormous credit, however, the international forest preservation organization did not stop with the acquisition and leave someone else to deal with the social fallout. Following Rochelle's lead, the fund-raisers not only recognized the potential of local interest in reinhabitation, but also developed a program that begins to address two of the outstanding flaws in the Wildlands Project strategy.

Once beyond the grandeur of the Wildlands Project vision, it becomes apparent that the challenge is much more complex than arrogant lines drawn on a map. Each biome—each microclimate, in fact—

presents a complex knot of relationships that requires exact knowledge of two functions or features of locale where a corridor might be located. What are the requirements of each plant, animal, or community native to that particular fold of the planet? Based on that knowledge (which can best be gathered over time by resident humans with help from professional ecologists), what kinds of economic activities are harmonious with those needs? Until the second question is answered, one doesn't have much to say to the people who inhabit the corridors one might be proposing.

The international forest preservation organization researched other sources of money and mounted a stewardship initiative in the area of the newly public wildlands. The skills of a half dozen local organizations, whose local expertise had been gained by systematic immersion in this unique biome, were put at the service of the people who lived in the area, providing information and experience needed for a cooperative effort in conservation-based land management. The group who had worked on salmon restoration for twenty years would train people to gather credible data on water quality and aquatic habitat. The sustainable forestry outfit would teach people to think about timber production in the long term and conduct workshops in fuel load reduction in the brushy forest effulgence that follows clearcutting. A local land trust would teach conservation easement potentials to those who had no interest in commercial production. The watershed council that had worked for fifteen years to reduce sediment flow into the waterways would systematically inventory poorly constructed and abandoned roads and seek public funds to help landowners repair or decommission them. Another local organization that concerns itself with the needs of terrestrial creatures would teach people how to track and identify their animal neighbors. The twenty square miles of subdrainages and their human inhabitants began to be understood as a reciprocally functional unit.

· · · · ·

The road Rochelle shows us is like a highway compared with the rutted roads we've traveled today. The State Parks Department, one of the public agencies involved in managing the newly protected areas, built the road in the last dry season. It is two lanes wide and well graveled and connects the assumedly private roads behind us with land recently acquired by conservation buyers, presumably for the protection of wildlife. "Parks" as the state agency is known, has a clear mandate to provide recreation for work-weary Californians. A draft land-use plan being circulated by Parks shows blue circles designating proposed campsite developments right on top of the largest population of northern spotted owls yet identified in the protected area. "Looks like we'll have to protect the land from the protectors," says Rochelle. She's received no clear answers to her inquiries about Parks' intentions, but she has managed to get a spur road closed for the winter with yellow plastic signs to protect against the spread of sudden oak death syndrome.

8.

He rode over Connecticut
In a glass coach.
Once, a fear pierced him,
In that he mistook
The shadow of his equipage
For blackbirds.

Sudden oak death syndrome is a plague that has appeared to the south of us and is spreading. It is a fungus, *Phytophthera*, currently believed to be water-borne, that rapidly kills tan oak, black oak, and coastal live oak. Three counties to the south, whole mountainsides present the grim panorama of standing dead trees, kindling for some catastrophic future fire. It has also been discovered to infect huckleberry bushes, another vector for the spread of the disease. It's been identified in nursery rhododendrons in Germany and the Netherlands and central California. Students of algae tell us *Phytophthera* is related to the fungus that caused the Irish potato blight of the nineteenth century. Journalists remind us of the chestnut blight of the twentieth century, which along with opportunistic cutting, eliminated that species from eastern woodlands. Two unconfirmed sightings of the disease have been made in the park to the east of where we are standing.

Some climatologists, using computer models, have projected that an increase of two degrees Fahrenheit in the global temperature will destroy the redwood forests nearby.

Four thousand or so years ago, during a warming cycle, salmon colonized rivers farther and farther to the south as the glaciers receded. Our little river is close to the southern extreme of that range. Salmon have a rather narrow temperature range in which they can flourish. As air temperatures rise on the planet, the ocean will heat up, and so will rivers. The range of the salmon will retreat back to the north where the waters are cooler. Russian scientists call the likely effects of climate change "ecosystem reorganization," unpredictable, chaotic. Watershed restoration? What can the words mean in a time of plagues? How shall we go on? What shall we restore?

These are not new questions. How could we have avoided asking them as we devoted ourselves to our tiny watershed at the same time as the larger world gave us Chernobyl, Bhopal, AIDS? Global warming hit the news around the same time we began work to enhance the spawning successes of our precious wild salmon. *We have never for a moment known if we would succeed.* But we have known that for any success to be enduring, changes would not be measured in numbers of wild creatures so much as in human attitudes toward the wild.

Plagues are a symptom of the human economies being institutionalized by treaties like NAFTA and GATT, which create supranational institutions that move us closer to what Wendell Berry calls the total economy. In the total economy there is no value but in personal wealth, no form of measurement but in numbers. In a total economy a marriage contract would be framed in deliverable ergs of sexual energy, hours of homemaking; profit-and-loss statements would take the form of tangible property, including children. What's clean water worth? A salmon run?

9.

The blackbird whirled in the autumn winds.
It was a small part of the pantomime.

Protection and preservation of "pristine" lands is no more than half a strategy. If the lands between the preserves are understood as economic sacrifice zones (which they will be until they are described otherwise), whose army will defend the preserves fifty years from now? The accommodation of wildness in the inhabited lands between the preserves is essential to the viability of the preserves themselves. Once a community of humans begins to understand itself as a functional part of the landscape, and learns how to act that way, the protected lands can be understood as sacred. Watersheds are more than museums with wildlands hanging on the walls.

10.

After another short haul in the truck, we can see a column of smoke. As we get closer, Rochelle grows positively gleeful. We pull into an opening in the doghair forest with an old homestead cabin in the middle of it. Two burn piles smoke and occasionally blaze up nearby. At least two chainsaws snarl away out of sight on the hillsides rising up steeply around the homestead. From a distance the work site looks like an anthill. A steady stream of people is pulling sections of wet green slash larger than themselves down out of the woods and onto the smoky fire.

I recognize one of the brush-pullers. I know her by her forest name, Velocity. The name fits. Velocity rarely stops moving, and if there is another human nearby, she's likely to be talking enthusiastically. "Isn't this great?" she cries. "We'll have two acres fireproofed by the end of the day."

Velocity is a forest defender, one of about twenty who have set up an encampment some fifteen miles to the north in order to resist the liquidation of the largest stand of undisturbed old-growth Douglas fir in the watershed and in the state. A rotating crew of twenty or so maintains the encampment, a trespass its residents call a "free state." Legal ploys to stop the cut have failed, and the young people will try to hold off the contract loggers while another group of residents looks for the money to purchase the forest.

Velocity had arrived in the watershed a couple of years earlier, when itinerant practitioners of nonviolent civil disobedience were defending the same forest. That time, the courts had agreed with the protestors. During both the earlier defense and the current one, the occupation had been augmented by legal blockades on public roads by residents of the valley. After that success, other activists moved on to other crises, but Velocity and two comrades had settled in the valley, recognizing the power of neighborly protest. They had found a place to live, grown gardens, performed odd jobs, and waited for the next move on the forest.

This time around, the blockades are larger and the free state has a different demographic. Some of its residents are young people who have grown up within twenty miles of the threatened forest. As residents, they have been encouraged over the years to become watershed paramedics, and they have independently intuited the cautionary words of the brilliant restoration ecologist Daniel Janzen: "An increasingly competent medical profession should not promote participation in potentially lethal acts."

Formulators of watershed restoration have a slogan: "Preserve the best and restore the rest." The formulas were developed on public land where decisions about saving the best could be part of administrative policy. I'm not sure the scientists who invented the catchy mnemonic phrase would recognize this local iteration of their excellent strategy. Preservation may be only half a strategy, but it's the first half.

Because the law requires the loggers to stay off the dirt roads for two days following a rain, the free state can be maintained by a skeleton crew. Today some forest defenders are taking advantage of the respite to earn a few bucks working on a fuel load reduction project.

This forest was cut over thirty years ago. Because it was cut before the law required replanting, and because of the aspect and microclimate of the slope, the site has grown back in a thick tangle of tan oak and coyote brush. The straw bosses are the guys with the chainsaws. One of them is Rochelle's husband, Thomas, who is smiling broadly. He describes the work of the day: Remove the highly flammable brush in the understory of the second-growth forest. Thin some of the spindly oaks to encourage the better trees to grow faster and straighter and to allow more sunlight into the grove so that the dominant Douglas firs can grow again. Cut the limbs up as high as the saws will reach, and burn them. When the next wildfire burns through here, there'll be a better chance that it will burn slow and cool and won't be able to leap to the crown. Salvage a little firewood while you're at it.

The other sawyer is an old friend. Drawn to the valley for its opportunities in restoration fifteen years ago, Dave has become a new-age gyppo logger, pouring months of work into resurrecting a self-loading log truck that had been abandoned in the fifties. He works at small logging and thinning jobs, promoting the promising new market in sustainably harvested California hardwoods. He has built a home out of lumber he has milled himself on a homestead carved out of a rehabilitated logging site. He is inventing a life and raising a family in what he hopes is a system of coherence, with the surrounding lands and waters as the binding medium.

11.
I was of three minds,
Like a tree
In which there are three blackbirds.

Jack Turner writes in *The Abstract Wild* that he believes ecological restoration to be a passing fancy. I think it's more likely it will turn out to be something else, incorrectly called ecological restoration, and resembling more the restoration of our relationship to the places where we live.

Ecological restoration is a natural process occurring wherever there has been ecological perturbation. When a clear-cut is allowed to recover according to the dictates of local natural succession, it is ecological restoration. In a Doug fir forest, the system sometimes recovers to the point that timber can be taken from it again in sixty to eighty years. It will take four times that long for the forest to recover its mature complex of flora, fauna, and habitat. When human inhabitants gain adequate knowledge (preferably through immersion) of the eccentricities of local natural succession, they may begin to take actions that hasten it toward more diverse and mature stages of development.

The truest value of this work called watershed restoration is measured in relationships that are difficult if not impossible to turn into numbers. Like new and ever-deepening relationships with portions of the landscape or another species. Like the coagulation of relationships with neighbors, which as they thicken begin to resemble the chaotic stew of community. What is restored is some aspect of watershed and ecosystem *function*. More importantly, we're rediscovering our own human species function as a natural part of life systems. This definition of ecological restoration cannot realize its potential except as it is practiced in community vernacular life. It should not be confused with the science of restoration ecology, which will likely endure as what William Jordan has called "experimental ecology," carefully controlled and isolated from human economic activity. We will continue to need the insights and methodologies of science, but if we allow the *practice* of restoration to become the exclusive domain of professional consultants and centralized government agencies, we will have lost its greatest promise, which is nothing less than a redefinition of human culture. It is equally possible for a fully professionalized concept of ecological restoration to become part of the price of doing extractive business as usual, a form of systematized mitigation that is one more cipher in a total economy.

12.
I do not know which to prefer,

. . .

The blackbird whistling
Or just after.

Sometime in the mid-eighties, I was occasionally offered the shelter of a retreat cabin at a Cistercian monastery near a remote watershed restoration work site. I enjoyed these respites, both for the calming simplicity of the cabin and for the opportunity to chat with the abbess, a wise and elderly Belgian woman. Once, when one of those plague signals had just erupted on the world—Bhopal, perhaps, or Chernobyl—I found myself in a state of despair. What was the sense, I asked her, of pursuing this difficult work in the face of a social order disintegrating so rapidly that it may well mean the end of the world?

"What does it matter?" she answered. Her Flemish consonants sounded like a stream working its way around an obstacle.

"Say you know the end of the world is coming tomorrow morning. How do you want to face it? With a clear mind and an open heart, yes? Now, say the world isn't going to end. How do you want to wake up in the morning and approach your work?" She pauses for effect, but not long enough for me to answer." "With a clear mind and an open heart!" She beams. "End of the world or not, same answer. Go on with your work."

The Spirit of Restoration

Thomas R. Petersen

The once-rich salmon watersheds in Oregon and the slumping, road-riddled hillsides of the Clearwater are slowly being restored. But Christopher Peters of the Seventh Generation Fund, a nonprofit group working for native people's issues, says we cannot restore the land, the physical makeup of the landscape, without also restoring the spirit of the land. To native peoples, "All things have life—rocks, trees, animals, and humans. The earth, mother of us all, has life." Judeo-Christian religions tend to see the natural world as separate from the spiritual world. Though they certainly appreciate rich sunsets, high mountains, and the sight of deer bounding across a field, these parts of the physical world are viewed more as the work of spirit and not spirit itself.

Can we restore the spirit of a place? Can we restore the spirit of that place once smothered in roads?

. . . . .

On the Fourth of July, two feet of snow obscured our view of the twenty-eight stone spokes radiating from a central rock-piled hub of the Medicine Wheel, sitting at 9,680 feet elevation, high in the Big Horn Mountains of northeastern Wyoming. All we could see was the central hub rising above the snow, and six rock cairns, small piles of limestone placed at intervals around the perimeter of the Wheel.

My son Evan, nine at the time, moved into the stiff wind, clockwise around the fenced perimeter of the Wheel, shuffling the deep powder. He paused at each of these peripheral cairns and sprinkled sage and cornmeal with gloved hands. The tokens barely reached the ground.

The wind stole his offerings and blew them across the face of the Wheel. It was an age-old ritual not his own, but he understood as much as any of us did: we were told we were guests in the presence of living spirits and we were there to honor and mingle with those spirits.

A sacred site to native peoples, the Medicine Wheel was built sometime between A.D. 1200 and 1700; but its makers and purpose remain a mystery. Some claim it was built as an astronomical observatory, used as a calendar to mark the alignment of the sun, stars, and celestial bodies with the spokes of the Wheel. Others says the early Plains tribes built the Wheel, its twenty-eight spokes being the exact number of poles or rafters used in the Sun Dance enclosures of the Cheyenne, Sioux, and Crow. Chief Joseph of the Nez Perce is said to have fasted at the Wheel after he had been imprisoned attempting to lead his people to Canada, fleeing from the pursuing U.S. Army troops in the Nez Perce war of 1877. Crows still remember the vision quest of Red Plum, their early chief, when he received eagle feathers and medicine at the Wheel to protect his people from harm.

Evan and I had trudged three miles through the deep snow to the Medicine Wheel on a winding road, recently improved to allow easier driving access all the way to the Wheel. Our hike in paralleled a 10,000-year-old travois trail, part of which was destroyed improving the road. As often happens in road development, increased access resulted in increased travel, and an increase in the number of visitors. In the past the Wheel had not been commonly known to the non-native world. Only 10,000 people visited this national historic landmark in 1988; after the road was improved, the number soared to 70,000 in 1992. And how would you say the spirit of the land fared? Thirty feet away from this sacred site were a makeshift parking lot and a porta-potty. Teepee rings in the area were vandalized or stolen. A seven-foot-high, barbed-wire fence with a locked gate was built around the Wheel to protect it from souvenir hunters who had stolen some of the spoked Wheel's stones. Thousands of tourists had circled the fence for a view, and a six-inch-deep pathway-trench was the result. Direct access to the Wheel was even restricted to native people during ceremonial events, who had to submit a written request for a key to the locked gate.

The day Evan and I visited the Wheel, the fence was adorned with traditional native offerings of raptor feathers, sun-bleached bone, and streaming bouquets of brilliant yellow, indigo blue, and blood-red ribbons. But clinging next to these offerings I saw big plastic cups, cigarette lighters, and spent condoms, "offerings" of another kind representing whatever a careless tourist could quickly grab from his or her nearby car.

Disturbed by the desecration, a coalition of native peoples asked the Forest Service, the agency responsible for national landmarks, to close the last mile and a half of the road to the Wheel and let visitors approach the Wheel on foot. The hope was that this would deter casual visitors, reduce visitor numbers, and therefore reduce the environmental and spiritual impacts to the Wheel.

This proved to be the case: after the last section of the road was closed, only 30,000 visitors came in 1993, in contrast with the 70,000 the year before. In 1994 only 15,000 visitors made the trek on foot the last mile and a half. It seemed it was easy access by car, not cultural interest, that drew so many non-natives to the Wheel.

The Seventh Generation Fund says more about sacred sites and the spirit they believe is there: "The destruction of these areas, or any significant alterations to their pure or pristine nature, adversely impacts the spiritual effectiveness of the area or the ability of Native people to access the energy there, whether, for example, through the use of ceremonies or vision quests."

In this belief, restoring these sacred sites renews the ability of the land to speak to all who are attentive enough to hear.

Non-native people are also considering spirit in restoration. William R. Jordan III, who was editor of "Restoration and Management Notes" (now called *Ecological Restoration*), says this about the act of restoration:

> It isn't enough, having caused harm, or just having caused change, to say, "We won't do it anymore." There should be recompense, in kind. What do you do to recompense for causing change in the case of nature? What you do should be some rich, deeply conceived act, carried out in terms that address the wrong.
>
> Having a landscape with lots of nature in it depends on finding a way to connect nature with culture. Restoration has a crucial component to bring to that relationship. Indigenous cultures generally tried to achieve some reciprocal relationship with nature, mediated into material and spiritual terms. Restoration, at the mechanical level, is the mechanical part of that reciprocal relationship.

But what is the spiritual part of that reciprocal relationship?

Bill TallBull was a Northern Cheyenne elder and member of the Medicine Wheel Alliance, a group of native and non-native people formed to protect the Wheel, especially in native people's use of the site for vision quests and sacred ceremonies. President Clinton selected TallBull as a member of the National Advisory Council on Historic Preservation for sacred sites.

Before he passed away, TallBull spoke with me about the spirits that inhabit not just the Medicine Wheel but all of Medicine Mountain in northeastern Wyoming. "All over Medicine Mountain," he explained, "native people see the rock spirits move from one piece of granite to another, they see the tree spirits dash from Douglas fir to ponderosa pine, and we see the plant spirits move among the sage when we collect materials for our ceremonies."

TallBull paused a moment and his coal-black eyes narrowed as if part of him saw the spirits even then.

"We have been taught to see these spirits since we were young children, and our elders were taught by their elders. This kind of seeing is a part of us. White people are not taught this way. No wonder we see the spirits and whites don't."

TallBull said the spirits have been active around Medicine Mountain for thousands of years, and they are active today.

TallBull told me of a time when he was walking to the Wheel on a vision quest, approaching quietly from the south along the same ridge Evan and I had walked. A quarter mile from the Wheel he came to a flat stone wall twelve feet high. He stopped. A blood-red wolf appeared from the stone wall as if materializing from the wall itself. It locked its amber-yellow eyes on TallBull like two steady flames in a bright red lantern. TallBull stared back at the red wolf. It turned in a circle, once. As suddenly as it appeared, the red wolf melted back into the wall, ghostlike.

"I don't know what the wolf was saying to me," TallBull reflected. "Maybe nothing. Maybe it was just the mountain's way of letting me know the spirits were with me, that they were joining me in my journey."

Another native elder says, "The trees, the four-leggeds, the wingeds, the insects, even stones, all are alive and conscious."

The spirit of restoration considers living spirits in the land, the idea that restoring the physical landscape somehow, with attentiveness and consciousness, also restores these living spirits. This is a different belief system and a different hope from those of most of the modern Western world. Archeologist Michael Wilson suggests that to fully comprehend a site like the Medicine Wheel "probably requires a worldview in which the secular/religious dichotomy simply does not exist."

But restoration is nothing if not pure possibility and the notion that you and I can give back to the land and to some extent reverse the mistakes of the past. Restoration is a positive belief system. William Jordan writes:

> Exact restoration is impossible. So is preservation. So let's get on with the conversation. We have all these influences on the ecosystem which are not only inadvertent, but *invisible* to us. What I'm driving at is that it's the commitment to restore the ecosystem that forces us to explore all that we've done to the system, and to uncover all of these hidden, unseen, or unrealized influences. *That's* how we get to know who we are in relationship to that system. That experience generates an ecological definition of who we are.

Although this idea of a living earth is new and difficult for many in our Western culture, it was not new to my more ancient ancestors, the northern European and Danish peoples. The Gauls referred to their spiritual faculties being awakened by the Wouivre, telluric (magnetic or cosmic) currents that move through the ground, represented symbolically by serpents. The ancients came to these places to receive what the earth could give them, literally "the Gift of the Earth." They came not only to be affected by them, but to actively awaken the earth's dormant energies. It was an exchange, a kind of sacred dialogue, and not a one-way taking. The earth was seen as a living being of matter, and energy currents and interchange took place with humans also possessing this spiritual energy. Dolmens or megaliths—large stones—were placed where these currents were particularly strong.

Large stones were gathered centuries ago at the top of Medicine Mountain, in a sacred place that had drawn sojourners there for millennium. The Wheel was formed and rock cairns built.

I think of these Celtic dolmens and the currents that course the earth and remember Evan on that snowy Fourth of July at the Wheel. His sky-blue rain jacket lit up the white landscape as he tossed light green sage and soft yellow cornmeal offerings to the wind.

But then, surprisingly, Evan fell to his knees at the Wheel and stared at the central cairn. Our family rarely prays in the traditional manner, and never on our knees, and yet Evan seemed pulled to the earth by the presence of something much greater than he or I consciously understood. In the blinding and blowing snow he remained kneeled and fixed.

Part Six: In Defense of Wild Places

"*If we hope to live in sane ways, we have no choice but to cherish and sustain those parts of the world that remain at least partways natural and intact.*"

—William Kittredge, "Sanity"

For all the good opportunities created by restoration, of course it would be better if these lands hadn't been damaged in the first place. We now understand the impacts of roads and the damage they can cause—we understand that they are not always an asset but can be an economic and ecological liability. It's important to realize that the possibility of restoring wildlands through road removal does not justify further road construction just because we now know how to clean up the mess afterward. It is incumbent upon us, as a society, to seriously consider what is and is not appropriate development, and to prevent additional damage to wild nature.

In this final section of the book, we hear from writers who passionately argue just this point. Road and motorized recreation issues, like all conservation issues, boil down to one simple concept, eloquently stated by Barry Lopez: "The wisest thing now, it seems to me, is to regard undeveloped lands as an asset and to protect every acre of land possible." This is the cornerstone of preservation—sustaining our wildlands and keeping our wild nature.

Tinker's Basin

Ted Kerasote

In the late afternoon, we turned the horses loose. Nearly sitting on their tails, they found their own way down a steep scree slope and into a basin lush with grass and running with a freshet. On the topographic map the drainage was unnamed, but geographically speaking, it was the east fork of the south fork of the Buffalo. An unwieldy name if there ever was one. So we called it Tinker's Basin, after the horse who had led us down.

The evening was so mild we didn't bother with the tent. Sitting on the grass by our panniers, we ate dinner and watched the moon rise over the divide, its full gold disk skating over the peaks. It was so quiet you could hear the horses rip grass from the earth.

Of all the many positive attributes of the preindustrial world—space, quiet, clean air, and potable water—this kind of quiet has been disappearing the fastest. Its balm has vanished from the secluded parks that once provided privacy in urban places. It has almost disappeared from rural landscapes, which once surrounded cities and are now interconnected suburbs. And it's no longer one of the defining attributes of our national parks and nonwilderness, multiple-use public lands, where timber production, fossil fuel extraction, mining, and motorized recreation share the turf. In fact, the only place you can find such quiet is in the roadless backcountry. Its possible elimination would be a major twofold loss: such quiet country is synonymous with intact, healthy wildlife habitat, and it's also the place in which many of us find sustenance for our souls. It is the nation's sacred places, akin to houses of worship.

For the latter reason, Congress passed the Wilderness Act of 1964. For the former, fish and game departments continue to set aside critical habitat, especially winter range, where wildlife is not to be disturbed by mechanized vehicles.

Of course, a few ATVs in all of Nevada or a few snow machines in all of Wyoming won't threaten the big banks of quiet—unless, that is, one goes by you when you're in the middle of talking with God or, more prosaically, stalking an elk. However, when mechanized vehicles number in the thousands and people in the tens of thousands, as they do in some of our national forests, not only does each individual's experience deteriorate, but wildlife becomes stressed. Scale—the cumulative effect of many individuals or the more massive effects of industry—matters. It matters enormously.

Today, about 90 percent of the United States has roads, most of the rivers are dammed, and nearly all of the wetlands in some regions have been filled. Given the scale of how we've changed nature, do we want to transform the remaining small slice of the unaltered continental pie—the remnant "wildernesses" such as Benj and I have been riding through—into what the other 90 percent looks and sounds like? This isn't merely an aesthetic question but a wildlife one. Put roads into unroaded country and you sign a warrant of ill health or even death for numerous species.

The following day found us on the Buffalo Plateau, straddling the headwaters of the continent. Far below and to our right the Shoshone River flowed toward the Atlantic. To the west the Snake curved toward the Pacific.

In twenty miles of riding, we saw not another person, and at sunset we dropped into the south fork of the Yellowstone River. Waterfalls like white mares' tails fell hundreds of feet to the valley floor. Leaving the trail behind, we rode deep into an amphitheater of tall grass. Above us, on the rim of the canyon, tiny pines were silhouetted against the violet sky. We hobbled the horses, built a fire, and sat listening to the river flow, its hush giving no indication as to what century or millennium we were riding through. Elk had left their hoofprints in the river gravel, and we decided that this would be our hunting valley for the fall. Then the moon rose over the divide, turning the waterfalls into silver plumes. You could have thought, sitting by that fire in the silence of the world, that the forest and rivers went on forever.

Of course they don't, which makes it imperative that those who act as their stewards be both competent and well intentioned.

Sanity

William Kittredge

The sun fell and left us with a long time to see the hills along the Big Blackfoot River as simply a dark and undulating subtext beneath a sky that was both spectacular and unsettling, close to frightening. We are nothing if not mystified amid glories.

Islands of cloud were silver to orange and occasional red. The pale sky beyond was perfect with infinities. In that moment I felt grief for the passing of our lives and recognized the possibility that we might come to find solace in the simple notion that we have no choice but to be part of such energies.

This last spring, in twilight across the upper meadow, thirty-seven thick-bodied elk were playing, limber and quick as they forgot their grazing and danced around chasing one another.

Annick and I stood in the strawberry garden, watching as a young mule came cantering toward them, trying to herd them or join them. The elk raised their heads and spooked away into the fringes of old-growth forest. They turned smokey in the twilight and then they were gone. The young mule was left prancing there, alone like us.

We have no choice but to understand ourselves and the movements of our lives in the run of evolving energies that is nature. The animal we are evolved in such connections; the need is built into our genetic makeup. Without intimacy with one another and with nature, we tend to slide off into insanities.

We have nowhere to live except in nature. Ruin that which is natural and we will soon lose entire track of ourselves. Lose contact with that which is wild and we fall out of touch with all that this animal we are is able to understand as actual.

We go dizzy trying to live inside a virtual, make-believe world (like cities in space). As individuals and as a society, when we are out of touch with that which is natural, we go literally insane. We see such craziness each day, reported in every newspaper we read.

The only story we really know how to inhabit is the ancient one about ourselves in the natural world. As the setting for that story vanishes, we begin to lose contact with our animal selves and become increasingly disoriented, disenfranchised.

Some of us are driven frantic and ultimately savaged by our anxieties. We don't know who we are; we don't know who we should want to be. Some of us begin to become monstrous.

If we hope to live in sane ways, we have no choice but to cherish and sustain those parts of the world that remain at least partways natural and intact. Without wilderness we start turning into not much of anybody; we lose track of our natural goodness, our capacity for compassion and empathy; we wander off in pursuit of unnatural desires. All cruelties are possible.

Like that young mule, we are alone, prancing around and out of love, impoverished, desperate in our isolation, driven to insanities of self-preoccupation and greed, literal indecencies. As we destroy that which is natural, we eat ourselves alive.

Miles . . . from Nowhere

Pepper Trail

When I was growing up, nourishing my imagination on a diet of *National Geographic* magazines and the narratives of real and fictional explorers, I had a special affection for anyplace that was described in those pages as "remote." The word itself stirred up a wind in my dreaming head. A wind was always blowing through the remote places of this earth, I felt sure, and it made no difference to me if the site in question was a cliff-top lamasery in Tibet, a sweltering rubber town along the Rio Negro, or an atoll in the Christmas Islands. Wind, a fierce sun to set a narrow-eyed look on my weather-beaten face, and some hard haggling with impassive headmen while children gazed big-eyed from the shadows. Such was remoteness in my twelve-year-old imagination.

As I grew older, it was a shock to realize that my own little hometown, surrounded by an utterly domesticated landscape of dairy farms and hedgerows, was considered remote by those city people who saw freeways and airports as necessary for civilization. My first trip across the country was a disillusioning journey through western towns where remoteness was measured in distance to the next gas station, and truck stops clustered around the interstate off-ramps like flies. In late-twentieth century America, I learned, a "remote" place was one that it took awhile to drive to.

I became a scientist, not an adventurer, and I have never made a trip anywhere simply because it was far away. Still, it gives me great satisfaction whenever my travels lead me somewhere that lives up to my childhood standards of remoteness. For years I carried out research at a place in South America where I could climb a vine-covered ridge and look out over a primeval landscape of unbroken rainforest. I once spent a week there completely alone. At the end of that week, when I heard the sound of human speech as I approached my campsite, my hair bristled like the pelt of a wild animal.

Probably the most remote place I have ever been, both in fact and in correspondence to my romantic imaginings, was an uninhabited atoll on the fringes of Polynesia. I will never forget my feelings as the ship that had dropped me there disappeared over the horizon. The wind did indeed blow ceaselessly, and I did indeed squint out of a weather-beaten face as I carried on my studies of the seabirds that hung over the island like smoke. Every moment I was there, I was conscious of the infinite weight and wildness of the unimaginably huge Pacific Ocean pressing in on all sides.

These places have given me something I don't think I was capable of receiving in any other way, a quietude and a sense of transcendent insignificance. For these permanent gifts I am ever grateful.

My thoughts were turned in this direction when I recently read about an effort to identify the most remote place in the lower forty-eight states, as determined by elaborate satellite imaging and computer analysis. In this instance, remoteness was defined in a way that even my twelve-year-old self would approve: distance from a road.

Now, pause. How far do you think this spot is from the nearest road? How far do you think a place should be, to be really and truly remote?

The lower forty-eight's remotest spot is in the southeastern corner of Yellowstone National Park. It is 20.3 miles from a road. From the ridge, the headlights of cars on the park's highways are clearly visible, and the glow from Jackson Hole's bars and boutiques smears the night sky. Three government patrol cabins are located within 3 miles.

So if a Wyoming grizzly bear or wolf wants to get away from roads, the farthest it can get is 20 miles. If a wolverine or a peregrine falcon or a human being would like to sit on a ridge at dusk and not see electric lights, it is almost impossible to do. Let there be no doubt: wilderness in America is almost extinct. Even a seemingly expansive area like the 180,000-acre Kalmiopsis Wilderness works out to only about 16 by 17 miles, a small box in which to fit a world.

We need wilderness because it is the world that made us. We need it to preserve a space where the human spirit can unfold and tentatively acknowledge the kinship and common fate that we share with the natural world. If we fail to protect the few remnants that exist, I fear a disconnected and tragic future for humanity.

A century ago, John Muir wrote: "The tendency nowadays to wander in wilderness is delightful to see. Thousands of tired, nerve-shaken, over-civilized people are beginning to find out that going to the mountains is going home; that wildness is a necessity; and that mountain parks and reservations are useful not only as fountains of timber and irrigating rivers, but as fountains of life. Awakening from the stupefying effects of the vice of over-industry and the deadly apathy of luxury, they are trying as best they can to mix and enrich their own little ongoings with those of nature, and to get rid of rust and disease." Muir wrote those words in a world before radio and television, before the airplane, before the computer, and before the chainsaw. How much more rust has civilization layered upon us in the last 100 years, and how little wilderness is left to wash us clean again!

Today I am no longer a twelve-year-old romantic; but my son is. His imagination is at least as easily ignited as mine ever was, but it flames in a world that harbors less mystery, less wilderness. My generation has much to answer for, and my generation and his have much work to do. It is my fervent hope that when the time comes, it will still be possible for my son and me to take *his* twelve-year-old for a walk into an unknown, uncontrolled, and uncontrolling place: wilderness, miles from nowhere.

Kith and Kin of the Wild

Phil Condon

About two years ago I stumbled across a worldwide writing contest on the Internet. Sponsored by British Shell Oil, it offered a prize of twenty thousand pounds, and the question under consideration was "Do we still need nature?" I tried to write a line or two or five, dispirited by the question and distrustful of its context. I wanted to believe the question was only intended to provoke, but I didn't enter the contest. I don't know anyone who did.

That contest theme still comes back to me now and again, especially when I talk with folks who strike me as if they might take the question seriously. Yet given who's out there cutting on all the cutting edges, those who seem to pull the rest of us along like so many field hands picking up the gleanings, maybe to all of us sooner or later it will have to be a serious question.

The need for nature, the defense of wildness. Many others have articulated both of these ideas better than I can, but in 2005, on the racing curve of change we're still trying to comprehend as history, it's likely good for each of us to take another run at thinking them through.

Yet here in the dark of a July morning, midway in the quick six hours between last and first light this time and latitude in Montana, it's difficult to feel coherent or logical, for more than a few minutes or a few sentences at most, about anything. Half a decade after the second coming didn't come and the calendar crash didn't crash, on this mind-muddled, bloody-handed, and soon-to-be unthermostatted planet, coherence feels close to impossible. The center is long loose—at worst gone, at best invisible—and the circumference, now surmised from sketchy evidence somewhere, I'm sure, to be only an erratic ellipse, won't hold either.

I slide to sleep most nights with a daylong brew of too much information and too little wisdom, in a slosh and surfeit of forlorn facts and faiths, trusting my dreams to the deep blue breath of wildness. And pressed, I find my waking self trusting truth deeper than logic and rationale, traces from waymarks along the paths I've come, most often found on foot and among trees, soil, and stone, alongside free-moving water, and beneath wide skies of all shapes and colors. Behold, the world. And I believe our species, we humans, are the beholden.

· · · · ·

The day was too hot for bushwhacking but that's what I was doing. I'd just cooled off in Rattlesnake Creek right where Bee Creek comes in. I nestled among wet stones, only my face, chest, and toes above water, as wands of sunlight wafted through cottonwoods. In ten minutes my jaw chattered and my shins ached. I was so cold I started hiking Bee Creek.

About the time I ascended into a hillside ravine of permanent midday shadow, the low arching limbs had me on hands and knees, half in the trickle creek, half out. I smelled a mix of dusts in the half distance—leaf dust, rock dust, grass dust—the summer heat and wind working on the mountain world, breaking it apart that afternoon like any other, molecule by molecule. When I came to thickets of coarse green straws, horsetail scouring-rushes, I stopped to sit on a boulder white-gray-green with lichen. It's impossible to move through the world without your weight falling on other life. The question, I guess, is how to be aware of it, how to move and carry it through a living world. It's so easy to throw our weight around, but throw it around enough and that's all we see, the world a mirror to our own poundage and force: tires and fumes, the blade and the dynamite, a bottomless concrete kiln and countless culverts.

As quickly as I'd chilled in the creek, I heated up in the rough, arbored crevice of Bee Creek. Ninety-five in the shade, I guessed, weather to stay still in. I slowed my breath, listening to the midday wind in the pines above the watery silence. It's a different sound in hot light than at cool night, higher-pitched and more uniform. I waited for nothing in particular, just glad to be out there alone. Except for the jets I expected, six miles up, and except for my breath, it was free of human sound. Learning time.

Nothing in particular came along soon enough, though, in the form of a whirr that could have been more wind but wasn't. A hummingbird whizzed by into the maze of a still-blooming syringa bush and then perched. Stunning. I'd seen them perch and tuck wings only a few dozen times in my life. This one seemed way too small, with its wings settled, to ever fly fast or far. And then more surprise: it had settled in right next to another who was already there apparently. For how long I didn't know.

The two sat an inch or so apart five feet from my forehead. I was sure they were black-chinned hummingbirds, but I couldn't see enough color to tell male from female. I tried not to tremble with my breathing, but something told me they knew I was there and were willing to sit still that close to me if I was willing to do the same. What did I look like to them? Too impossibly big for locomotion of any kind? Each of us lived and moved in a world scaled beyond the other's understanding.

Then, transcending my speculations, why I remember all this enough to tell happened. They turned, one to the other, their beaks in profile seeming as narrow as tenpenny nails and as long as the birds were tall. I took this in, made my mental comparisons, just in time to see the bird on the right open its beak wide, maybe two inches, while the one on the left moved its closed beak down and into the other's. Something rare was happening in that four o'clock heat on a steep slope in western Montana, and I wanted to slow it down but couldn't. The first bird kept poking its long beak all the way down into the second's throat, and I could think, of course, only of what I really know, which is love, and sex, and eating, and I wondered if I was seeing two mates or two siblings or a parent with offspring. The breeze winked sunlight between the arms of Douglas fir and fingers of river birch for a long clock-gone moment, and then it all stopped; the beaks closed up and the birds turned back, both facing me again. Just as I decided that, yes, it must be feeding, the first bird lifted, its wings a dynamo blur again, and hovered off to disappear in green. I wanted to feel lonely for the one remaining behind, or for myself, but before I could do either, the second one's wings changed too. It rose, turned, and vanished.

Both birds seemed about the same tiny size, no clear distinction, and I wasn't sure who was feeding whom, one regurgitating a nectary syrup or mashed insects for the other or one retrieving food from the other's throat. I couldn't tell the feeder from the fed, but maybe that's just a line the mind draws through the fleshy fabric of wild time where every living thing, and maybe every dead thing, too, is both, over and over again.

I'm sure somebody somewhere knows, in general, what's likely, what's known, about what I saw, but no one really does because those two very particular hearts the size of peas beating two hundred times a minute, those tiny moments with wings, showed me something one time only and then took it with them back into their folded forest life.

No matter how I name and number, it still comes out the same: four o'clock, Bee Creek, ninety-five degrees, forty-two hundred feet above sea level, Rattlesnake Mountains, two birds, a thousand-odd trees, one human.

Wildness.

. . . . .

These days I don't much attempt to define that word, *wildness*, much less *wilderness*. Frankly—and I get the idea I'm not alone in this—I'm tired of trying. The wild is either defined narrowly, in which case the words become exclusive and soon contentious and arbitrary, or the wild is defined so broadly it's all-inclusive, everything we've woken into and everything we do, because yes, we're part and parcel of the dream, but this begs the question and erases all distinctions.

Yet something large is changing, something vital is being lost. We can keep right on arguing, keep splitting the last hairs on a chemo patient. Or what? We could look in her eyes, ask her how she feels, try to learn the language she answers in, try to remember why we love her. We could try to quit hurting her.

No, I can't say exactly what wildness is; I only point to part of it when I sense it, like two tiny hummingbirds in a quiet moment of sharing. Yet there is a useful category we can measure and define: roadless. And when we examine the patient earth, it seems to me that roadless is close enough to wildness for diagnosis and treatment: less *is* more, and road*less* is *more* wild. Because on the ground, where most of us have to live and walk and drive, one thing we can clearly see and demonstrate is that where roads go, the life there in its million forms suffers, shrinks, pales, dies. Where roads go, motors and fumes and the hard edges and stiletto points of civilization follow close by. Wildness is changed and challenged, diminished, divided, and de-diversified. Even extinguished.

I admit, like most of you I'd guess, that I've spent the bulk of my life near roads, within a few dozen or a few hundred feet from some kind of road, and then, too, a fair share of my life right out on the pavement. I was born and bred and grown entirely in the century of the automobile and its roads. So how can I criticize them, renounce them, now? It's true: my life has been mostly graded and paved, bull-dozed and banked.

But neither I nor anyone else is suggesting an end to roading. The suggestion, which some see as nature's demand, is only for a forbear-ance. Only a stopping of the grading or paving that we already have and use.

What does that Cat Stevens song from the early 1970s say? Some-thing like, "We build the roads / for our lorry loads / but they just go on and on / and you can't get off." Maybe this is as good a time as any to ask again that song's title question: "Where do the children play?" The literal children of this or any generation, of course, but what I'm thinking of are the children in all of us who—if detoured, merged, bypassed, and trafficked long and hard enough—could disappear entirely. And where would that leave us? Lose the close-to-ground wonder and the pure first-morning curiosity that have at their core a humility before the words for it, lose this and I fear we're just going through the motions. I'm talking about the children in us who love animals and plants and turn to them for comfort and lessons without being told to—until told not to in classrooms and magazines—the ones who find sustenance in skies and clouds when given time and space to stare at them, the ones who first sense their souls and the souls of others from watching and playing among plants and stones and puddles and raindrops. Those children.

· · · · ·

Walking in the Sapphire Mountains, in the Rock Creek watershed, I followed a trail up a feeder stream from the east called Grizzly Creek, though like almost everywhere else, grizzlies were murdered out of here decades back. This was a late morning in April like honey, clear water with a twist of lemon. In a small meadow near the creek's mouth, a black hawthorn tree held a giant twig nest, three feet across, barely above my eye level. It looked clumsy, unuseful, playful, as if kids built it and in a hurry, yet I startled two magpies from the nest. They dove out, those heavy three-tone corvids, falling halfway to the earth before their wings held and gave them rise. I peered in, couldn't even see an opening, yet this was someone's home.

The canyon narrowed, scree and talus swooping up and away on both sides, aspen stands working toeholds in the boulder fields, ponderosa and larch and fir wild-patterned across both slopes. At a creek crossing, I retrieved a daypack lunch and ate, staring at a stony slope. It was an irregular triangular shape, maybe two hundred feet high and several hundred feet across at its base, with only the odd wild raspberry bushes and aspens growing here and there and a few fallen logs, sunbleached and wind-silvered, broken across it. I climbed up just far enough to know the stack and slide of it all, feeling the stored heat rising around me. I found a niche, like an awkward open-air rock coffin, and eased down into the hard heat for a postlunch nap. The creek notes were a liquid xylophone below me, a hawk cried in the thermal distance, a warbler called from chokecherry thickets. I squinted against the bright sunlight, amazed at the gravity those jumbled stairs of stone defined by defying. Imagine. Thousands of boulders, in one field on one side only of one small creek. Abundance. Multiplicity. Unseen powers, unknown uses.

In the narrowed light of my squint and the slow rush of my daydreams, I finally saw the spider lines. First near me, between two stones by my right arm. Then at my feet, linking two medicine-ball boulders twice across a two-foot gap. I rolled over, craned my neck, sighting up the tossed angles of the talus slope. And then I saw more, gossamer weavings, almost invisible, mostly connected low down on the sides of each boulder, hooked to small crevices, to lichen, to rocky shelves. The landscape of each stone had been surveyed on a spider scale for likely tie-off points. They were everywhere, webs across and among these thousand rocks, in quality and physicality the opposite of stone, wind-fragile and light-ray-thin against these harsh tons of unwieldable weight, yet I realized they must be helping to hold the mountainside up, to keep the slide at bay, however slightly. Silk-stone mountains.

I saw no spiders, could raise none in this midday sun, even when I moved small stones, upturning them behind me as I worked my way up the slope. Yet the webs told the tale, one stone at a time, their connections everywhere, trapping and seining the surfaces of the world.

Spider silk, real as quarks or photons, fine as emotion, holds our wild world together. Keeps this world apart long enough for us to pass through.

. . . . .

Think of the change in the places of your lifetime, however old you are and wherever you might have come from. Holding that vision, can you have any idea what the city you live in, or the county, state, nation, or certainly this planet, will be like in five decades? Isn't it true that no matter what we do or don't do, individually or together, we can't imagine what awaits us in 2055? I know the best trust I can muster is that an understanding of the effects of the twentieth century, the century of the automobile, the oil well, and electricity, may be clearer then. Might we then, in the face of our inability to foresee anything clearly even fifty years from today, modestly propose to make the twenty-first, at least partly, a century of patience?

Why not a moratorium on road construction for fifty years? Why not restore all the thousands of abandoned miles in our forests, deserts, and mountains? Why not a wait-and-see on using vehicles of any kind on any unroaded land—just for fifty years. Give it a rest for two short generations and, if I'm wrong, if the wiser folks from whom I get this kind of idea are wrong, well, then let that third generation have at it. But give them a choice. And give the land a chance.

Pull the camera back very far at all for perspective and the truth is that all roads are one road, and that this single road of progress has mostly been one-way. The one way of thinking we know best, the one way of building it and seeing if they come—and can survive it—the one way of letting our descendants deal with the results of our vision, no matter how myopic, tunneled, or rose-colored history may later reveal it to have been. What about letting the third generation have a vision, too? Trust them and be patient for them, even if we can never meet, but let them have something to work with when they come, something left of the world we found when we came, only twenty-five or fifty years ago, rather than nothing but the world we've constructed.

This kind of moratorium would simply say that patience *is* a virtue—and mean it. It would honor the wisdom in an old phrase: "saving it back." It would exercise our ability to forgo and forbear, an ability that many of us tell our children distinguishes us from them.

Does fifty years of forbearance sound radical? Are our lives and times so desperate that we can't even contemplate fifty years of patience? Do we live so close to the edge that we don't have even a half century of leeway to adjust to the magnitude of what we've already accomplished and wait to see how unintended consequences might catch up to complex causes? That isn't how we portray ourselves to one another, from what I see. On the contrary, I would think that these last hundred years of breakneck pace and incessant invention, if anything were ever to give us some breathing room, would have done so by now.

. . . . .

I call it Arrowleaf Mountain, but that's not a name anyone but I would know it by. I like to rename, ever since I tried an exercise with field trip students. We each inventoried a small-radius circle, describing, sketching, and measuring plants, flowers, leaves, trees, needles, stones, insects. And then made up a name for each thing. Later, back home, we could look up the world's names and compare. It's a curious practice. I recommend it.

On one of these trips this early June, sauntering across a slope on the south side of a mountain near Missoula, I was struck still by that familiar and somewhat coarse flower, arrowleaf balsamroot. Struck still by so many of them together that they seemed a single organism the size of the whole hillside. Arrowleaf Mountain.

After a morning of examining small intricate flowers, consulting guidebooks, counting stamens and pistils, and exploring leaf vein patterns, this landscape-scale arrowleaf organism was so distinct. Flowers bright and lurid, leaves large and dull, the plants so prolific and common.

How can plain flowers stir such emotion? This way: The yellow hallelujahs of the arrowleaf, fielded beyond counting in casual yet careful profusion. The sky so blue and domed as a flower itself, the bloom that makes all other blooms possible, stringing the sun each day on a changing track, mustering the rain from four directions, containing the wind that connects mountains on every continent. What could more uplift a human spirit than these flowers in this place on this morning? The rising shape of the hill I stood on, the slant of yellow above me, the thrust of the leaves, each skyward and all displayed to stars, but subtly, as if pointing a hundred ways to the same crest or constellation. Everything lifting toward the top, toward the sky, toward the sun, and each yellow flower a sun you can stare at. All this upward brightness, reminding, reminding.

They're so different, reminding and remembering. Reminding happens out there, right then, or not at all, the work and play of single moments. I can't prepare for them and often miss them when they come. That morning I stood a long while, rising without moving, closing my eyes and opening them again. I almost came to a point when I couldn't tell open from closed.

Back here, I try to remember that almost moment: yellow hope rising blue eye.

· · · · ·

There's a sign for a wild animal zoo just south of Glacier National Park: YOUR CAR IS YOUR CAGE. The drive-thru zoo is a simulacrum of wildland, a place captured and encapsulated, all its vision out of focus on a few big animals neutered by fences they can't cross and confused by cars they can't flee. How could the irony of the billboard come-on not occur to the owners? Maybe it has and they're already a level of winking beyond me. I bring it up here, though, letting its literal truth ring through my life, and yours, in the moment of its first reading, for another reason.

I hope it's clear I've chosen not to speak for the intrinsic value of wildness, which I believe in though I can't see it, or the value of unroaded places to the inhabitants themselves, which I also believe in though I can't know the perspectives that confer that value. Instead, I've wanted to explore the need for wild places, full of first lives, for us humans ourselves, and to examine an even tighter focus within that human need for wildness, not for its materials but for our spirits.

Granted, I'm lucky. I've been able to get off-road and off-vehicle here and there in my life. Yet surely these essential, unquantifiable benefits are not limited to those who walk off-road, who see and sense firsthand an unroaded place. I believe this because I sense so surely, below the surface of our civilized lives, those levels that connect us all, the deepest kith and kin of wildness. If you don't share that sense of things, I'm not sure I can convince you, although I've been doing my best to show how the living world reveals its unseen levels to me. Still, if I'm anywhere near right, the *big* spirit in the *big* all-of-us is either nurtured or starved by whatever happens between all the roads of our world. In Montana or Manhattan, even in those generations to come, all are touched by wildness and how we participate in it.

Caged wild animals, believing they know how to steer, believing they know where they're going. To me there's little that's more sad. And nothing more dangerous.

. . . . .

The "it" run through by roads is the wild. Wildness, wildity, wildination, wildority: we can Latinate and noun it for all we're worth and we won't get any closer. It's the wind that works the world, blowing across all political names and lines and respiring on both sides of every live membrane, be it skin or lung or tongue. Hummingbird wings power it. Spider silks hold it together. Flower blooms remind it.

Perhaps we can yet find a way to ask these meek inheritors what to do. To ask our grandchildren, fifty years out. To ask our own child-souls.

The catch-21, the caveat of our century, is that to hear these voices we'll need a great and humble quiet, a quiet we can't build or intend. Such a quiet escapes all our cleverness and software, is more subtle than any equation or engine.

The wild is its own quiet engine, alive and patient as sunrise, waiting for each of us to take a few steps away from the road. And hear it.

Resources

Wildlands CPR: www.wildlandscpr.org. A site full of photos, dozens of resource materials, and an online, 12,000 citation database, all on the ecological effects of wildland roads and motorized recreation.

Conservation Biology (journal), special section on the ecological effects of roads, 14, no. 1, February 2000.

Natural Trails and Waters coalition: www.naturaltrails.org. A nonprofit coalition of more than 100 conservation groups concerned about the rising abuse of dirt bikes, four-wheelers, and other off-road vehicles on our public and private lands.

No Place Distant: Roads and Motorized Recreation on America's Public Lands, by David Havlick. An excellent book written in lay language on the ecological impacts of roads, motorized recreation, and what lies ahead for our roaded, public landscape.

Divorce your Car! Ending the Love Affair with the Automobile, by Katie Alvord. A well-written book filled with humor and hubris that gives compelling reasons to walk away from our romance with cars.

Contributors

Edward Abbey was the scrappy author of more than a dozen nonfiction books, including *Desert Solitaire*, and eight novels, including *The Monkey Wrench Gang*. In Abbey's own words, "I am a redneck myself, born and bred on a submarginal farm in Appalachia, descended from an endless line of dark-complected, lug-eared, beetle-browed, insolent barbarian peasants, a line reaching back to the dark forests of central Europe and the alpine caves of my Neanderthal primogenitors." (From "In defense of the Redneck," *Abbey's Road*.)

Katie Alvord, author of *Divorce Your Car: Ending the Love Affair with the Automobile*, has been a transportation reform activist for more than ten years. She is a freelance environmental writer and has contributed to *E Magazine*, *Sierra*, *The Urban Ecologist*, *Library Journal*, and *Wild Earth*, and she is an advisor for *Car Busters* magazine. She resides in Michigan and is a cofounder of Wildlands CPR.

Susan Cerulean is the director of the Red Hills Writers Project and a writer, naturalist, and activist living in Florida. Her latest book is a nature memoir, entitled *Tracking Desire: A Journey After Swallow-tailed Kites*.

Phil Condon teaches environmental writing and literature at the University of Montana. Author of *Clay Center* and *Montana Surround*, he is a winner of the William Faulkner Award for Creative Writing.

Carolyn Duckworth is a writer, editor, and naturalist living in Gardiner, Montana. She is one of Yellowstone National Park's publications managers.

Rosalie Edge is described by environmental historian Stephen Fox as "the first woman to have a considerable impact on the conservation movement." As the chairman of the Emergency Conservation Committee, she was one of the foremost environmental advocates in the United States in the 1930s and 1940s. Her accomplishments include leadership in the successful efforts to create Olympic National Park and Pennsylvania's Hawk Mountain Sanctuary.

Guy Hand is a freelance writer and NPR correspondent living in Boise, Idaho whose work has appeared in *Sierra*, *Audubon*, *Northern Lights*, *Orion*, and *High Country News*.

David Havlick is author of *No Place Distant: Roads and Motorized Recreation on America's Public Lands*, and co-founder of Wild Rockies Field Institute. He teaches in the Environmental Studies program at Brandeis University.

Freeman House is a co-founder of the Mattole Salmon Group and the Mattole Restoration Council and author of the award-winning *Totem Salmon: Life Lessons from Another Species*.

Derrick Jensen is the author of *Railroads and Clearcuts; Listening to the Land: Conversations About Nature, Culture, and Eros*; and *A Language Older Than Words*. He lives in Crescent City, California.

Ted Kerasote has written for many national and international magazines and is author of a half a dozen books, including *Bloodties* and *Out There: In the Wild in a Wired Age*, which won a National Outdoor Book Award for literature. He lives by the Tetons in Wyoming.

William Kittredge grew up on and then managed his family's cattle ranch in the Great Basin in southeastern Oregon. He has taught in the English department at the University of Montana for twenty-five years and lives in Missoula. His books include the short story collections *The Van Gogh Field* and *We Are Not in This Together* and a memoir, *Hole in the Sky*.

Kraig Klungness is a wilderness advocate and cofounder of Wildlands CPR.

Barry Lopez, essayist, short-story writer, and international traveler, is the author of *Arctic Dreams*, for which he received the National Book Award. Among his other nonfiction books are *About This Life*, and *Of Wolves and Men* (a National Book Award finalist). Lopez is considered one of the nation's premier nature writers. In his nonfiction he often examines the relationship between human culture and physical landscape. Most recently, he has published a collection of stories, *Light Action in the Caribbean*.

Tom Lyon is retired from the University of Utah, where he has been a professor since 1964. He edited the classic anthology *This Incomparable Land: A Book of American Nature Writing*, and was editor of the journal *Western American Literature*. He has been honored with conservation awards from the Utah Wilderness Association and the Bridgerland Audubon Society.

Stephen J. Lyons is the author of *Landscape of the Heart, Writings on Daughters and Journeys*. He lives and writes in Illinois.

Peter Matthiessen has authored more than twenty works of fiction and nonfiction spanning fifty years, including *At Play in the Fields of the Lord, Far Tortuga*, and *The Snow Leopard*, which won the National Book Award in 1978. Twenty-five years into his writing career, Matthiessen began Zen practice and has since become an ordained Buddhist priest. Today he lives with his wife in Sagaponack, New York, where he runs a small Zen center.

Stephanie Mills is author of *In Service of the Wild: Restoring and Reinhabiting Damaged Land* and editor of "Turning Away from Technology: A New Vision for the Twenty-First Century." She lives in the upper Midwest.

Mary O'Brien is an environmental consultant and activist, and a founding and past member of Wildlands CPR's board of directors. She lives in Eugene, Oregon and Castle Valley, Utah.

David Petersen resides year-round in "a little cabin on a big mountain" in southwestern Colorado. David's many books include the anthology *A Hunter's Heart: Honest Essays on Blood Sport*, and *Heartsblood: Hunting, Spirituality, and Wildness in America*.

Thomas R. Petersen is development director of Wildlands CPR. His writing has appeared in *Utne Reader, Orion*, and other publications. He lives with his two sons in Missoula, Montana.

David Quammen, a former Rhodes scholar, wrote the highly acclaimed *Song of the Dodo, Monster of God*, a series of books based on his columns for *Outside* magazine, and three novels. All of his nonfiction books are still in print. His writing for *Outside* garnered that magazine a National Magazine Award. Although he is likely to be found conducting research anywhere from Rumania to Congo, he lives in Bozeman, Montana.

Janisse Ray is a naturalist, environmental activist, and winner of the 1996 Merriam Frontier Award. She wrote *Ecology of a Cracker Childhood* and *Wild Card Quilt: Taking a Chance on Home* and is a nature commentator for Georgia Public Radio.

Mary Sojourner, novelist (*Sisters of the Dream*), prize-winning fiction and essay writer (*Story, Nimrod, Sierra*), columnist for *High Country News*, and NPR national commentator, came to the Southwest in 1985 to write and fight for what is left of the wild places and people. She continues to do both from her home in Flagstaff. Her books include *Solace: Rituals of Loss and Desire, Delicate: Stories*, and *Bonelight: Ruin and Grace in the New Southwest*.

Scott Stouder lives in Pollock, Idaho, and is a writer, an avid hunter, and a sportsman. He is the western field director for Trout Unlimited and works to protect roadless public land in Idaho.

Pepper Trail is a biologist and writer in Ashland, Oregon, where he has worked on wildlands protection in the Soda Mountain region. His writing has appeared in *National Geographic*, *High Country News*, and *Open Spaces Quarterly*.

T. H. Watkins was a prominent writer about the American West and the environment. He was the editor of *Wilderness*, the quarterly magazine of the Wilderness Society; was selected as the first Wallace Stegner Distinguished Professor of Western American Studies at Montana State University–Bozeman in 1997; and was the author, coauthor, or editor of twenty-five books and more than 250 articles. His book on Harold Ickes, *Righteous Pilgrim*, was a finalist for the National Book Award.

Brooke Williams is the author of *Halflives* and executive director of the Murie Center in Moose, Wyoming. He also lives in Utah with his wife, author Terry Tempest Williams.

Permissions

P.O. Box 7516 • Missoula, MT 59807 • wildlandscpr.org

All royalties from the sale of this book will be donated to Wildlands CPR.

Founded in 1994, Wildlands CPR is the only national conservation group in the United States that specifically targets off-road vehicle abuse of public lands and actively promotes wildland restoration, road removal, and the prevention of new road construction.

Respected by citizens, grassroots conservation groups, decision-makers, and public land management agencies alike, Wildlands CPR provides scientific resources, strategy consultations, workshops, slide shows, and other professional resource materials on the ecological effects of wildland roads and off-road vehicles. As an advocacy support and clearinghouse organization, they are bringing people together to protect and restore our public lands.

For more information on Wildlands CPR and how to join in the efforts toward a quieter, more roadless landscape, please see Wildlands CPR's website, www.wildlandscpr.org.